AMERICAN POLITICAL, ECONOMIC, AND SECURITY ISSUES

POLITICAL ECONOMY

THEORIES, PRINCIPLES AND POLITICS

CALEB M. CLARK
AND
EVELYN A. CLARK BENAVIDES
EDITORS

nova science publishers
New York

https://doi.org/10.52305/LZDN5428

NOTICE TO THE READER

Library of Congress Cataloging-in-Publication Data

ISBN: 978-1-68507-106-6

Published by Nova Science Publishers, Inc. † New York

For our beloved spouses, Janet and Carlos

CONTENTS

INTRODUCTION

***Caleb M. Clark*[1,*] *and Evelyn A. Clark Benavides*[2]**
[1]Department of Political Science, Auburn University, Auburn, AL, USA
[2]Department of Sociology, SUNY, Oswego, Oswego, NY, USA

ABSTRACT

The academic literature on political economy includes many models and theories. The contributions to this volume illustrate four basic principles that many exhibit. First, many different types of political economies exist. There are large differences between not just developed and developing countries but between early and late developers (Gerschenkron, 1962); and substantial differences are easy to discern even among superficially similar ones, such as the East Asian developmental states (Clark and Roy, 1997). Second, most political economies are marked by a myriad of interdependencies among market, state, and civil society. Third, change, both incremental and fundamental, occurs regularly in many. Fourth and as a result of the first three, the analysis of political economies is often quite complex. Chapter 1 focuses on change by analyzing the ongoing Great Reset in the U.S. political economy in the early 21st century. Chapters 2-4 discuss how China differs from western models: in particular, models for international relationships, Confucianism

[*] Corresponding Author's E-mail: clarkcm@auburn.edu

and the Belt and Road Initiative, and China's cooperation with the Central and East European Countries respectively. Chapter 5 also covers variety and complexity with an in-depth theoretical treatment of Marx's theory of value. Chapter 6 raises issues of interdependence by highlighting the social bases of political economies. Chapters 7 and 8 touch upon interdependence and complexity by demonstrating how the U.S. political economy marginalizes minorities in the areas of education and health care respectively. Chapter 9 focuses upon interdependence by linking fiscal policy to subsequent election outcomes. Finally, Chapter 10 relates workforce development policy to changes in the 21st century American economy.

Keywords: political economy, change, complexity, interdependence, variety

The academic literature on political economy includes many models and theories. The contributions to this volume illustrate four basic principles that many exhibit. First, many different types of political economies exist. There are large differences between not just developed and developing countries but between early and late developers (Gerschenkron, 1962); and substantial differences are easy to discern even among superficially similar ones, such as the East Asian developmental states (Clark and Roy, 1997). Second, most political economies are marked by a myriad of interdependencies among market, state, and civil society. Third, change, both incremental and fundamental, occurs regularly in many. Fourth and as a result of the first three, the analysis of political economies is often quite complex.

Chapter 1 focuses on change by analyzing the ongoing Great Reset in the U.S. political economy. Chapters 2-4 discuss how China differs from western models: in particular, models for international relationships, Confucianism and the Belt and Road Initiative, and China's cooperation with the Central and East European Countries respectively. Chapter 5 also covers variety and complexity with an in-depth theoretical treatment of Marx's theory of value. Chapter 6 raises issues of interdependence by highlighting the social bases of political economies. Chapters 7 and 8 touch upon interdependence and complexity by demonstrating how the U.S. political economy marginalizes minorities in the areas of education and health care respectively. Chapter 9 focuses upon interdependence by linking fiscal policy to subsequent election outcomes. Finally, Chapter 10 relates workforce development policy to changes in the 21st century American economy.

Chapter 1 by Cal Clark and Evelyn A. Clark discusses "The Great Reset and the 'Back to the Future' Vision of Donald Trump." In *The Great Reset*, Richard Florida defines Great Resets as "broad and fundamental transformations of the economic and social order that involve much more than economic or financial events." In this chapter, we expand Florida's model to give a much greater emphasis to politics and power and then argue that, while the Trump administration can be viewed as a response to America's ongoing Great Reset in the 21st century, its efficacy appears to be highly problematic, in large part because it represents a "Back to the Future" vision of where America should go. In particular, the Great Reset that has transformed the political economy of the United States after World War II is composed of a complex set of interacting economic, political, and social phenomena. Economic resets include: 1) the transformation of the economy from an industrial to an information-age one; 2) the communications and transportation revolutions that spurred globalization; 3) the *laissez-faire* international order after World War II; 4) the transformation of the impact of globalization from positive to negative on many aspects of the economy; 5) deindustrialization; 6) the changing nature of employment; 7) a changing business philosophy; 8) the marginalization of labor; 9) slower economic growth; and 10) the Covid-19 crisis. Political and social resets include: 1) the replacement of Keynesianism by neoliberalism as the nation's public philosophy; 2) the rise of cultural issues in domestic politics; 3) the abjuring of large-scale government interventions in the economy, such as the GI Bill and Great Society Programs; 4) the "Great Risk Shift" in social insurance; 5) the decline of the educational system; 6) a financialization of economy; 7) a limited reduction in barriers facing marginalized members of society; 8) the escalating polarization of domestic politics; 9) escalating inequality; and 10) the creation and then decline of broad middle class. The Trump administration has had a mixed response to the threats and opportunities that these resets create for continuing and expanding the "American Dream." It has clearly tried to reverse: 1) globalization's changing impact on the American economy; 2) the changing nature of employment; 3) deindustrialization; 4) slower growth; 5) the changing fortunes of the middle class; 6) macroeconomic neoliberalism; 7) the role of public education; and 8) the negative impact of the Covid-19 crisis on the economy. In addition, it has accelerated: 1) the rise of cultural issues; 2) the polarization of American politics; 3) the barriers facing marginalized members of society; 4) the financialization of the U.S. economy; and 5) the marginalization of labor. In contrast, it has generally ignored: 1) the transformation from an industrial to an information-age economy; 2) the postwar communications and transportations revolutions; 3) the change in business philosophy; 4) direct government interventions, like the Great Society and G.I. Bill; 5) the Great Risk Shift; and 6) rapidly rising inequality.

In Chapter 2, R. James Ferguson develops a new perspective on "Adaptive Confucian Relationships: Models for International Relations." Chinese thought has a sophisticated concept of human relations, in the Confucian tradition based on core ideas of benevolence (*ren*), social customs (*li*), harmony (*he*) and reciprocity (*shu*). Five relationships have been identified as the basis of a stable society: between ruler and minister, father and son, husband and wife, older to younger brothers, and among friends. Likewise, in China's historical international relations, diverse relational models have been propounded including the 'tribute system' (asymmetrical relations supporting China's primacy), *Tianxia* as an inclusive empire embracing 'all-under heaven', and the idea of Chinese culture as an attractor and stabilizer. These relations imply a degree of prescriptive hierarchy that is at odds with equal respect for sovereign nations (the legal basis of the current interstate system), modern liberalism and socialist egalitarianism. In contrast, contemporary Chinese foreign policy mobilizes principles that emphasize harmony and cooperation: the Five Principles of Peaceful Coexistence, notions of co-governance (*guojia gongzhi* and *quanqiu gongzhi*), and building communities of 'common destiny.' These general formulations do not provide detailed guidelines for positive and nuanced interactions. However, when combined with an active understanding of *zhong* (contextualized as 'equilibrium' or the 'mean'), creative and positive relations among nations can be postulated as a Confucian political norm. This line of thought provides insights for beneficial and benevolent relations among states, institutions and diverse actors, even when they have unequal power levels and different cultures, e.g., the PRC's relations with smaller states in Central Asia.

Chapter 3 by Rosita Dellios discusses "When Geopolitics Meets Development on the Belt and Road: A Confucian Journey." As China's Belt and Road Initiative (BRI) traverses the decade that began with a global pandemic, big infrastructure plans are not enough. The coronavirus pandemic, as in many sectors, has hastened the imperative for adaptive change. Development in its wider sense needs to be rediscovered. This is where Confucian philosophy can help. As with the BRI itself, there are in fact many routes and directions to development. In cultivating/developing ourselves and others, Confucius would concur that we can live harmoniously without being the same or privileging a more narrowly economic version of development. This change would amount to a culturally-infused political economy within the BRI, where infrastructures of the mind matter as much as the nuts and bolts of ports and transport links. More specifically, the BRI is well positioned to spread a different ontology of development at a time when a virus has forced the world into re-examining its old assumptions.

Chapter 4 by Katarzyna A. Nawrot proposes "New Directions in Theoretical Discussions, Empirical Research and Practical Cooperation for China-CEEC Cooperation in a Global Framework." The dialogue and cooperation between China and the Central and Eastern European countries (CEEC) have evolved significantly since the first China-Central Europe-Poland Economic Forum held in Warsaw on the 26th of April 2012. A decade after the beginning of the 16+1 formula of cooperation and of rejuvenation of the Silk Road, it seems crucial to assess the current state of the relations between China and the CEECs, as well as to make an attempt to identify and indicate possible future directions for practical cooperation and to highlight the relevant theoretical discussions and empirical research. First, an overview of the historical background and current directions of the relations between China and the CEECs will be presented. Furthermore, the institutional mechanisms of the bilateral and multilateral relations will be discussed as a crucial setting on which the cooperation is evolving. In particular, the evolution of trade patterns and the investment flows between China and the CEECs will be examined in the broader context of the EU and Europe. Finally, the possible new directions, dimensions, and fields of cooperation will be discussed for enhancing the relations between China and the Central and Eastern European countries.

Chapter 5 by Miguel D. Ramirez on "Marx's Theory of Value: A Sympathetic Yet Critical Perspective" critically analyzes the important notion of value or exchange-value from a Marxian perspective as opposed to a neoclassical one. It is argued that the value of a commodity is a historically determined social relation between producers, rather than a subjective relation between man and commodities á la Eugen von Böhm-Bawerk and Stanley Jevons. Value, in the Marxian scheme, tends to assume certain specific forms more often than others depending on the particular stage of economic history, reaching its fullest expression under capitalist production—the highest form of commodity production based on private property. In turn, exchange value—a quantitative relation--is the manner in which value expresses its character of being the product of social (abstract) labor. The chapter highlights the classical view of value as expounded by David Ricardo and focuses on how Marx develops and attempts to resolve key problems in Ricardo's labor theory of value. It is argued that Ricardo dealt not only with the problem of relative value but, like Marx, also grappled with the concept of positive (absolute) value. This work also reviews important challenges to Marx's theory of value, ranging from the role of the composition of aggregate demand in determining "socially necessary labor" to the issue of whether the transformation of labor values into prices of production is an unnecessary and irrelevant exercise. Finally, the chapter turns its attention to the economic role of time from a Marxian perspective as it relates to the determination of interest-bearing (loan) capital and Adam Smith's important distinction between productive and unproductive labor—one whose clear comprehension rests on viewing value as a social relation.

In Chapter 6, Katie Mills and Alexander C. Tan develop a theory about "Social Bases and the Political Economy of Development." Much has been said about the relationships among violence, policy, institutions and development. Are there social bases for development? What is the role of social bases for economic and political development? In this essay, they consider how social bases will constrain the ability to consolidate polities as well as to restrict regime choice options that may have implications and consequences for political and economic development. They also consider how ideological and social factors in the developed nation of the United States of America are perhaps changing or no longer serve to maintain the development of the country, threatening to undermine the state's stability and, therefore, economic growth. This underscores the extent to which development is not linear, even for so-called "developed" states. This essay fundamentally calls into question the use of the term "developed" in the discourse for the way in which it suggests the possibility for completing "development."

Chapter 7 by Marcus Bell on "The Color-Line and the Classroom: Racialized Space and the Making of Neoliberal Schools" examines the policies of the Brick City School District in Upstate New York. The BCSD has responded to student poverty in a number of ways. Similar to schooling in other neoliberal cities, the BCSD has prioritized elevating standardized test scores and improving skills, as opposed to combating poverty and reducing racial segregation. In recent years—and spanning the tenure of multiple school superintendents—the Brick City School District has begun a "renewed emphasis" on student achievement. The district has adopted what it terms an "all hands on deck" approach to closing the racial *and* economic achievement gaps. This "new" approach includes more money for technology, teachers and staff, corporate and nonprofit partnerships, and an ambiguous "commitment to innovation." Comparatively, there have been few district-wide efforts to combat, or even mitigate, the effects that concentrated poverty has on its student body. What is ignored is the hyper-segregation, concentrated poverty, and chronic joblessness that characterized the schools and the communities that housed them. This reflects a firm commitment to neoliberalism, a political and economic regime that elevates individualism, self-help, and market forces as preferable solutions to any number of institutional inequities. Unfortunately, the practice of crafting neoliberal solutions to neoliberal problems has become routine, ensuring that systemic, more comprehensive solutions to the racialization of space, racial segregation, and concentrated poverty are likely to remain elusive.

Chapter 8 by Charles Menifield and Cal Clark explores "Race and Influenza Deaths in the United States." In recent months, we have watched COVID-19 spread across the planet like an out-of-control tsunami. As the deaths mount, evidence suggests that minority communities have been hit harder by the virus in every respect. However, influenza type viruses are not new in the United States or other parts of the world. In fact, the Centers for Disease Control and Prevention estimated that influenza caused 34,000 deaths in the U.S. during the 2018-2019 season. While much of the literature examines the incidence of death from influenza from a medical perspective, this research takes a social science perspective with the goal of influencing public policy. The analysis addresses two important questions. Are certain states and regions of the U.S. more prone to deaths from influenza? Are non-whites more likely to die from influenza than whites? Our analysis demonstrates that certain U.S. states, regions, and racial groups are more likely to die from influenza than other groups.

In Chapter 9, Alfred G. Cuzan and Richard J. Heggen present "A Derivative-Based Model of U.S. Presidential Elections: 1880-2020," which explains electoral outcomes by whether government spending increased or decreased during the previous four-year administration. In particular, as a hike in the price of any good reduces the quantity purchased, we conjecture that as spending increases support for the incumbent party falls at the ballot box, thereby reducing its chances of re-election. A variety of analyses over the past forty years have strongly supported this hypothesis. In this chapter, we describe the core model, its variations, uses, and results, and then return to the original model to compare the effect of fiscal policy on American presidential elections between two periods, 1880-1980 and 1880-2020.

Chapter 10 by Nicholas Bolden examines "Workforce Development in the Age of COVID-19: Implications for Policymakers." Since the beginning of the 21st Century, America has been engaged in an ongoing attempt to overturn the effects of deindustrialization and a waning middle class with innovative policy strategies aimed at restoring America's workforce to its global position following the Cold War. Unfortunately, the 21st century has produced more educated citizens than previous decades but has turned out to be much less favorable than the industrial period for maintaining a viable middle class. In particular, the period of deindustrialization left many local economies victim to the impact of capital flight and unprepared to attract and retain jobs for their citizenry. Manufacturing jobs have declined more over the past two decades than during the Great Depression of the 1930s. This is especially harmful because manufacturing has a larger multiplier effect than any other economic sector. A more positive trend is building up with state and federal workforce development policy, however. Over the past decade, there has been a growing interest in work-based learning in the US. Through bi-partisan efforts, American states have embraced the need for modern workforce development strategies to mitigate the effects of capital flight and respond to the demands of 21st-century technological advancements. However, the novel COVID-19 virus introduced new complexities to modern workforce development efforts in the US.

REFERENCES

Clark, C, and K.C. Roy. 1997. *Comparing Development Patterns in Asia.* Boulder, CO: Lynne Rienner.

Florida, R. 2010. *The Great Reset: How the Post-Crash Economy Will Change the Way We Live and Work.* New York: Harper Collins.

Gerschenkron, A. 1962. *Economic Backwardness in Historical Perspective: A Book of Essays*, Cambridge: Harvard University Press.

In: Political Economy
Editors: Caleb M. Clark et al.
ISBN: 978-1-68507-106-6

Chapter 1

THE GREAT RESET AND THE 'BACK TO THE FUTURE' VISION OF PRESIDENT DONALD TRUMP

Caleb M. Clark[1,*] and Evelyn A. Clark Benavides[2]
[1]Department of Political Science, Auburn University, Auburn, AL, USA
[2]Department of Sociology, SUNY, Oswego, Oswego, NY, USA

ABSTRACT

In *The Great Reset*, Richard Florida defines Great Resets as "broad and fundamental transformations of the economic and social order that involve much more than economic or financial events." In this chapter, we expand Florida's model to give a much greater emphasis to politics and power and then argue that, while the Trump administration can be viewed as a response to America's ongoing Great Reset in the 21st century, its efficacy appears to be highly problematic, in large part because it represents a "Back to the Future" vision of where America should go. In particular, the Great Reset that has transformed the political economy of

* Corresponding Author's E-mail: clarkcm@auburn.edu

the United States after World War II is composed of a complex set of interacting economic, political, and social phenomena. Economic resets include: 1) the transformation of the economy from an industrial to an information-age one; 2) the communications and transportation revolutions that spurred globalization; 3) the *laissez-faire* international order after World War II; 4) the transformation of the impact of globalization from positive to negative on many aspects of the economy; 5) deindustrialization; 6) the changing nature of employment; 7) changing business philosophy; 8) the marginalization of labor; 9) slower economic growth; and 10) the Covid-19 crisis. Political and social resets include: 1) the replacement of Keynesianism by neoliberalism as the nation's public philosophy; 2) the rise of cultural issues in domestic politics; 3) the abjuring of large-scale government interventions in the economy, such as the GI Bill and Great Society Programs; 4) the "Great Risk Shift" in social insurance; 5) decline of educational system; 6) financialization of economy; 7) limited reduction in barriers facing marginalized members of society; 8) the escalating polarization of domestic politics; 9) escalating inequality; and 10) the creation and then decline of broad middle class. The Trump administration has had a mixed response to the threats and opportunities that these resets create for continuing and expanding the "American Dream." It has clearly tried to reverse: 1) globalization's changing impact on the American economy; 2) the changing nature of employment; 3) deindustrialization; 4) slower growth; 5) the changing fortunes of the middle class; 6) macroeconomic neoliberalism; 7) the role of public education; and 8) the negative impact of the Covid-19 crisis on the economy. In addition, it has accelerated: 1) the rise of cultural issues; 2) the polarization of American politics; 3) the barriers facing marginalized members of society; 4) the financialization of the U.S. economy; and 5) the marginalization of labor. In contrast, it has generally ignored: 1) the transformation from an industrial to an information-age economy; 2) the postwar communications and transportations revolutions; 3) the change in business philosophy; 4) direct government interventions, like the Great Society and G.I. Bill; 5) the Great Risk Shift; and 6) rapidly rising inequality.

Keywords: economic development, great reset, industrial age, information age, middle-class society, Trumponomics

INTRODUCTION

In *The Great Reset*, Richard Florida (2010: 2) defines Great Resets as:

> "broad and fundamental transformations of the economic and social order that involve much more than economic or financial events. A true reset transforms not simply the way we innovate and produce but also ushers in a whole new economic landscape."

Florida argued that the financial collapse of 2008-2009 constituted the third Great Reset in the United States during the century and a half following the Civil War, with the other two being the Depression during the 1870s and the Great Depression. Florida's analysis was optimistic since these other two resets ushered in prolonged periods of economic dynamism and transformation (Clark and Clark, 2020; Florida, 2010; Gordon, 2016). Indeed, Mancur Olson (1982) in *The Rise and Decline of Nations* developed a theory that Great Reset-like transformations (he did not use the term) created the conditions for economic success by destroying the institutional rigidities that economic elites had constructed to preserve their economic "rents" and self-interest. However, there is no guarantee that a depression will be followed by an economic resurgence, as the case of Japan illustrates (Koo, 2009).

This chapter extends Florida's analysis in two ways. First, it puts more emphasis on the political and social factors that are part of the Great Reset in the early 21st century; and second, it includes events over a longer time frame. In particular, it focuses the response of the administration of President Donald Trump to the challenges thrown up by this Great Reset. The first section provides an overview of the economic factors involved in America's changing political economy; the second focuses upon the political and economic dynamics; and the third analyzes the nature and efficacy of "Trumponomics."

THE ECONOMIC RESET IN POST-WORLD WAR II AMERICA

The Great Reset that has transformed the political economy of the United States after World War II is composed of a complex set of interacting economic, political, and social phenomena. Ten important economic resets can be discerned. First, the transformation of the economy from an industrial to an information-age one commenced in the 1980s and was well underway by the early 21st century. Second, the communications and transportation revolutions of the 1950s and 1960s spurred globalization. Third is the creation of a postwar *laissez-faire* global economic order. Fourth is the transformation of the impact of globalization from positive to negative on many aspects of the economy from the 1980s on. Fifth, deindustrialization started in the 1960s and has increasingly hurt the economy since the 1980s. Sixth, the changing nature of employment was another major shift that started in the 1960s and continues today. Seventh, a major change in business philosophy started in the 1970s and has clearly impacted economic outcomes since then. Eighth, labor became increasingly marginalized in the U.S. political economy from the 1970s-1980s on. Ninth, economic growth has slowed appreciably since the 1960s. Tenth, the Covid-19 crisis had a major negative impact on the economy in 2020.

A fundamental transformation in the U.S economy during the late 20th century was the emergence of what Alvin and Heidi Toffler (1980, 1995) have called the Third Wave of massive economic change. Following the first two waves of economic transformation in human history (the development of agriculture and the Industrial Revolution), the Third Wave encompasses a technological revolution which is creating an information-age society. One key component of this is the growing importance of what has been called "advanced manufacturing" (Drucker, 1989; Reich, 1991; Thurow, 1992, 1996). Advanced manufacturing and services require a much different type of employee than those who work in mass production. In contrast to the physical labor of mass production, advanced production requires discretion and innovation (mental work) even in physical work. Likewise, mass production is focused on individual work, while advanced production emphasizes collaborative teamwork. In mass production a specific technical expertise is usually sufficient, but advanced production relies on employees learning new skills periodically. Finally, mass production values a predictable workforce, while advanced production requires a highly flexible and learning one (Luke, Ventress, Reed, and Reed, 1988). In particular, two types of employees, who had previously been paid well, have been especially victimized by the transformations of information-age economies: 1) semiskilled industrial workers whose jobs migrated overseas and 2) middle managers who fell victim to the cutting away of bureaucratic layers in more decentralized management schemes (Gordon, 2016; Harrison, 1994; Smith, 2012). Thus, the evolution of the information-age had sharply contrasting effects, benefitting people with certain skills and educational credentials and limiting the opportunities for many others who lack them, including a growing number of professionals. For example, 40% of those 22–27-year-olds with a BA are underemployed, and many of them have enrolled in training programs for the skilled trades (Marcus, 2020).

In general globalization means that, over the second half of the twentieth century, much of the world has become substantially more interlinked in a variety of mutually reinforcing ways that have had profound consequences for economic performance, social stratification, and public policy. Globalization refers to growing economic interdependence (i.e., trade and capital flows, multinational corporations, transnational corporate alliances, and international networks in the making of specific products) across national borders that marked the late twentieth century. Two important causes for globalization should be distinguished. First, the transportation and communications revolutions of the second half of the century have made it possible to ship goods, funds, and information around the world cheaply and quickly (Gilpin, 1987; Greider, 1997; Thurow, 1992). By themselves, though, these technological changes would not have created an integrated global economy. Consequently, a second revolution was vital as well. This was that national borders have become much more porous to economic transactions as part of the U.S.-led effort to establish a free-trade global economy (Gilpin, 1987, 2001).

Globalization's impact on the U.S. has evolved very significantly over time. The dynamics of globalization played a central role in creating and sustaining America's golden age. During the 1950s and 1960s, globalization provided growing markets abroad for American exports, both manufactures and agricultural products; and U.S. MNCs found many lucrative sites for investment. America also became the financial center of the non-communist world which certainly created a more robust financial system. This led to growing profits for domestic businesses, rising wages for workers, and growing prosperity in many areas of the country. Indeed, many workers even achieved middle-class incomes and lifestyles (Bennett, 1996; Garfinkle, 2006; Thurow, 1992). The dynamics of globalization in regard to the United States changed dramatically during the 1970s, however. The rest of the developed world had recovered from their devastation during World War II, creating more intense competition for America, particularly from Japan and Germany. Furthermore, domestic corporations, starting in the 1960s, took advantage of the rapidly evolving international product cycle to move labor-intensive production to developing countries (Gilpin, 1987; Harrison, 1994; Reich, 1991).

A key component of growing economic and social stress was the deindustrialization of the U.S. economy. While it was not much noticed until the 1980s, deindustrialization can be traced back to the 1970s. For example, America's share of the world's manufacturing exports fell more than 25 percent in the 1970s (Bluestone, 1984). Beginning in the 1960s, American industry began moving some of its labor-intensive production offshore, primarily to East Asia with its much lower labor costs (Harrison and McMillan, 2011). High-paying manufacturing jobs were replaced by low-paying service ones; and a lack of retraining or adjustment programs resulted in downward mobility for a substantial number of Americans (Brill, 2018; Gordon, 2016; Greider, 1997; Reich, 1991; Rifkin, 1995; Thurow, 1996). The decline of manufacturing is well summarized by Duesterberg and Preeg (2003: 44):

> Manufacturing uses less and less of the economy's resources. Manufacturing's value-added in current dollars was 18.7% of the economy in 1987, 18.4% in 1989, and 15.9% in 2000. The same declining trend is apparent in gross output. Manufacturing gross output in current dollars was 34.6% of the economy in 1973 and rose to 35.4 percent in 1979 before falling to 29.2% in 1989 and 26.4% in 2000. Gross output in manufacturing is projected to continue to lose share over the next decade, falling to 24.9% in 2010.

These economic changes turn our attention to the shifting composition of the American workforce, which is reported in Table 1. Overall, agricultural workers probably faced the least favored conditions. Thus, the continuous drop in their share of employment from 46% in 1870 to 17% in 1940 to just 3% in 1970 represents a very positive trend. Blue collar workers constituted between 34% and 39% of the workforce throughout the century of 1870 to 1970. Their relative position improved dramatically in the 1950s and 1960s, as many attained middle-class wages and lifestyles. Thus, the fact that their share of the labor market was almost halved between 1970 and 2010, as it fell from 36% to 20%, clearly represents a major setback. White-collar jobs include clerical and many service occupations. They were probably better than blue-collar occupations until the postwar era and equivalent since then. Their share of the workforce grew steadily from 13% in 1870s to 38% in 1970 and 41% in 2010. Until recently, this was a positive trend. However, since both white-collar and blue-collar occupations have suffered in the transition to the information-age, the fact that in combination they now represent just over 60% of working Americans is not good news. Finally, managers and professionals occupy the elite positions in the American economy. Their share of the workforce increased slowly but steadily from 8% in 1870 to 15% in 1940. The managerial revolution of the 1950s and 1960s increased their numbers to 23%. Then the emerging information age created many more such jobs, as managers and professionals composed 38% of the workforce in 2010 (Gordon, 2016).

Table 1. Distribution of U.S. Workforce, 1870-2010 (in %)

	1870	**1910**	**1940**	**1970**	**2010**
Agriculture	46	31	17	3	1
Blue Collar	34	38	39	36	20
White Collar	13	20	28	38	41
Managers & Professionals	8	12	15	23	38

Source: Gordon. 2016. p. 255.

Another significant change in the economic environment was that business became much more aggressive and assertive in dealing with labor and government and much more interested in achieving greater flexibility, promoting cost minimization, and increasing the rewards ("incentives") of top management and investors starting in the 1970s. At that time, corporate America faced growing stress from several sources. First, the increasing international competition created financial stress. Second, union victories during the 1960s at the bargaining table generated fears starting in the early 1970s that business was under threat. Third, publicly held corporations were under intense pressure from Wall Street to maximize short-term profits. Fourth, the rapid escalation of healthcare costs that commenced in the 1980s threatened the bottom line of many businesses (Reich, 2015; Smith, 2012; Vogel, 1989, 1996). Furthermore, the nature of the business elite changed considerably. In the 1970s, conservative Sunbelt entrepreneurs, especially in the energy sector, became much more powerful (Sale 1975); and by the 1980s and 1990s, the "meritocratic" businesspeople, who were much more skillful, innovative, and energetic in pursuing their business goals than traditional business leaders, had reached top management positions (Brill, 2018). This represented a fundamental revolution in the corporate approach to labor relations. By the time the U.S. had reached the stage of advanced industrialization in the 1960s, many American corporations evidently viewed their workers as "human capital" whose skills and long-term loyalty were worth significant investments. Over the last several decades, in contrast, the dominant corporate strategy became what Harrison (1994) calls the "low road" of seeking competitiveness and increased profits by squeezing the work force through downsizing, pressure for enhanced productivity, holding the line on salaries, and so forth. This can be seen, for example, in the often cited statistic that CEO pay skyrocketed from 40 times the wages and salaries of the average employee in 1980 to almost 400 times in 2000 (Smith 2012: 110).

Starting in the early 1970s, economic growth in the U.S. has clearly decelerated as part of the normal process of economic evolution. For the last several centuries, economic development has been generally associated with industrialization or the transition from an economy based on agriculture and the work of artisans to one based on industry. In fact, through World War II the few countries that industrialized generally grew rich, while the rest of the world remained mired in massive poverty. The nature of industrialization, of course, changed dramatically over the 19th and 20th centuries in terms of what industry was the most advanced or technological driver. The Industrial Revolution started with light industries, such as textiles and shoes, moved forward to such heavy industries as iron and steel, then moved into mass production with automobiles and other consumer durables, and finally peaked with the high-tech industries and high quality industrial products. By the last third of the 20th century, post-industrial societies began to emerge in the developed world whose economies centered on services and the processing of information.

Figure 1 sketches an overview of how these changes in leading industry constitute an "S-curve" in terms of the rate of increase in productivity and GDP, where a steeper curve represents more rapid growth -- the curve in Figure 1 is viewed, at least by economists, as looking like an S. In traditional economies, productivity increases are relatively small, but productivity (and consequently GDP) growth "take off" (Rostow, 1960) once industrialization starts. However, the advantages of the most advanced industrial nations will eventually be undercut as they move beyond high tech industry to a postindustrial society whose economy is dominated by the service sector where productivity gains come much more slowly than in manufacturing (Gilpin, 2001; Kuznets, 1976; Rostow, 1960; Thurow, 1992; Toffler and Toffler, 1980, 1995).

The covid-19 crisis of 2020-2021 will almost certainly have a significant impact on the U.S. economy. As of late February 2021, three waves of Covid-19 had produced 21 million cases and 410,000 deaths in the United States. The first wave occurred in February and March in the Northeast, which was the primary entry point for infected people from Europe; the second in June as infected people in the Northeast spread out across the country; and the third in October due to the changing conditions brought by cold weather. This health crisis will have both short- and long-term effects on the economy which are generally negative. First, the increased unemployment resulting from the pandemic reduces consumer spending on which economic vitality depends in a postindustrial society. Second, the pandemic has accelerated businesses drive to replace employees with technology which extends the unemployment problem into the future. (COVIDUSA, 2021; Patton, 2020; Worldometer, 2021).

Figure 2 summarizes a model of how these ten factors interacted to produce a Great Reset in the economic realm. The most important drivers were globalization (which was stimulated by the postwar the technological revolutions in transportation and communications) and by the *laissez-faire* economy). Together, they forced the increasing deindustrialization of America. In turn, deindustrialization combined with the change in business philosophy to produce the changing nature of employment and the marginalization of labor, while the COVID-19 crisis accelerated some of the shifts in employment patterns as well. Finally, the growing importance of the postindustrial economy and deindustrialization resulted in a significant decline in the rate of growth in the United States.

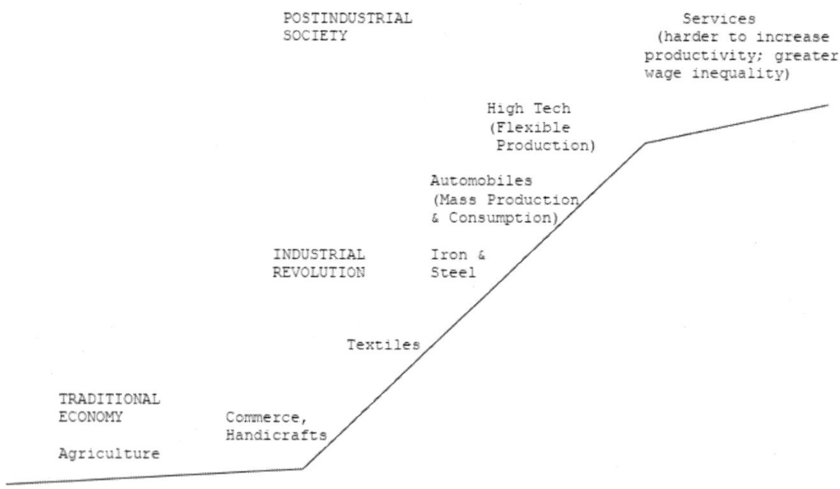

*Line signifies rate of annual GDP and productivity growth.

Figure 1. Changes in Leading Economic Activity and the "S-Curve" of Productivity and GNP Growth.

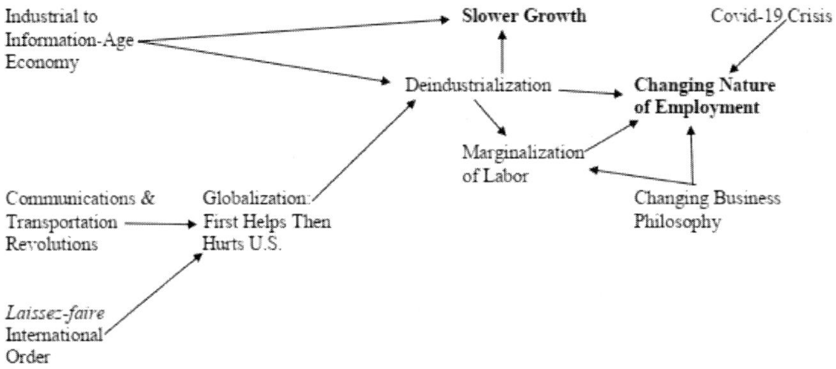

Figure 2. Economic Dynamics of Great Resets in the Post W.W. II United States.

THE POLITICAL AND SOCIAL RESETS IN POST-WORLD WAR II AMERICA

Ten important political and social resets also occurred to transform the politics of postwar America. First, the replacement of Keynesianism by neoliberalism as the country's public philosophy in the 1980s brought fundamental change to the nation's political economy, as did the second factor of the rise of cultural issues in domestic politics that started in the 1970s and has been intensifying since then. A third important political change has been the abjuring of large-scale government interventions in the economy, such as the WPA, GI Bill, and Great Society programs since the 1960s. Fourth, there also has been a "Great Risk Shift" in social insurance that started in the 1980s in which government and business have reduced their role considerably. Fifth, America's educational system has been declining since the 1960s. Sixth, the financialization of economy that started in the 1980s has had major effects as well. Seventh, only a limited reduction in barriers facing marginalized members of society can be discerned. The escalating polarization and gridlock in domestic politics has clearly altered the political dynamics in America. Finally, the postwar United States has been marked by declining then escalating inequality and by the creation and then decline of broad middle class.

An important political reset was the transformation of the nation's public philosophy from Keynesianism to neoliberalism in the 1980s. While Keynesianism is technically just the use of fiscal and monetary policy to narrow the swings in the business cycle, it is often used to denote an activist economic policy by the state (Clark and Clark, 2020). The New Deal ushered in a much more interventionist approach to managing the economy which continued in the post war era. One of the most dramatic examples was the GI Bill that was adopted near the end of World War II. As the end of the war came into sight, there were fears in the Roosevelt administration that the returning troops would flood the job market and create large-scale unemployment, as occurred after World War I. To avoid such a situation, the GI Bill provided support for veterans who wanted to attend college or purchase homes, which helped stimulate the postwar economic dynamism in two distinct ways. First, it contributed to the housing boom; and second, veterans taking advantage of the GI Bill created a huge surge in college enrollments. This turned out to be quite fortuitous because of the postwar managerial revolution which created a strong demand for more educated people for the rapidly expanding well-paid, white-collar jobs (Chandler, 1977). Overall, therefore, the GI Bill made an important contribution to the postwar economy and society (Bennett, 1996). The Great Society programs of the mid-1960s provide an even more sweeping illustration of governmental activism, albeit one that is much more controversial. These programs were initiated by President Lyndon Johnson and included the War on Poverty, expanded public support for public school education, the pre-school Head Start program, Medicare, Medicaid, urban renewal, the Job Corps, measures to produce racial equality, urban renewal, consumer product safety, measures to help depressed rural areas, public housing, measures designed to reduce inequality, anti-crime measures, and improving transportation. The extremely broad scope of these programs was likened by many to Roosevelt's New Deal; however, some showed few or even counterproductive results (Kaplan and Cuciti, 1986; Milkis and Mileur, 2005; Zeitz, 2018). For example, even many liberals now concede that the massive increases in both military and social spending along with a refusal to raise taxes of the Democratic Johnson administration (1963-68) set off an inflationary spiral that culminated in the "stagflation" (i.e., simultaneously high inflation and unemployment) of the 1970s which discredited the Keynesian approach (Garfinkle, 2006). The policies of the conservative Republican Reagan administration (1981-88) then ushered in an era of "neoliberalism" or the strong preference for market solutions over government intervention in the economy (Clark and Clark, 2020; Mirowski and Plehwe, 2009).

During most of the New Deal era in U.S. politics (i.e., the 1930s through the 1970s), political life was dominated by economic issues concerning the role of government and the distribution of resources in American society. This issue dimension had its roots in the Great Depression and focused upon the *Politics of Rich and Poor* (Phillips, 1990). At the time of the Great Depression and into the 1950s, these issues stimulated bitter partisan polarization between the advocates and opponents of Roosevelt's New Deal. Growing prosperity in the 1950s and 1960s gradually weakened their divisiveness, however. Starting in the 1980s, in contrast, new issues, such as abortion, crime, gay marriage, guns, immigration, race, and religious freedom arose which changed the nature of American politics dramatically by creating a new cleavage concerning social and cultural values developed that has become increasingly central to partisan conflict and competition. This second set of issues was rooted in the social upheaval of the 1960s and 1970s when the "traditional values" of American society came under increasing challenge by insurgent political and social groups trumpeting a "new morality" (Brewer and Stonecash, 2006; Frum, 2000; Hunter, 1991; Leege, Wald, Krueger, and Mueller, 2002).

Two other important resets represented a reversal of progress that had occurred during the first part of the postwar period. First, growing problems in education over the postwar era have hurt America. Until recently the United States was the undisputed world leader in education, which was widely credited as an important reason for its economic success (Thurow, 1992). Since the 1960's, the country's educational system clearly declined so that by the 1990s its pre-college education was only average at best for the developed world. The reasons for this were quite complex and include great inequalities among local education systems, decreasing student and parent interest in quality education, growing spending limits, and the resistance to reforms by teachers' unions (Buckley and Schneider, 2007; Kozol, 1991; Ravitch, 2010). Second, the rise of neoliberalism has been associated with an absence of governmental activism on economic matters for the last 40 years (Clark and Clark, 2020).

More indirectly, government policy contributed to what Jacob Hacker (2006) has called the "Great Risk Shift" in protecting individual Americans. The two central pillars of social insurance in the United States, pensions and health insurance, were based on a combination of public and private initiatives that, despite some conflict in the early stages, ultimately created an effective system that worked quite well in the early postwar era. The Social Security Act of 1935 established a mandatory publically run pension system; and over time business built a system of private pensions on top of it. The Social Security Act explicitly omitted health insurance because of fears that including it would doom Social Security, but in the postwar era business provided tax-subsidized health insurance for most employees. Then in 1965, the U.S. government inaugurated Medicare to provide health insurance for the elderly and Medicaid, a joint federal-state program, of health insurance for low-income people (Hacker, 2006; Skocpol, 2000).

For the first three decades of the postwar era this system worked tolerably well, but starting in the late 1970s it faced growing pressure which over time led to a very significant unraveling. Corporate America faced growing stress from several sources. The increasing international competition created financial stress; the accelerating decline in lifetime or long-term employees made private-sector pensions more questionable; and the rapid escalation of health care costs that commenced in the 1980s threatened the bottom line of many businesses. More subjectively, the tacit contract that companies offered their workers changed from one of shared fate to one of individual gain (Hacker, 2006; Smith, 2012; Vogel, 1989, 1996). In the public sphere, the change was even more dramatic and perhaps more than a little unexpected since the growing insecurity of the late 20th and early 21st century would have seemingly called for more, not less, social insurance. However, increasing budget deficits, rising medical expenses, and the growth of structural (as opposed to cyclical) unemployment all pushed a conservative drive to cut the size and scope of government (Hacker, 2006).

Another growing problem of the last four decades is that deregulation of the financial sector by both the Republican Reagan administration in the 1980s and the Democratic Clinton administration in the 1990s led to two major crises. First, the "casino capitalism" of the 1980s in which speculation and financial games (e.g., leveraged buy outs, junk bonds, insider trading in stocks, and the $300-$500 billion Savings & Loan collapse) seemingly replaced production as the best way to make money in America (Burrough and Helyar, 1990; Foroohar, 2016; Greider, 1997; Lewis, 1989; Mayer, 1990; Miller, 1989). Second, in the early 21st century, the financial sector engaged in increasingly risky speculation that ultimately precipitated the financial collapse of 2008 which, in turn, caused massive dislocations both in the U.S. and globally. These speculative activities, while enormously profitable in the short run, became increasingly risky and almost sure to fail over the longer term. One was the increasing use of "derivatives" (securities based on some other security). A second practice was that subprime housing loans to people who ordinarily would not qualify for them assumed an unimaginably central role in the financial system. These were bundled into securities by the loan originators (who received large fees and were able to get them off their books) and were in high demand by Wall Street investment banks who were, ironically, both able to camouflage the risk to a considerable extent and to make the higher rate of return on these securities very attractive to investors. However, when the subprime market began to unravel in 2007, a panic soon developed over anything tied to mortgage-based securities, leading to the collapse of Bear Stearns and Lehman Brothers in 2008 which, in turn, set off the financial collapse and the Great Recession (Brill, 2018; Foroohar, 2016; McLean and Nocera, 2010; Philippon, 2012; Reich, 2015; Sorkin, 2009; Smith, 2012; Stiglitz, 2010). Finally, this "financialization" brought a reduction in business investment and research and development, despite the normal function of the financial sector to promote business activity and growth. Instead, by the early 21st century financialization had produced what might be termed the "tyranny of stockholder value and short-term stock prices." It was estimated, for example, that only 15% of investment went to support economic activities, as opposed to 85% for the "financial engineering" of enhancing stock prices. Thus, Wall Street pressured corporations to reduce payrolls and R & D spending in order to improve their bottom lines. For example, privately held companies invest twice as much as publicly held ones. Relatedly, many corporations bought back their stock in order to increase share value by reducing the total number of shares. To do this, many relied on borrowing the necessary funds, thereby increasing corporate debt (Brill, 2018; Day, 2019; Foroohar, 2016).

The rise of cultural issues discussed above was associated with the polarization of American politics. These new issues are much more directly caught up in the cultural identity of people and groups. Therefore, their growing salience in American politics has resulted in the rise of the highly emotional symbolic politics associated with conflicts over basic identity. Significant minorities take polar-opposite positions, refuse even to consider compromise, and are constantly on the lookout for new issues. For example, prochoice and prolife groups on abortion became mobilized, respectively, for and against stem cell research. This results in issues being presented as highly symbolic ones on which compromise is impossible (Edelman, 1985; Hunter, 1991; Leege, Wald, Krueger, and Mueller, 2002). Because the partisan balance in the U.S. has been fairly even for almost half a century, this has also resulted in a growing gridlock in policymaking (Abramowitz, 2011; Brewer and Stonecash, 2006; Brownstein, 2007).

The postwar era has also witnessed a radical reversal in the trend of income inequality over time (Bartels, 2008; Gordon, 2016; Hacker and Pierson, 2010; Harrison and Bluestone, 1988; Phillips, 1990; Smith, 2012). Figure 3 provides a long-term perspective by charting the share of income going to the top one percent and half of a percent of Americans from 1913 to the present. Income inequality peaked in the Roaring 1920s, when the top 1% astoundingly received slightly over half of all income in the United States. It then declined steadily for half a century. By the start of the postwar era in the early 1950s, the share of the top 1% had dropped by a half to approximated 30%; and it continued to decline by another third over the next quarter of a century, as America became the first nation to develop a broad middle class that encompassed the majority of its citizens. However, the concentration of wealth jumped precipitously to more than 40% over the next quarter century. Escalating inequality, in turn, brought with it a sharp diminishment of the middle class.

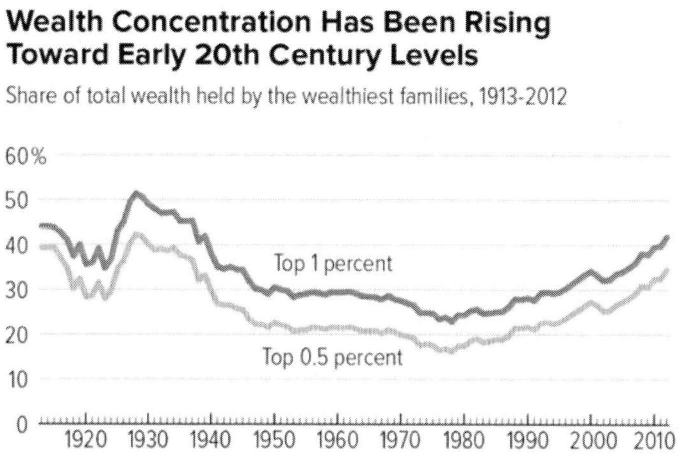

Source: Saez and Zucman, May 2016.

Figure 3. Changing Wealth Concentration in United States.

Moreover, the barriers facing marginalized members of American society remained daunting throughout the postwar era. Gender and racial inequality continued to skyrocket, with wage inequality remaining high and with a low level of raises and promotions for workers of color and women compared to white men, even controlling for education, skills, years on the job, and productivity. For example, the benefits from the G.I. Bill were much more likely to be granted to white veterans, whereas veterans of color faced strict restrictions on education and housing (Lui, Robles, Leondar-Wright, Brewer, and Adamson, 2006). Consequently, as both women and workers of color increased their participation in the workforce, they had only limited opportunities to support a middle-class lifestyle (Johnston, 2015; Pager and Shepherd, 2008; Pager, Western, and Bonikowski, 2009).

Figure 4 presents a model of how the factors included in this section interacted. The two initial causal features are the transformation of Keynesianism to neoliberalism as Americas' dominant public philosophy and the growing importance of cultural issues in domestic politics. The former brought financialization, the Great Risk Shift, the abjuring of governmental activism, and the decline in education, while the latter stimulated the sharp increase in political polarization and gridlock, the very limited reduction in the barriers facing marginalized sectors of society, and the decline of public education (the last of which helped prevent marginalized groups from improving their situation). All of these second-stage factors, along with the changing nature of employment discussed in the last section, then contributed to growing inequality and the decline of the middle class.

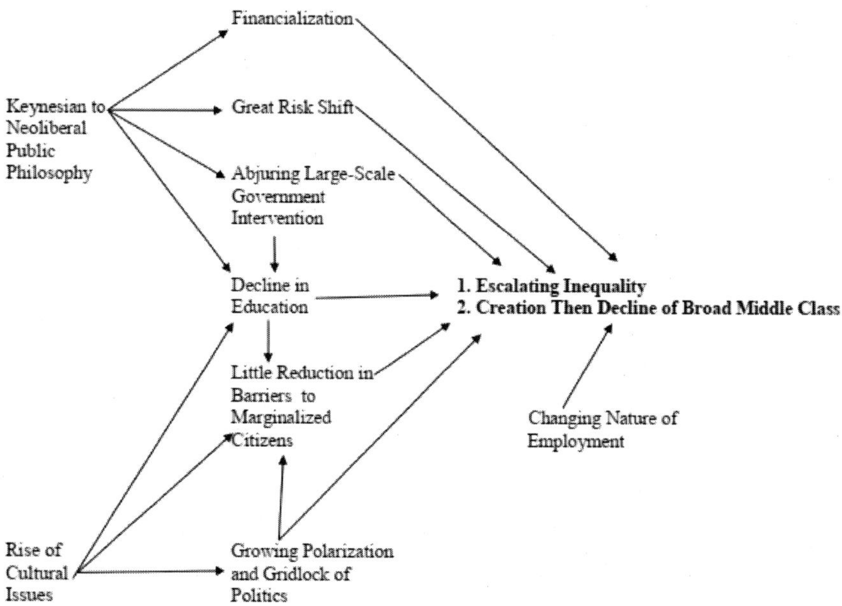

Figure 4. Political and Social Dynamics of Post W.W. II Great Resets in the United States.

TRUMPONOMICS AS A RESPONSE TO THE GREAT RESET

Donald Trump won the presidency in 2016 by promising to Make America Great Again (MAGA). He clearly recognized that economic and social change had undercut the lives of many Americans and that neither major party (Democrats or Republicans) had made much of an effort to counteract these negative trends. The Republicans' commitment to neoliberalism and globalization meant that they did not even consider this a problem, while the Democrats focused primarily on expanding social welfare programs (Brewer and Stonecash, 2006). Trump ran for President of the United States in 2016 as a Republican on a platform that included a strong appeal to the white working class. He promised to use the power of government to overturn the forces of globalization to bring "good jobs" back to the U.S. and restore prosperity to the victims of globalization and neoliberalism. Indeed, this group pushed him to victory in the key Midwestern states that were pivotal in his presidential victory (Cillizza, 2016; Edsall, 2017; Jones, 2017; Long 2017a, 2017b; Sides, Tesler, and Vavreck, 2018). Trump was, in fact, the only presidential candidate who has promised "good jobs" to the less educated and less skilled who have lost out to the processes of deindustrialization over the last four decades. Indeed, the term "Trumponomics" was soon coined to describe his distinctive, if not unique, economic strategy. This section, hence, analyzes how well Trumponomics has responded to the Great American Reset of the 21st century.

Table 2 summarizes how the Trump administration attacked the 20 challenges discussed in the first two sections. The three columns in the table contain the problem, the administration's position, and the overall effect so far. The first 16 are related to the traditional Republican support for free-market capitalism. Here, Trump's response was rather muddy about neoliberalism as he accepted some of its principals and rejected others. On the one hand, he rejected a *laissez-faire* world order, believed that globalization was hurting America, decried deindustrialization, promised to reverse the decline of the middle class, and argued that his MAGA policies would increase America's economic performance considerably. On the other hand, he simultaneously championed some aspects of global capitalism and neoliberalism, such as the changing business philosophy, financialization, the privatization of education, and rising inequality He also ignored the rise of the information age, the communications and transportation revolutions, the changing nature of work, and the barriers facing marginalized Americans. As a result, his strategy was highly ambiguous about government's role in the economy as he advocated an activist government in some areas and condemned it in others.

Table 2. Trump Administration's Responses to Challenges of Great Resets

Challenge	Trump Response	Effect
Free-Trade Capitalism		
Rise of Neoliberalism	Ambiguous	Not Much Effect
Laissez-faire Global Order	Opposes	Some Success
Rise of Information Age	Ignores	No Progress
Communications & Transportation Revolutions	Ignores	Problems Worse
Globalization Hurts US	Supports	Not Much Effect
Deindustrialization	Opposes	Not Much Effect
Changing Nature of Work	Ignores	Not Much Effect
Abjuring Govt. Intervention	Ambiguous	Enhances
Changing Bus. Philosophy	Promotes	Not Much Effect
Financialization	Promotes	Not Much Effect
Decline in Education	Promotes	Enhances
Barriers to Marginalized Citizens	Ambiguous	Enhances
Rising Inequality	Promotes	Enhances
Decline of Middle Class	Opposes	Situation Worsens
Slower Growth	Opposes	Positive Until COVID Crisis
Political Transformations		
Rise of Cultural Issues	Promotes	Enhances
Political Polarization & Gridlock	Promotes	Enhances
Great Risk Shift	Ignores	Enhances
COVID-19	Downplays	Somewhat Negative

Trumponomics includes a variety of initiatives to provide more jobs in manufacturing and other fields for low- and medium-skilled workers. The most fundamental was Trump's commitment to use protectionist measures to revive manufacturing, which sharply challenged the traditional Republican support of free trade and free markets. Donald Trump, as both a candidate and the President, has strongly rejected neoliberalism's advocacy of free trade and capital flows throughout the global economy. Instead, he views international economics as a competition among nations, whose outcomes are shaped by the "deals" that they make with each other and promised that he would use the U.S.'s economic and political power to force concessions from other countries. Examples of this include his withdrawal from the nascent Trans-Pacific Partnership (TPP), renegotiation of NAFTA to benefit several American industries, employing tariffs and the threat of tariffs in a fairly wide variety of instances and calling himself "Tariff Man." In doing so, he has roundly been criticized by many economists, businesspeople, and Republicans.

While Trump immediately removed American from the emerging Trans-Pacific Partnership and sounded quite aggressive, his actual economic nationalism remained fairly restrained through his first year in office. However, in the first half of 2018, he began announcing tariffs that threatened to set off a trade war with China and perhaps several other countries. The first tariffs were structured to help revive the steel and aluminum industries and were popular with workers in steelmaking and mining regions. Conversely, they raised fears and opposition in the sectors that used these products, such as automobiles, or were the targets of foreign retaliation. These were followed by broad-ranging and expanding tariffs on Chinese products aimed at forcing China to make concessions in its economic behavior. By late 2020, little progress had been made; and both sides seem to have concluded that nothing dramatic would occur until after the 2020 presidential election. The trade war with China has had a very wide impact on America. For example, Chinese cuts in the purchase of U.S. agricultural goods hurt U.S. farmers considerably -- which led Trump to provide aid in the form of farm subsidies (Abbott, 2019; Borak, 2018, 2019a; Brownstein, 2018 Douma, 2017; Graham, 2018; Henney, 2019; Kirby, 2018; Palmer, 2018; Shih and Telford, 2019; Smith, 2018; Teleford, Paletta, and Lynch, 2019; Tesfaye, 2018; Warner, 2018). The growing ripples of the trade war have even led Fareed Zakaria (2019) to conclude that "Trump's trade strategy has turned into a politicized wrecking ball." For example, China's much quicker economic rebound from the COVID crisis in comparison to America's reinforced the conclusions of some analysts that it may be winning the trade war (*Bloomberg Business Week*, 2021; Haas and Denmark, 2020; He, 2021).

The next two issues concerning the promotion of manufacturing also diverge greatly from Republican orthodoxy. One is Trump's personal and public jawboning of CEOs to maintain and bring back working-class jobs, which is certainly inconsistent with Republicans' normally business-friendly position (Graham, 2016; Kiley, 2019). In addition, Trump's proposal to spend $1 trillion on restoring America's infrastructure was opposed by many Republicans because of their traditional concerns about government spending and the national debt. Later, he sought to promote a primarily privately funded infrastructure program with little success. In the Spring of 2019, he seemingly was moving toward an agreement with Democrats for a $2 trillion infrastructure upgrade, but this was soon derailed by partisan fighting over other economic and budgetary issues (Campbell, 2017; Kettl, 2018; Snyder and Cook, 2019; Zanona, 2017).

Trump's crackdown on immigration was partially justified by the need to create more jobs for Americans, although it was primarily justified by national security considerations and definitely appealed to those who believe that America is undergoing disastrous cultural change. In contrast to the other issues in this group, this represents a growing Republican position. Once elected, Donald Trump made this a high priority in his administration, being quite forceful and implementing a much more restrictive policy regime. He has continued to denounce immigrants in extremely harsh and controversial terms, devoted substantial resources to border security, led the Bureau of Immigration and Customs Enforcement to become more aggressive, barred immigration from specific countries, instituted a "family separation" policy that took children away from their parents, curbed legal immigration, sought to deport illegal immigrants who came to the United States as children (the so-called Dreamers), increasingly cracked down on asylum seekers, and advocated, with only partial success, the building of a wall along the entire length of the U.S.-Mexican border (Ainsley, 2017; Amadeo, 2019b; Foer, 2018; Graham, 2016, 2018; Hurley, 2019; Kopan, 2018; McCarthy, 2017; Pierce, Bolter, and Steele, 2018; Pierce and Sellee,

2017; *The Economist*, 2018). Somewhat ironically, Trump has America following the lead of Europe, which is generally despised by U.S. conservatives, in which politicians push strong immigration restrictions in order to appeal to the working-class victims of globalization (Chua, 2002; Sassen, 2005).

Many components of Trumponomics, in direct contrast, are quite consistent with the tenets of neoliberalism and globalization. First, massive tax cuts for business and the wealthy, according to their advocates, should produce more resources for savings and investment in what is called "supply-side economics" (Nunns, Burman, Rohaly, and Rosenburg, 2016; Rozsa, 2017). Indeed, perhaps the biggest legislative success of the Trump administration was the Tax Cuts and Jobs Act of December 2017 which reduced the corporate tax rate from 35% to 21%, doubled the minimum amount of estates that are taxed, and cut many individual tax rates (Cohen and Cohen, 2018). Despite the massive changes included in the Act, two studies by the Congressional Research Service and International Monetary Fund in the summer of 2019 found that its economic impact during 2018 was surprisingly small. The effective tax rate (what they actually paid) for corporations was cut in half from 24% to 12%. Yet, the estimated contribution that this made to economic growth in 2018 was only 0.3% out of 2.9%; and the estimated contribution to investment growth was also fairly marginal. Also, U.S. companies spent $1 trillion on stock buybacks, which raise stock prices by reducing the amount of stock in circulation rather than by improving corporate performance (Cox, 2019; Scott, 2019; Smith, 2019).

Second, Republicans argue that deregulation should free business to operate more efficiently and, in particular, create more jobs in the energy sectors, such as coal (as opposed to President Obama's "War on Coal") (Horsley, 2017; Johnson and Mui, 2017; Pisani, 2017). President Trump promised business that his administration would activate a massive deregulation program and stated the goals of abolishing two regulations for every new one that was adopted and of scrapping 70% of regulations on business (Belsie, 2018; Horsley, 2017; Johnson and Mui, 2017; Klein, 2018; Pisani, 2017). This clearly has been a central thrust of his administration. In terms of the ratio of abolished to adopted regulations, he exceeded expectations, as the ratios were 22 to 1 in 2017 and 12 to 1 in 2018. The deregulation campaign was concentrated on seven federal agencies: the Environmental Protection Agency, the Department of Education, the Department of Health and Human Services, the Department of the Interior, the Department of Labor, the Department of Agriculture, and the Department of Transportation. More recently, the administration gave greater scrutiny to the Federal Reserve, the Federal Election Commission, the Consumer Product Safety Commission, the Security and Exchange Commission, and the Futures Trading Commission. Also, several agencies have radically changed their behavior during the Trump administration. For example, the Consumer Financial Protection Bureau cut its enforcement actions in half during Trump's first two years in office compared to the Obama era. The deregulation realm has not been entirely rosy for the President, however. The administration has lost about 90% of the court challenges it faced in this area; and the fact that the Federal Aviation Agency streamlined the approval of the Boeing 737 Max 8, which was subsequently grounded after two major crashes, was not exactly a ringing endorsement of the deregulation campaign (Brookings, 2019; *Conservapedia*, 2019; Garland, 2019; Graham and Belton, 2019; Hunter, 2017; Jones, 2018; Stole, 2019; Wolf, 2019).

Third, neoliberals urge government support for the financial sector since it provides the resources for business expansion and economic growth. In America, for example, the financial sector almost doubled in size from 5% to 9% of GDP between 1980 and 2010. America's large financial institutions (Wall Street) reached the brink of ruin over the first decade of the 21st century by engaging in increasingly speculative activities that, while enormously profitable in the short run, became increasingly risky and almost sure to fail over the longer term (McLean and Nocera, 2010; Paletta, 2019; Philippon, 2012; Reich, 2015; Smith, 2012; Sorkin, 2009; Stiglitz, 2010). Candidate Trump promised to reduce the regulation of the finance industry (Hohmann, 2017; Zeleny and Murray, 2017). Once in office, he then pursued this agenda aggressively. The highpoint of this campaigned was the passage of the Economic Growth, Regulatory Relief, and Consumer Protection Act of 2018; and actions against corporations by the Security and Exchange

Commission have dropped very precipitously during the Trump administration. The President has even advocated repealing the requirement that public corporations issue quarterly reports (Garofalo, 2018; Lebovitch and Said, 2019; Valladares, 2019).

Fourth, neoliberals advocate transferring resources from the public to the private sector to increase economic efficiency by privatizing government services. Here, the Trump administration has been quite active, but at least so far, the results are fairly mixed. Perhaps, Trump's most broad-reaching initiative was his proposal to privatize the U.S Postal Service, but this attempt was killed by bipartisan opposition in Congress. Also, his proposals for a primarily private-invested infrastructure upgrade and for selling off a variety of federal assets including Dulles and Reagan Airports were largely unsuccessful. Still, Trump has increased the share of private care in the services provided by the Department of Veterans' Affairs from 22% in 2014 to 36% in 2018, with an ultimate goal of 54%. The Trump administration has actively supported using more public resources to help private schools, opening land on Public Monuments for private economic activities, and reversing Obama's policy of deprivatizing the federal prison system, as well as indicating its intention to privatize Fannie Mae and Freddie Mac (Arnsdorf, 2018; Carroll, 2017; DePillis, 2018; Dominguez, 2019; Guerin, 2019; Katz, 2018; Strauss, 2017; Weber, 2018).

Fifth, neoliberals demand substantial cuts in the budget for domestic spending and a general downsizing of government in order to create more resources for productive investments. With a few exceptions, such as his initial support of Social Security and Medicare, President Trump has enthusiastically supported this agenda. The Trump administration has certainly lived up to the neoliberal dictum for cutting government spending with substantial budget and personnel cuts outside the security realm and repeated attacks on the "deep administrative state." For example, by the end of the 2016-2017 fiscal year, all the cabinet agencies except the Departments of Homeland Security, Veterans' Affairs, and Interior had lost fulltime staff positions. Trump appeared to double down on downsizing as he entered the second half of his first term in 2019. First, he proposed to abolish the Office of Personnel Management by transferring its various functions to the

General Services Administration, the Office of Management and Budget, and the Department of Defense, making it the first major federal agency to be abolished since World War II, and then threatened furloughs and layoffs in OPM if Congress failed to adopt this plan. Second, he ordered a one-third cut in advisory committees. Third, his budget for the 2019-2029 fiscal year projected a 25% cut in discretionary domestic spending for the decade of 2019-2029. Fourth, the Department of Agriculture announced that it was moving most of the employees in its Economic Research Service and National Institute of Food and Agriculture from Washington, D.C. to Kansas City, which was expected to result in massive resignations (Bach, 2019; Blitzer, 2019; Brownstein, 2017; Clark, 2017; Drum, 2019; Edwards, 2019; Goldshan, 2019; Hardy, 2019; Liptak, 2017; Matthews 2018; McCausland, 2019; Price, 2019; Rein and Tran, 2017; Rucker and Costa, 2017; Scholtes, 2019).

Sixth, Republicans and trade unions have long had a mutually antagonistic relationship, with the former arguing that reducing the power of trade unions should allow corporations to operate more efficiently and profitably. Donald Trump's commitment to courting the white working class might have created some strains here, but so far at least he has seemed successful in representing himself as a champion of working men and women while continuing traditional Republican policies. For their part, the leadership of labor unions has tried to survive in a "delicate dance" with the President. In the area of labor relations, the Trump administration has been active in curtailing the power of unions but also jawbones CEOs to keep or create blue-collar jobs. Furthermore, President Trump also has shown little, if any, concern about business's "low road" strategy for treating their employees. For example, many corporations are now contracting out a significant number of functions to temp firms with very low wages to get around commitments to unionized workers and other permanent employees (Alemany, 2017; Brown, 2019; Marvit, 2019; Porter, 2017; Walter, 2018).

Seventh, candidate Trump strongly endorsed the Republic demands for increased military spending. While this is not an economic policy per se, it should help the economy through huge defense procurements and increased economic activities in communities near military bases. Trump's administration has implemented a steady increase in total military spending, which includes both the Defense Department and other agencies involved in national security. This rose by 30% between the last full fiscal-year Obama budget (2015-2016) of $768 billion to the Trump budget for the 2019-2220 fiscal year of $989 billion. President Trump has consistently praised and supported the armed forces, culminating in his designing the nation's 2019 4th of July event to honor the military. It's not surprising, consequently that veterans are much more supportive of the President than the general public is (Amadeo, 2019b; Barria, 2017; Berman, 2017; Buford, 2018; Frum, 2017; Hakim and Wee, 2017; Horsley, 2017; Igielnik, Parker, and Cilluffo, 2019; Johnson and Mui, 2017; Miller and O'Hanlon, 2019; Mullen, Isidore, and Todd, 2017; Nunns, Burman, Rohaly, and Rosenburg, 2016; Pisani, 2017; Rozsa, 2017; Seligman, 2019; Shafer and Claggett, 1995; Superville, 2019; Venook, 2017).

Eighth, as both candidate and President, Donald Trump strongly advocated repealing and replacing President Obama's Affordable Care Act. This would result, according to neoliberals, in decreased government spending on health, cut overall health care costs by increasing market competition, and increase personal freedom of choice. The ACA or Obamacare to Republicans has three important components. First, it provided insurance coverage to about half the people who were uninsured before its implementation; second it mandated reforms by health insurance companies in how they treat their clients that included preventing them from not offering insurance to those with "pre-existing health conditions" and ending annual and lifetime limits on payouts; and third it expanded Medicaid to provide some of the coverage, although the Supreme Court ruled that states could opt in or out of expanded Medicaid. Currently, 14 states have not adopted expanded Medicaid.

Donald Trump made the repeal and replacement of Obamacare one of his highest priorities. His first Executive Order on his first day in office directed the Department of Health and Human Services to waive any parts of the ACA that "impose a fiscal burden on individuals or states." One of his highest priorities was to have the Republican Congress pass legislation that would repeal and replace the ACA. However, the Republican Congress was never able to succeed in this endeavor, much to the President's frustration. Trump did succeed in including a provision in the December 2017 Tax Cut Act that eliminated the "individual mandate" that people who did not buy health insurance would be assessed a penalty on their taxes. This created a financial problem because the people who continued to buy insurance tended to be those with significant medical conditions. More indirectly, this led to a serious challenge to the entire ACA in 2018 when a federal District judge in Texas ruled that the abolition of the individual mandated invalidated the entire Act; and in the Spring of 2019 President Trump ordered the Department of Justice to oppose the appeal of this decision to the Circuit Court. Finally, in June 2020, Trump demanded that the DOJ support repealing all of the ACA despite concerns raised by administration officials and Republicans in Congress (Alonso-Saldivar and Sherman, 2020; Cesca, 2019; Hiltzik, 2019; Kaiser Family Foundation, 2019; Kamal, Cox, Fehr, Ramirez, Horstman, and Levitt, 2018; Shaw, 2017).

Ninth, neoliberals believe that private education should be emphasized because it is more effective and gives parents freedom of choice. Also, by the second decade of the 21st century, it had become a significant investment opportunity. The new President signaled his active support for using more public resources to help private schools by appointing Betsy DeVos, who had long been an ardent promoter of private charter schools. DeVos certainly lived up to her reputation in pushing for transferring more resources to private schools, reversed the Department's support for civil rights and student protections, and refused to enforce the Borrower Debt Repayment rule which the Obama administration had enacted to help students at for-profit universities that had misled their applicants (Carroll, 2017; Faux, 2012; Leonard and Nasiripour, 2019; Lobosco, 2019; Strauss, 2017).

Finally, neoliberals contend that monetary policy should be favored over fiscal policy for stabilizing the economy because the latter involves inefficient subsidies during recessions that are politically hard to end when the economy improves. At least superficially, this is true because Trump definitely has a monetary policy, while he is silent on applying a fiscal stimulus. However, this should be taken with the caveats provided by the two issues on which the President breaks with Republican orthodoxy. First, while Republican policy is generally associated with tight money and high interest rates because they are presumed to benefit the financial sector, Trump pressured the Federal Reserve to keep interest rates low because, in actuality, Wall Street and business prefer low interest rates to provide more liquidity (Harrison, 2019). The last policy of stimulating the economy by running up the national debt is termed "implicit" because it reflects a strategy which has not been claimed by the Trump -- increasing government spending to make more resources available in the society and economy. This is a Keynesian countercyclical policy to get a country out of a recession that is largely anathema to Republicans. Still, the Trump administration increased the national government's deficit in 2017 by 13% over the last year of Obama's presidency; and his tax cuts and omnibus budget acts in December 2017 and March 2018 both mandated much larger deficit spending (Buford, 2018; C. Jones, 2018, 2019). For example, the budget deficit for the first three quarters of the 2019 fiscal year was 23% or $140 billion dollars greater than the same period in the previous fiscal year; and the national debt is projected to rise from 78% of GDP in 2017 to 92% in 2029, to 144% in 2049. Finally, in July 2019 Trump reached an agreement with congressional leaders that would eliminate the caps on spending that had been imposed in 2011 and suspend the debt ceiling until mid-2021, thereby almost insuring a massive jump in the federal deficit (Amadeo, 2019a; Borak, 2019b, 2019c; Mattingly and Zeleny, 2019).

Turning to the effects of Trumponomics, the aggregate performance of the American economy was quite good during the first three years of the Trump administration before the devastation of the COVID-19 pandemic in 2020, as demonstrated by the data on the U.S.'s economic growth, unemployment rate, and the value of the Dow Jones stock-market index in Table 1.3. America's performance on economic growth and unemployment during 2017-2019 is part of a long-term recovery from the Great Recession of 2008-2010. Still, the economic record in the first half of the Trump era has clearly been significantly better than during the second Obama administration. The overall growth rate of 2.5% during Trump's first three years in office was considerably higher than the approximately 2.0% growth of Obama's second term. Similarly, at the time of Trump's presidential victory (November 2016), unemployment stood at 4.6% (down from 6.9% three years earlier), while by April 2018 it had decreased significantly to 3.5%, the lowest level since 1969. Furthermore, the stock-market boom during the first half of Trump administration was clearly an atypically spectacular performance. Between November 2013 and November 2016, the stock market climbed 2,600 points from 15,594 to 18,200. Over just the following 12 months, though, it jumped just over 5,000 to 23,584 before stabilizing in the 25,000 – 27,000 range. Indeed, the Republicans trumpeted this good economic news as a validation of Trump's presidency and economic strategy (Kopan, 2018).

Table 3. Economic Indicators for Trumponomics

	Annual Economic Growth	**Unemployment Rate (Nov)**	**Dow Jones Stock Index (Nov 7)**
2019	2.3	3.5	27,492
2018	2.9	3.7	26,180
2017	2.2	4.1	23,548
2016	1.5	4.6	18,260
2015	2.9	5.0	17,910
2014	2.2	5.8	17,554
2013	1.7	6.9	15,594

*April 1, 2019.

Sources: NASDAQ. 2019. Solberg. 2020. *Statistica*. 2019. U.S. Bureau of Labor Statistics. 2019.

President Trump's responses to the other 15 challenges in this category are, surprisingly, more ambiguous for several reasons. First, he basically ignored three of them, the rise of the information age, the communications and transportation revolutions, and the changing nature of work. Consequently, there ill effects on American society have probably intensified a little. Second, his policies to reverse globalization's negative impact on the U.S., the *laissez-faire* global order, deindustrialization, and the declining middle class have yet to improve the situation in America noticeably. Third, he promoted several of the challenging trends, including the changing business philosophy, financialization, the decline of education, and the barriers to marginalized Americans. Here, the effects varied somewhat from little to clearly enhanced. Finally, his opposition to neoliberalism and promise to use an activist government have been ambiguous because his administration has acted both consistently and inconsistently with these principles.

The other four issues included in Table 2 concern political challenges that faced the incoming Trump administration. As indicated in the second section, the rise of cultural issues and the growing polarization and gridlock of the political system in the United States long predated the Trump campaign for President; or in the words of Alec Tyson (2018b), "America's Polarized Views of Trump Follow Years of Growing Political Partisanship." However, Trump during both the campaign and his term in office strongly emphasized cultural issues and divisiveness. This is at least partially explicable by the fact that in the 2016 election cultural issues were considerably more important than economic ones in stimulating support for Trump at the polls (Clark and Clark, 2020; Sides, Tesler, and Vavreck, 2018). For example, recent political science research indicates that the President may be correct in this strategy. Republican voters respond more to cultural issues than to economic ones, while the reverse is true for Democrats; a quarter of Democrats are closer to Republicans than to other Democrats on cultural and a quarter of Republicans are closer to Democrats than to other Republicans on economic issues (Bartels, 2018). In addition, Trump's emphasis on preserving conservative social and religious values probably account for his improvement in support among Latinos as opposed to Mitt Romney, the Republican who lost the 2012 presidential election (Caputo, 2020). Overall, therefore, political polarization primarily based upon an intensification of the culture wars in America seemed to have peaked late in the Trump administration (Bacon, 2019; Bump, 2019; Caputo, 2020, Cillizza, 2020; Klar, 2020; Liasson, 2020; Tyson, 2018a, 2018b).

Another source of stress on the working and middle classes is the *Great Risk Shift* (Hacker, 2006) that has increasingly placed the burden for health and retirement security on the individual as the government and business have reduced their previous support. Here, President Trump has shown some sympathy to the problem as he has expressed support for Medicare and Social Security despite the plans of Congressional Republicans to move toward their privatization. Still, several of his policies are likely to increase the economic stress on the working class. First, his strong commitment to repeal and replace the Affordable Care Act or Obamacare (Bade, 2017; Pear, 2017) may well exacerbate the financial problems facing the working class in both direct and indirect manners. Directly, abolishing the ACA would deprive a large number of working-class people of health insurance. More indirectly, Republican opposition to expanded Medicaid has led to the growing crisis facing rural hospitals, which brings both medical and economic loss to these generally pro-Trump communities (Kacik, 2019). A second problem in this area is that the major reductions in domestic spending included in the Trump budgets will almost certainly have a major negative impact on working-class citizens (Alcindor, 2017; Brownstein, 2017; Flegenheimer, 2017; Goldstein, 2017; Liptak, 2017; Nunns, Burman, Rohaly, and Rosenburg, 2016; Shapiro, Trisi, and Chaudhry, 2017; Shear, 2017). Third, the strong opposition of the Trump administration and Republicans to increasing the minimum wage means that a substantial number of workers will continue to be marginalized economically. Fourth, Trump's approach to education, which emphasizes expanding private and charter schools (Elder, 2017) may not help the working class much for several reasons. First, the effectiveness of charter schools remains controversial (Buckley and Schneider, 2007; Ravitch, 2010). Second, regardless of the quality of the new private schools that may develop under Trump's program, most working-class children will remain in public schools. Thus, despite the fact that high-paying jobs are linked to advanced skills and expertise, the Trump administration has yet to show much interest or planning for helping working-class citizens become equipped for better jobs.

Finally, Trump's response to the COVID-19 crisis was ambiguous, to say the least. He was widely criticized for understating the threat throughout 2020, thereby leading many of his strong supporters to simply deny that COVID was real and engage in risky behaviors that helped spread the pandemic.

However, he claimed that he was doing this to save the economy from a massive collapse. The record of the U.S. economy gave some support to his claims. The stock market fell to 19,000 but then surged back to an all-time high of over 30,000 in early January 2020; the unemployment rate skyrocketed to 14.7% in August but then dropped to 6.7% in November; and the U.S. growth rate plummeted 34% in the second quarter before skyrocketing 33% in the third (Trading Economics, 2021). Similarly, the President was rather confusing about what he wanted in terms of relief packages to mitigate the economic effects of the COVID crisis but ultimately signed several major pieces of legislation (Liptak, 2020; Pearson, 2020). However, the strong surge of the pandemic in late 2020 and early 2021 led to a new closing of the economy that led to a jump in unemployment and a significant number of people leaving the job market. Minorities and women were particularly hard hit by this economic downturn (Cambon and Lang, 2021; Ember, 2021; Peterson, 2021; Rushe and Sainato, 2021).

IMPLICATIONS

Donald Trump used his presidency to try to implement what might be term a "Back to the Future Strategy." On social and cultural issues, he sought to turn back time to an era when traditional values prevailed; and in the economic realm he sought to go back to a society in which basic manufacturing provided good jobs with middle-class wages for people who did not have an advanced education or training. In contrast, as argued in the Introduction, Great Resets, such as the one occurring in early 21st century America, provide an opportunity to move on to new economic and social institutions. At least so far, Trump's attempts to recreate the past do not appear to be very successful, thereby suggesting that the efficacy of such a strategy is decidedly limited.

References

Abbot, C. 2019. "Trump Tariffs Could Triple Farm Subsidies This Year." *Successful Farming*. May 28, www.agriculture.com.

Abramowitz, A.I. 2011. *The Polarized Public: Why American Government is so Dysfunctional*. New York: Pearson.

Ainsley, J.E. 2017. "Trump Moves Ahead with Wall, Puts Stamp on U.S. Immigration, Security Policy." *Reuters*. January 26, www.Reuters. com.

Alcindor, Y. 2017. "In Ohio County that Backed Trump, Word of Housing Cuts Stirs Fear." *New York Times*. April 2, www.nytimes.com.

Alemany, J. 2017. "Big Labor's Delicate Dance with Donald Trump." *CBS News*. April 25. www.cbsnews.com.

Alonso-Saldivar, R. and M. Sherman. 2020. "Trump Administration Urges End to ACA as Pandemic Surges." *PBS News Hour*. June 26, www.pbs.org.

Amadeo, K. 2019a. "Donald Trump on Immigration: Pros and Cons of Donald Trump's Immigration Policy." *The Balance*. June 25, www.thebalance.com.

Amadeo, K. 2019b. "Trump and the National Debt." *The Balance*. May 30, www.thebalance.com.

Arnsdorf, A. 2018. "President Trump Pushes the Department of Veterans Affairs Toward Increased Privatization." *Pacific Standard*. November 19, www.psmag.com.

Bach, N. 2019. "USDA Faces Exodus of Scientists as Employees are Forced to Move to Kansas City." *Fortune*. July 17, www.fortune.com.

Bacon, P., Jr. 2019. "Is Trump's Use of Identity Politics Strategic?" *Fivethirtyeight*. July 25, www.fivethirtyeight.com.

Bade, R. 2017. "Ryan and Trump Set for Medicare Showdown." *Politico*. January 17, www.politico.com.

Barria, C. 2017. "US CEOs Meet with Trump amid Tensions over his Policies." *Reuters*. February 3, www.cnbc.com.

Bartels, L.M. 2008. *Unequal Democracy: The Political Economy of the New Gilded Age*. Princeton: Princeton University Press.

Bartels, L.M. 2018. "Partisanship in the Trump Era." *Research Papers*. Center for the Study of Democratic Institutions. Nashville: Vanderbilt University.

Belsie, L. 2018. "Trump's Reregulation Scale is Epic in Scale and Scope. And Yet ..." *Christian Science Monitor*. January 5. www.csmonitor.com.

Bennett, M. J. 1996. *When Dreams Come True: The G.I. Bill and the Making of Modern America*. New York: Brassey's.

Berman, R. 2017. "The Donald Trump Cabinet Tracker." *The Atlantic*. February 16, www.theatlantic.com.

Bluestone, B. 1984. *Is Deindustrialization a Myth? Capital Mobility versus Absorptive Capacity in the U.S. Economy. Annals of the American Academy of Political and Social Sciences*. 475.

Blitzer, R. 2019. "Trump Administration Threatens Layoffs to Eliminate Major Federal Agency." *Fox News*. June 20, www.foxnews.com.

Bloomberg Business Week, 2021. "How China Won Trump's Trade War and Got Americans to Foot the Bill." *Bloomberg News*. January 12, www.bloomberg.com.

Borak, D. 2018. "US Business to Trump: Don't Go Through with Tariffs." *CNN*. April 4, www.cnn.com.

Borak, D. 2019a. "Trump Defends Trade War Against China Despite Risks." *CNN*. June 25, www.cnn.com.

Borak, D. 2019b. "U.S. Budget Deficit Jumps 23.1% Over Last Year as Debt Crisis Looms." *CNN*. July 11, www.cnn.com.

Borak, D. 2019c. "US Debt Projected to Hit Unprecedented Levels Over Next 30 Years." *CNN*. June 25, www.cnn.com.

Brewer, M.D. and J.M. Stonecash. 2006. *Class and Cultural Divides in American Politics*. Washington, DC: CQ Press.

Brill, S. 2018. *Tailspin: The People and Forces Behind America's Fifty-Year Fall -- and Those Fighting to Reverse It*. New York: Alfred A. Knopf.

Brookings Institution. 2019. *Tracking Deregulation in the Trump Era*. Washington, DC: Brookings Institution. www.brookings.edu.

Brown, 2019. "Trapped in a Union: Trump Administration Works to Change the Rules for Railroad and Airline Workers." *Washington Examiner*. April 16, www.washingtonexaminer.com.

Brownstein, R. 2007. *The Second Civil War*. New York: Penguin.

Brownstein, R. 2017. "Trump's Budget Proposal Threatens Democratic and Republican Ambitions." *The Atlantic*. February 28, www.theatlantic.com.

Brownstein, R. 2018. "Trade War Threatens GOP Firewall in 2018." *CNN*. April 10, www.cnn.com.

Buckley, J. and M. Schneider. 2007. *Charter Schools: Hope or Hype?* Princeton: Princeton University Press.

Buford, J. 2018. "The American Economy: From Whence It Came; Where It Might be Headed." *The Auburn Villager*. February 8, www.auburnvillager.com.

Bump, P. 2019. "Trump is the Most Polarizing Person Around – And Almost Nobody's Opinion on Him is Changing." *Washington Post*. January 16, www.washingtonpost.com.

Burrough, B. and J. Helyar. 1990. *Barbarians at the Gate: The Fall of RJR Nabisco*. New York: Harper Row.

Cambon, S.C. and H. Lang. 2021. "U.S. Unemployment Claims Elevated Last Week." *Wall Street Journal*, January 21, www.wsj.com.

Campbell, T. 2017. "Are Trump's Infrastructure Plans Crumbling?" *The Motley Fool*. April 13, www.fool.com.

Caputo, M. 2020. "Culture Wars Fuel Trump's Blue Collar Latino Gains." *Politico*. November 21, www.politico.com.

Carroll, T. 2017. "Trump's School Choice Victory is Just Beginning." *The Hill*. December 31, www.thehill.com.

Cesca, B. 2019. "Trump's Attack on Obamacare Goes Critical: Surprisingly It's Built on Enormous Lies." *Salon*. July 9, www.salon.com.

Chandler, A.D., Jr. 1977. *The Visible Hand: The Managerial Revolution in American Business*. Cambridge: Harvard University Press.

Chua, A. 2002. *World of Fire: How Exporting Free Market Democracy Breeds Ethnic Hatred and Global Instability*. New York: Anchor.

Cillizza, C. 2016. "The 13 Amazing Findings in the 2016 Exit Poll." *Washington Post*. November 10. www.washingtonpost.com.

Cillizza, C. 2020. "Yes, Things are Worse Now Than Ever Before." *CNN*. January 21, www.cnn.com.

Clark, C. and E.A. Clark. 2020. *Preserving Basic U.S. Industries: The Implications of Trumponomics*. New York: Nova Science.

Clark, C.S. 2017. "Deconstructing the Deep State." *Government Executive*. August 15, www.govexec.com.

Cohen, P. and M. Cohen. 2018. *Tax Cuts and Jobs Act: The Complete Bill*. New York: Skyhorse Publishing.

Conservipedia. 2019. "Donald Trump Achievements: Deregulation and Government Size." *Conservipedia*. www.conservipedia.com.

COVIDUSA. 2021. *COVIDUSA*. February 24, www.covidusa.net.

Cox, T. 2019. "Tax Cuts Did Little to Boost Economic Growth in 2018: Study Shows." *CNBC*. May 29, www.cnbc.com.

Day, K. 2019. *Broken Bargain: Bankers, Bailouts, and the Struggle to Tame Wall Street*. New Haven: Yale University Press.

DiPills, L. 2018. "White House Backs Off Privatizing the Postal Service." *CNN*. December 4, www.cnn.com.

Dominguez, L. 2019. "Trump's Stance on National Monuments is Straight out of the 19th Century." *Los Angeles Times*. February 22, www.latimes.com.

Douma, M. 2017. "Unintended Effects of Trump's Trade Policy Beginning to Emerge." *The Hill*. February 9, www.thehill.com.

Drucker, P.F. 1989. *The New Realities*. New York: Harper & Row.

Drum, K. 2019. "Why is Trump Hellbent on Dismantling OPM?" *Mother Jones*. June 19, www.motherjones.com.

Duesterberg, T.J. and E.H. Preeg, Eds. 2003. *U.S. Manufacturing: The Engine for Growth in a Global Economy*. West Port, CT: Praeger Publishers.

Edelman, M. 1985. *The Symbolic Uses of Politics*. Champaign-Urbana: University of Illinois Press.

Edsall, T.B. 2017. "Reaching Out to the Voters the Left Behind." *New York Times*. April 13, www.nytimes.com.

Edwards, C. 2019. "Trump Budget 2020." *Downsizing Government*. March 11, www.downsizinggovernment.org.

Elder, S. 2017. "Trump Weighs School Choice, Vouchers in his Education Policy." *Newsday*. January 18, www.newsday.com.

Ember, S. 2021. "Unemployment Claims Rise Sharply, Showing New Economic Pain." *New York Times*. January 14, www.nytimes.com.

Faux, J. 2012. "Education Profiting: Wall Street's Next Big Thing?" *Huffington Post*. October 1, www.huffpost.com.

Flegenheimer, M. 2017. "Trump Voters in a Swing District Wonder When the 'Winning' Will Start." *New York Times*. April 18, www.nytimes.com.

Florida, R. 2010. *The Great Reset: How the Post-Crash Economy Will Change the Way We Live and Work*. New York: Harper Collins.

Foer, F. 2018. "How Trump Radicalized ICE." *The Atlantic*. September, www.theatlantic.com.

Foroohar, R. 2016. *Makers and Takers: The Rise of Finance and the Fall of American Business*. New York: Crown Business.

Frum, D. 2000. *How We Got Here: The 1970s, the Decade that Brought You Modern Life (for Better or Worse)*. New York: Basic Books.

Frum, D. 2017. "How to Build an Autocrat." *The Atlantic*. March, www.theatlantic.com.

Garfinkle, N. 2006. *The American Dream vs. the Gospel of Wealth: The Fight for a Productive Middle Class Economy*. New Haven: Yale University Press.

Garland, E.G. 2019. "The Trump Deregulation Scorecard Will Impact Public Health and the Economy for Generations." *Yale Journal of Regulation*. April 15, www.yalejreg.com.

Garofalo, P. 2018. "Trump's Learned Nothing from the Financial Crisis, and his Deregulation Spree Could Trigger Another." *NBC*. September 16, www.nbcnews.com.

Gilpin, R. 1987. *The Political Economy of International Relations*. Princeton: Princeton University Press.

Gilpin, R. 2001. *Global Political Economy: Understanding the International Economic Order*. Princeton: Princeton University Press.

Goldshan, T. 2019. "Trump's 2020 Budget Proposal Seriously Cuts the Nation's Safety Net." *Vox*. March 11, www.vox.com.

Goldstein, A. 2017. *Janesville: An American Story*. New York: Simon & Schuster.

Gordon, R.J. 2016. *The Rise and Fall of American Growth: The U.S. Standard of Living Since the Civil War*. Princeton: Princeton University Press.

Graham, D. 2016. "Trump's Threats Chill Corporate Investment Plans in Mexico." *Reuters*. December 9. www.reuters.com.

Graham, D. 2018. "The Tenacity of Trump." *The Atlantic*. April 6, www.theatlantic.com.

Graham, J. and K. Belton. 2019. "Will Trump's Deregulation Survive?" *Politico*. March 26, www.politico.com.

Greider, W. 1997. *One World, Ready or Not: The Manic Logic of Global Capitalism*. New York: Simon & Schuster.

Guerin, J. 2019. "WSJ: Trump Administration Set to Release Plan on Fannie, Freddie Privatization." *Housing Wire*. May 31, www.housing wire.com.

Haas, R. and A. Denmark. 2020. "More Pain Than Gain: How the US-China Trade War Hurt America." *Brookings Reports*. August 7, www.brookings.edu.

Hacker, J.S. 2006. *The Great Risk Shift: The Assault on American Jobs, Families, Health Care, and Retirement; And How You can Fight Back*. New York: Oxford University Press.

Hacker, J.S. and P. Pierson. 2010. *Winner Take All Politics: How Washington has Made the Rich Richer and Turned Its Back on the Middle Class*. New York: Simon & Schuster.

Hakim, S. and S. L. Wee. 2017. "From Trump the Nationalist, a Trail of Global Trademarks." *New York Times*. February 21, www.nytimes. com.

Hardy, K. 2019. "'Mixture of Outrage and Resignation:' Why USDA Employees Aren't Thrilled with Kansas City Move." *Kansas City Star*. June 23, www.kansascity.com.

Harrison, A. and M. McMillan 2011. "Offshoring Jobs? Multinationals and U.S. Manufacturing Employment." *Review of Economics and Statistics* 93: 857-875.

Harrison, B. 1994. *Lean and Mean: The Changing Landscape of Corporate Power in the Age of Flexibility*. New York: Basic Books.

Harrison, B. and B. Bluestone. 1988. *The Great U-Turn: Corporate Restructuring and the Polarizing of America*. New York: Basic Books.

Harrison, D. 2019. "President Trump's Criticism of the Fed Hasn't Shifted Perception of Its Independence, Economists Say. *Wall Street Journal*. July 12, www.wsj.com.

He, L. 2021. "China is Winning the Trade War and Its Exports Have Never Been Higher." *CNN*. January 14, www.cnn.com.

Henney, M. 2019. "US-China Trade Talks Could Hit Rut as Beijing Takes Harder Stance." *Fox Business*. July 8, www.foxbusiness.com.

Hiltzik, M. 2019. "Trump's Assault on Obamacare was Much More Damaging Than Previously Thought." *Los Angeles Times*. June 18, www.latimes.com.

Hohmann, S. 2017. "The Daily 202: Trump's Lurch Toward Globalism, Corporatism Shows Why Bannon's Marginalization Matters." *Washington Post*. April 13, www.washingtonpost.com.

Horsely, S. 2017. "Trump Orders Agencies to Reduce Regulations." *NPR*, www.npr.com.

Hunter, B. 2017. "Trump is Quietly Deregulating All the Things." *Forum for Economic Education*. November 1, www.fee.org.

Hunter, J.D. 1991. *Culture Wars: The Struggle to Define America*. New York: Basic Books.

Hurley, L. 2019. "U.S. Supreme Court to Hear Trump Appeal to Ditch 'Dreamers' Program." *Reuters*. June 28, www.reuters.com.

Igielnik, R., K. Parker, and A. Cilluffo. 2019. "Trump Draws Stronger Results from Veterans Than from the Public on Leadership of U.S. Military." *PEW Research Center*. July 10, www.pewsocialtrends.org.

Johnson, J. and Y Q. Mui. 2017. "Trump to CEOs: Stay Here and I'll Wipe out 75% of Regulations, Fast-track Factories." *Washington Post*. January 23, www.washingtonpost.com.

Johnston, D.C. 2015. *Divided: The Perils of Our Growing Inequality*. New York: The New Press.

Jones, C. 2018. "Trump's Federal Budget Deficit: $1 Trillion and Beyond." *Forbes*. February 9, www.forbes.com.

Jones, C. 2019. "Trump's Budget Deficits Could Almost Double Obama's." *Forbes*. July 29, www.forbes.com.

Jones, J.M. 2017. "Race, Education, Gender Key Factors in Trump Job Approval." *Gallup Daily*. March 13, www.gallup.com.

Jones, T. 2018. "Deregulation Nation: President Trump Cuts Regulations at Record Rate." *Investors' Business Daily*. August 14, www.investors.com.

Kaiser Family Foundation. 2019. "Status of State Medicaid Expansion Decisions: Interactive Map." *Kaiser Family Foundation*. May 13, www.kff.org.

Kamal, R., C. Cox, R. Fehr, M. Ramirez, K. Horstman, and L. Levitt. 2018. "How Repeal of the Individual Mandate and Expansion of Loosely Regulated Plans are Affecting 2019 Premiums." *Kaiser Family Foundation*. May 13, www.kff.org.

Kaplan, M. and P.L. Cuciti, Eds. 1986. *The Great Society and Its Legacy: Twenty Years of Social Policy*. Durham, NC: Duke University.

Katz, E. 2018. "Trump's Postal Privatization Plan Met with Bipartisan Rebuke in Congress." *Government Executive*. June 22, www.govexec.com.

Kettl, D.L. 2018. "Trump's Failed Infrastructure Plan is a Wasted Opportunity." *Governing*. October, www.governing.com.

Kiley, D. 2019. "GM Tries to Fend Off Trump Tweets About Ohio Plant Closure." *Forbes*. March 18, www.forbes.com.

Kirby, J. 2018. "Trump Called Himself 'Tariff Man:' The Internet Did the Rest. *Vox*. December 14, www.vox.com.

Klar, R. 2020. "Party Polarization Hits New High in Trump's Third Year: Poll." *The Hill*. January 21, www.thehill.com.

Klein, E. 2018. "Republicans Are About to Deregulate Banks -- With Democratic Support." *Vox*. March 8, www.vox.com.

Koo, R.C. 2009. *The Holy Grail of Macroeconomics: Lessons from Japan's Great Recession* Hoboken: NJ: John Wiley.

Kopan. T. 2018. "How Trump is Quietly Rewriting Immigration Law." *CNN*. March 30, www.cnn.com.

Kozol, J. 1991. *Savage Inequalities: Children in America's Schools*. New York: Crown.

Kuznets, S. 1976. *Modern Economic Growth: Rate, Structure, Spread*. New Haven: Yale University Press.

Lebovitch, M. and J. Spaid. 2019. "In Corporations We Trust: Ongoing Deregulation and Government Protections." *Harvard Law School Forum on Corporate Governance and Financial Regulation*. February 6, www.corpgov.law.harvard.edu.

Leege, D.C., K.D. Wald, B.S. Krueger, and P.D. Mueller. 2002. *The Politics of Cultural Differences: Social Change and Voter Mobilization in the Post-New Deal Period*. Princeton: Princeton University Press.

Leonard, D. and S. Nasiripour. 2019. "Trump Picked His Perfect Education Secretary in Betsy DeVos." *Bloomberg Business*. July 17, www.bloombergbusiness.com.

Lewis, M. 1989. *Liar's Poker: Rising Through the Wreckage on Wall Street*. New York: Penguin.

Liasson, M. 2020. "As the Culture Wars Shift President Trump Struggles to Adapt." *National Public Radio*. June 20, www.npr.org.

Liptak, K. 2017. "Budget Proposal Will Focus on Spending Cuts." *CNN*. February 27, www.cnn.com.

Liptak, K. 2020. "Trump Chooses Chaos with Signing of Covid Relief Bill." *CNN*. December 28, www.cnn.com.

Lobosco, K. 2019. "Betsy DeVos Faces New Lawsuit Over Student Debt Forgiveness." *CNN*. June 25, www.cnn.com.

Long, H. 2017a. "NAFTA is Killing the 'American Dream,' Michigan Workers Say." *CNN*. February 16, www.cnn.com.

Long, H. 2017b. "Rust Belt Voters Made Trump President. Now They Want Jobs." *CNN*. March 3, www.cnn.com.

Lui, M., B. Robles, B. Leondar-Wright, R. Brewer, and R. Adamson. 2006. *The Color of Wealth: The Story Behind the U.S. Racial Wealth Divide.* New York: The New Press.

Luke, J.S., B. Ventress, B.J. Reed, and C.M. Reed. 1988. *Managing Economic Development: A Guide to State and Local Leadership Strategies*. San Francisco: Jossey-Bass.

Marcus, J. 2020. "More People with Bachelor's Degrees Go Back to School to Learn Skilled Trades." *"Washington Post*. November 20, www.washingtonpost.com.

Marvit, M. Z. 2019. "Trump's Labor Law: Heads Workers Lose, Tails Workers Lose." *The American Prospect*. January 31, www.prospect.org.

Matthews, D. 2018. "Congress's New $1.3 Trillion Omnibus Spending Act, Explained." *Vox*. March 23, www.vox.com.

Mattingly, P. and J. Zeleny. 2019. "Trump, Congressional Leaders Clinch Sweeping Deal on Budget and Debt Ceiling." *CNN*. July 22, www.cnn.com.

Mayer, M. 1990. *The Greatest-Ever Bank Robbery: The Collapse of the Savings and Loan Industry*. New York: Charles Scribner's Sons.

McCarthy, A.C. 2017. "Trump's New Guidance Calls for Vigorous Immigration Enforcement." *National Review*. February 21, www.nationalreview.com.

McCausland, P. 2019. "Trump's Order to Slash Number of Science Advisory Boards Blasted by Critics as Nonsensical." *NBC News*. June 15, www.nbcnews.com.

McLean, B. and J. Nocera. 2010. *All the Devils are Here: The Hidden History of the Financial Crisis*. New York: Penguin.

Milkis, S.M. and J.M. Mileur, Eds. *The Great Society and the High Tide of Liberalism*. Amherst: University of Massachusetts Press.

Miller, J.N. and M.E. O'Hanlon. 2019. "Quality Over Quantity: U.S. Military Strategy and Spending in the Trump Years." *Brookings Policy Brief Series on the New Geopolitics*. www.brookings.edu.

Miller, L.M. 1989. *Barbarians to Bureaucrats: Corporate Life Cycle Strategies - Lessons from the Rise and Fall of Civilizations*. New York: Potter.

Mirowski, P. and D. Plehwe, Eds. 2009. *The Road from Mont Pelerin: The Making of the Neoliberal Thought Collective*. Cambridge: Harvard University Press.

Mullen, J., C. Isidore, and B. Todd. 2017. "China Grants Trump a Trademark He's Been Seeking for a Decade." *CNN*. February 27, www.cnn.com.

NASDAQ. 2019. *NASDAQ Data*, www.nasdaq.com.

Nunns, J., L. Burman, J. Rohaly, and J. Rosenburg. 2016. *Tax Policy Center*. www.taxpolicycenter.org.

Olson, M., Jr. 1982. *The Rise and Fall of Nations: Economic Growth, Stagflation and Social Rigidities*. New Haven: Yale University Press.

Pager, D. and H. Shepherd. 2008. "The Sociology of Discrimination: Racial Discrimination in Employment, Housing, Credit, and Consumer Markets." *Annual Review of Sociology* 34: 181-209.

Pager, D.B. Western and B. Bonikowski. 2009. "Discrimination in a Low-Wage Labor Market: A Field Experiment." *American Sociological Review* 75: 777-799.

Paletta, D. and D. Lynch. 2019. "Surge in Risky Loans to Corporations Sparks Fears of Another Financial Crisis." *Washington Post*. April 7, www.washingtonpost.com.

Palmer, D. 2018. "Trump's Trade Policies Slammed by GOP Lawmakers." *Politico*. March 21, www.politico.com.

Patton, M. 2020. "The Impact of Covid-19 on U.S. Economy and Financial Markets." *Forbes*, October 12, www.forbes.com.

Pear, R. 2017. "Trump Threatens Health Subsidies to Force Democrats to Bargain." *New York Times*. April 13, www.nytimes.com.

Pearson, 2020. "Hidden in the New House Coronavirus Relief Bill: Bills for Defense Contractors." *ProPublica*, May 25, www.propublica.org.

Peterson, M. 2021. "*Unemployment Claims Remain High as Labor Market Stalls*." New York: Peter G. Peterson Foundation, January 21, www.pgpf.org.

Philippon, T. 2012. "Finance vs. Wal-Mart: Why are Financial Services so Expensive?" pp. 235-246 in A.S. Blinder, A.W. Lo, and R.M. Solow, Eds. *Rethinking the Financial Crisis*. New York: Russell Sage.

Phillips, K. 1990. *The Politics of Rich and Poor: Wealth and the American Electorate in the Reagan Aftermath*. New York: Random House.

Pierce, S., J. Bolter, and A. Steele. 2018. *U.S. Immigration Policy Under Trump: Deep Changes and Lasting Impacts*. Washington, DC: Migration Policy Institute.

Pierce, S. and A. Sellee. 2017. "Immigration Under Trump: A Review of Policy Shifts in the Year Since the Election." *Policy Briefs*. Migration Policy Institute. December, www.migrationpolicy.org.

Pisani, B. 2017. "Wall St. is Excited about Trump's First Step Toward Deregulation." *CNBC*. March 17, www.cnbc.com.

Porter, E. 2017. "Shaky Jobs, Sluggish Wages: Reasons are at Home." *New York Times*, February 25, www.nytimes.com.

Price, M. 2019. "President Trump is Eliminating a Major Federal Agency. The White House Told Us Why." *Daily Caller*. April 12, www.daily caller.com.

Ravitch, D. 2010. *The Death and Life of the Great American School System: How Testing and Choice are Undermining Education*. New York: Basic Books.

Reich, R. B. 1991. *The Work of Nations: Preparing Ourselves for 21st-Century Capitalism*. New York: Alfred A. Knopf.

Reich, R. B. 2015. *Saving Capitalism: For the Many, Not the Few*. New York: Alfred A. Knopf.

Rein, L. and A. Tran. 2017. "Trump Keeps His Pledge to Shrink the Size of Government." *Washington Post*. December 30, www.washington post.com.

Rifkin, J. 1995. *The End of Work: The Decline of the Global Labor Force and the Dawn of the Post-Market Era*. New Books.

Rostow, W.W. 1960. *The Stages of Economic Growth: A Non-Communist Manifesto*. Cambridge: Cambridge University Press.

Rozsa, M. 2017. "Donald Trump, Representatives, Plan Enormous Tax Cuts, Even though it's Going to Balloon the Deficit." *Saloon*. January 25, www.salon.com.

Rucker, P. and R. Costa. 2017. "Bannon Vows Daily Fight for 'Deconstruction of the Administrative State.' *Washington Post*. February 23, www.washingtonpost.com.

Saez, E. and G. Zucman. 2016. "Wealth Inequality in the United States Since 1913: Evidence from Capitalized Income Tax Data." *Quarterly Journal of Economics* 131: 739-798.

Sale, K. 1975. *The Rise of the Southern Rim and the Challenge to the Eastern Establishment*. New York: Random House.

Sassen, S. 2005. "Regulating Immigration in a Global Age." *Parallax* 11(1): 35-45.

Scholtes, J. 2019. "Trump's Budget: Winners and Losers." *Politico*. March 11, www.politico.com.

Scott, D. 2019. "The GOP Tax Law's Lopsided Give Away to Corporations Explained in One Sentence." *Vox*. May 29, www.vox. com.

Seligman, L. 2019. "Pentagon Eyes Windfall as Trump Seeks $750 Billion Defense Budget." *Foreign Policy*. March 10, www.foreignpolicy.com.

Shafer, B.E. and W.J.M. Claggett. 1995. *The Two Majorities: The Issue Context of Modern American Politics*. Baltimore: Johns Hopkins University Press.

Shapiro, I., D. Trisi, and R. Chaudhry, 2017. "Poverty Reduction Programs Help Adults Lacking College Degrees the Most." *Center for Budget and Policy Priorities*. www.cbpp.org.

Shaw, G.M. 2017. *The Dysfunctional Politics of the Affordable Care Act*. Santa Barbara, CA: ABC Clio.

Shear, M.D. 2017. "Trump Takes a Gamble Cutting Programs his Base Relies On." *New York Times*. March 16, www.nytimes.com.

Shih, G. and T. Telford. 2019. "Global Markets Plunge After China Slaps Back at U.S., Escalating Trade War with No End in Sight." *Washington Post*. August 5, www.washingtonpost.com.

Sides, J., M. Tesler, and L. Vavreck. 2018. *Identity Crisis: The 2016 Presidential Campaign and the Battle for the Meaning of America.* Princeton: Princeton University Press.

Skocpol, T. 2000. *The Missing Middle: Working Families and the Future of American Social Policy*. New York: Century Foundation.

Smith, H. 2012. *Who Stole the American Dream?* New York: Random House.

Smith, M. 2018. "Trump is 'Saving Us.' Minnesota Workers Love Trump's Tariffs: Minnesota Mining Country Warms to Trump and GOP." *New York Times*. April 4, www.nytimes.com.

Smith, M. 2019. "Trump's Tax Cuts Failed to Deliver." *Bloomberg*. June 7, www.bloomberg.com.

Snyder, T. and N. Cook. 2019. "Trump to Democrats: No Infrastructure without Trade Deal." *Politico*. May 21, www.politico.com.

Solberg, A. 2020. "U.S. Economy Finishes 2019 on Strong Fourth Quarter." *U.S. News and World Report*. January 30, www.usnews.com.

Sorkin, A.R. 2009. *Too Big to Fail: The Inside Story of How Wall Street and Washington Fought to Save the Financial System - and Themselves.* New York: Viking Press.

Statistica. 2018. *Statistica*, www.statistica.com.

Stiglitz, J.E. 2010. *Freefall: America, Free Markets, and the Sinking of the World Economy*. New York: W. W. Norton.

Stole, I. 2019. "Blame Trump's Deregulation for Boeing's Crashes." *New Boston Post*. March 29, www.newbospost.com.

Strauss, V. 2017. "What 'School Choice' Means in the Era of Trump and DeVos." *Washington Post*. May 22, www.washingtonpost.com.

Superville, D. 20019. "Trump to Honor U.S. Military During Fourth of July Address." *Military Times*. July 19, www.militarytimes.com.

Teleford, T., D. Paletta, and D.J. Lynch, 2019. "Trump Backpeddles on China Threats as Trade Deal Shows Signs of Slipping Away." *Washington Post*. July 30, www.washingtonpost.com.

Tesfaye, S. 2018. "Trump's Trade War Will Punish Trump Country Worst of All." *Salon*. April 3, www.salon.com.

The Economist. 2018. "Donald Trump Takes a Hard Turn on Immigration." *The Economist*. April 5, www.theeconomist.com.

Thurow, L. 1992. *Head to Head: The Coming Battle Among Japan, Europe, and America*. New York: Warner.

Thurow, L. C. 1996. *The Future of Capitalism: How Today's Economic Forces Shape Tomorrow's World*. New York: Morrow.

Toffler, A. and H. Toffler. 1980. *The Third Wave*. New York: Morrow.

Toffler, A. and H. Toffler. 1995. *Creating a New Civilization: The Politics of the Third Wave*. Atlanta: Turner.

Trading Economics. 2021. *Trading Economics*. www.tradingeconomics.com.

Tyson, A. 2018a. "Disagreements About Trump Widely Seen as Reflecting Divides Over 'Other Values and Goals.'" *Fact Tank*. March 15. www.pewresearch.org.

Tyson, A. 2018b. "America's Polarized Views of Trump Follow Years of Growing Political Partisanship." *Fact Tank*. October 14, www.pewresearch.org.

U.S. Bureau of Labor Statistics. 2019. *Bureau of Labor Statistics Data*, www.data.bls.gov.

Valladares, M.R. 2019. "The Weakening of Big Regulations Under Trump is the Seed for the Next Financial Crisis." *Forbes*. May 2, www.forbes.com.

Venook, J. 2017. "Donald Trump's Conflicts of Interest: A Crib Sheet." *The Atlantic*. April 7. www.theatlantic.com.

Vogel, D. 1989. *Fluctuating Fortunes: The Political Power of Business in America*. New York: Basic Books.

Vogel, D. 1996. *Kindred Strangers: The Uneasy Relationship between Politics and Business in America*. Princeton: Princeton University Press.

Walter, K. 2018. "New NLRB Rule Undermines American Workers." *The Hill*. November 2, www.thehill.com.

Warner, E. 2018. "Ohio Workers Love Trump's Tariffs, and That's Making Trouble for Republicans." *Washington Post*. April 4, www.washingtonpost.com.

Weber, P. 2018. "Trump Proposes Privatizing Federal Assets Including Airports, Freeways, and the International Space Station." *The Week.* February 13, www.the week.com.

Wolf, Z.B. 2019. "Trump Wants Radically Less Government: Here's What That Looks Like." *CNN.* June 15, www.cnn.com.

Worldometer. 2021. "Regeneron's Study for COVID-19 – Treatment Research Study." *Worldometer*, January 5, www.worldometer.info.

Zakaria, F. 2019. "Trump's Trade Strategy has Turned into a Politicized Wrecking Ball." *Washington Post.* August 8, www.washingtonpost.com.

Zanona, M. 2017. "Trump's Infrastructure Plan: What We Know." *The Hill.* January 13, www.thehill.com.

Zeitz, J. 2018. *Building the Great Society: Inside Lyndon Johnson's Whitehouse.* New York: Penguin.

Zeleny, J. and S. Murray, 2017. "Trump Diminishes, But Does Not Dismiss, Bannon." *CNN.* April 12, www.cnn.com.

In: Political Economy
Editors: Caleb M. Clark et al.
ISBN: 978-1-68507-106-6

Chapter 2

ADAPTIVE CONFUCIAN RELATIONSHIPS: MODELS FOR CONTEMPORARY INTERNATIONAL RELATIONS

R. James Ferguson
Centre for East-West Cultural and Economic Studies,
Bond University, Gold Coast, Australia

ABSTRACT

Chinese thought has a sophisticated concept of human relations, in the Confucian tradition based on core ideas of benevolence (*ren*), social customs (*li*), harmony (*he*) and reciprocity (*shu*). Five relationships have been identified as the basis of a stable society: between ruler and minister, father and son, husband and wife, older to younger brothers, and among friends. Likewise, in China's historical international relations, diverse relational models have been propounded including the 'tribute system' (asymmetrical relations supporting China's primacy), *Tianxia* as an inclusive empire embracing 'all-under heaven', and the idea of Chinese culture as an attractor and stabilizer. These relations imply a degree of prescriptive hierarchy that is at odds with equal respect for sovereign nations (the legal basis of the current interstate system), modern liberalism and socialist egalitarianism. In contrast, contemporary Chinese foreign policy mobilizes principles that emphasize harmony and cooperation: the Five Principles of Peaceful Coexistence, notions of co-governance (*guojia gongzhi* and *quanqiu gongzhi*), and building communities of 'common destiny'. These general formulations do not provide detailed guidelines for positive and nuanced interactions. However, when combined with an active understanding of *zhong* (contextualized as 'equilibrium' or the 'mean'), creative and positive relations among nations can be postulated as a Confucian political norm. This line of thought provides insights for beneficial and benevolent relations among states, institutions and diverse actors, even when they have unequal power levels and different cultures, e.g., the PRC's relations with smaller states in Central Asia.

Keywords: China, Confucianism, five relationships, international relations, tribute system

Nuanced Relationships as the Basis of Sustainable Societies

International relations theory has often been view through the dominant axes of Western political thought, deriving much of its terminology from the idealist, realist, liberal and Marxist traditions that evolved through the 16th-20th centuries. However, it is also possible to analyse international politics as a matrix of power *relations*, with a focus on how those relationships are shaped, formed and interpreted, paralleling modern constructivism with its focus on identity and socially-constituted relations (Qin, 2000, 2010, 2011). Within the wider framework of Chinese philosophy, Confucianism has developed sophisticated concepts of human relations based on the values of benevolence (*ren*) and harmony (*he*), regulated by social customs (*li*) and reciprocity (*shu*). Traditionally, the five cardinal relationships (*wulun*) were seen as the basis of society: those between ruler and minister, father and son, husband and wife, older to younger brothers, and among friends. In more generalized forms, they can be taken as the relationships of ruler to subject, parent to child, older to younger sibling, older to younger friend (Dallmayr, 2003; Chan, Chu, and Young, 2012). In the *Doctrine of the Mean* (Zhongyong), a fundamental Confucian education text influential from the

Han period on (206 BCE-220 CE), the five cardinal relations are viewed as universal paths, but with varying degrees of understanding and practice:

> There are five things that extend throughout the world and three means of practicing them: ruler and minister; father and son; husband and wife; elder and younger brother; friend meeting friend. These five form a universal Dao for the world. Wisdom, humanity, valor: these three form the universal virtues for the world. There is but a single means of putting them into practice.
>
> Some are born understanding it, some study to understand it, some come to understand it only in circumstances of duress. But once they understand it, they are all one. Some practice it through natural ease, some practice it to benefit thereby, some practice it by forcing themselves. But once they succeed by means of it, they are all one (Eno, 2016: 374).

Confucian relationships are often interpreted as hierarchical and asymmetrical, and politically as implicitly paternalistic and communitarian or authoritarian (Spina, Shin, and Cha, 2011; Lo, 2016). In the five relationships, one person tends to have a higher level of power in each relationship: the ruler, the father, the husband, and the older brother. These relationships can be seen as 'three bonds' (*san gang*) with "the dependency of the son on the father, of the wife on her husband, and of the minister on the ruler" (Dallmayr, 2003). However, the asymmetry of authority is supposed to be moderated by the overall context of benevolence (*ren*), by concern and reciprocity, and by the 'rectification of names' which ensured that persons should fulfil their social roles, e.g., rulers as caring leaders rather than tyrants (Zhang, 2005; Dallmayr, 2003). Put another way, these relationships are hierarchical, but not 'necessarily authoritarian' (Elstein, 2012).

Confucian ethics do not divide up the private and public spheres, mixing political and non-political issues within a wider perception of human nature (Dallmayr, 2003). Taken as a political philosophy, *ren* when combined with proper social ritual (*li*) would allow a harmonization of family and state interests, reinforcing a hierarchical political system focused on evolving roles and duties. In the *Doctrine of the Mean* (Chan 1963), this was not seen as de-humanizing: indeed, the humane family was seen as the basis of the state and of humanity itself. For Confucius, the family was the training ground for political relationships, with filial piety (*xiao*) and respect (*jing*) for elders or superiors the basis for political obedience and humane conduct (Confucius, 1979, 1993; Connolly, 2012).

The relationship among friends was not always asymmetrical. It could be a dialogue among peers, but elsewhere was focused on learning among elders and juniors (Confucius, 1979; Chan, 1963). Friendship is ideally based on mutuality and trust, paralleling the Confucian idea of the relationship between teachers and students. Mutual learning and self-cultivation rather than emotional bonds were the main justifications for friendship in early Confucian thought (Confucius, 1979; Kutchner, 2000). As noted by Confucius, worthy and learned friends improve a person, though he also welcomed those who were straightforward and sincere (Confucius, 1979). Friendship is unique in that it lies outside of state and family, is voluntary, and could be based on equality, therefore leading to it being viewed suspiciously if it interfered with other relationships (Kutchner, 2000; Huang, 2007). Indeed, some sections of Confucius' *Analects* can be taken to suggest that friendship should be based on a certain type of equality, at least an equality based on shared loyalty and trust (Confucius, 1979; Connolly, 2012).

Powerful friendships abound in the historical and poetic records, many of them involving self-sacrifice e.g., Guan-Bao friendships based on the interwoven careers of Guan Zhong and Bao Shuya, which was at once a professional and deeply personal and emotive relationship (Nylan, 2001). However, official and family duties were held to override personal affiliations, though conflicts could occur among different familial and state duties, e.g., a son would not normally be expected to testify against his father (Confucius, 1979, 1993; Kutchner, 2000). There was an effort to lift the status of friendship among some intellectuals in China from the 16th century onwards, especially among philosophical circles that linked travel, debate and peer networks into a new social force (Huang, 2007). Reformers such as Tan Sitong (late 19th century) sought to position friendship within the context of egalitarianism, equality (*pingdeng*) and moral autonomy, rejecting patriarchal and authoritarian relationships (Gao, 2010; Li, 2017). Modern modes of friendship in China are now more diverse, with special links to work comrades, room-mates, graduation groups, hometown associations, and business circles.

As we shall see below, 'friendships' and 'friendly relations' are concepts that have been re-invoked in international relations, in spite of the dominance of state interests in realist political analysis, itself being challenged by constructivist and relational theories (Koschut and Oelsner, 2014; Digeser, 2016). The historical 'lessons' we can take are that such 'friendships' involve mutual learning processes, can evolve and change, may exist among equals or unequals so long as there is a shared positive intent, and may be over-ridden by other governance or relational needs. At the least, however, friendship involves reciprocity and expectation of future exchange and engagement.

From the viewpoint of Confucianism, a particular kind of reciprocity (*shu*) is involved in all these relationships. *Shu* is a complex, nuanced concept, in some contexts embracing the idea of kindness and forgiveness. *Shu* contains the notion of reciprocity based on the universal golden rule. As stated in the *Analects* 15.24:

> Tzu-kung asked, 'Is there a single word which can be a guide to conduct throughout one's life?' The Master said, 'It is perhaps the word "*shu*". Do not impose on others what you yourself do not desire.' (Confucius, 1979).

This is placed into a wider context in the *Doctrine of the Mean*:

> Therefore the superior man governs men as men, in accordance with human nature, and as soon as they change [what is wrong], he stops. Conscientiousness (*chung*) and altruism (*shu*) are not far from the Way. What you do not wish others to do to you, do not do to them (Chan, 1963).

Even *shu* (reciprocity) may still seem limited by the frame of traditional relationships, e.g., the benevolence of rulers is reciprocated by loyalty of their ministers, with the father being compassionate to a filial son (Chang,

2005). However, we should not take this as a purely negative or limiting reciprocity. *Shu* in wider contexts emerges as an inner quality of "doing one's best" when extending help to others. There is an active component of mutually-developing relations that is powerfully outlined in the *Doctrine of the Mean*:

> Only those of utmost creativity (*zhicheng*) in the world are able to make the most of their natural tendencies (*xing*). Only if one is able to make the most of one's own natural tendencies is one able to make the most of the natural tendencies of others; only if one is able to make the most of the natural tendencies of others is one able to make the most of the natural tendencies of processes and events (*wu*); only if one is able to make the most of the natural tendencies of processes and events can one assist in the transforming and nourishing activities of heaven and earth; and only if one can assist in the transforming and nourishing activities of heaven and earth can human beings take their place as members of this triad (Ames and Hall, 2000; Chan, 1963).

It is here that we find the link between human relationships and the wider development of the world affairs. In the history of Chinese thought, these are both ethical and cosmological interactions. Since human relations are mutually transforming and developmental, we can see that this engages much more than rote behaviour, formal ritual or functional outcomes. This is why wisdom (*zhi*), benevolence (*ren*) and courage (*yong*) are needed to actively fulfil these complex social roles, working within the context of sincerity (*cheng*) (An, 2004).

The 'Mean' in a Governance Context

An active understanding of *zhong* (equilibrium or the 'mean') might point us toward creative and positive relations that can be developed among nations. A few caveats are needed when mobilising the thought of the *Doctrine of the Mean*. The word *zhong* in different contexts can suggest 'focus', 'focussing', 'equilibrium', 'centre', 'impartiality', 'average' or 'mean' (Xu, 2012). Philosophically, the 'mean' (*zhong*) referred to is certainly a dynamic balancing or 'ceaseless rebalancing.' The word usually translated as doctrine (*yong*) is not so much a rigid formulation as a regular usage, hinting at the idea of putting the mean 'into practice in modes of behavior that trace from the lowest to the highest' across the range of human capacities (Plaks, 2014). The *Doctrine of the Mean* uses this approach to explore filial piety and benevolent rulership, leading onto the notion of an ideal, informed 'sagehood.' However, realisation of the self can only be achieved when actualized 'in the sphere of human action' (Plaks, 2014). Within the context of political philosophy, it suggests a cultural or political awareness that involves inclusive, applicable judgements that take into account the history and culture of a given person or country, allowing unique relationships to be formed (Xu, 2012).

Zhong as a cluster of meanings and practical understandings is found in a number of early Chinese texts and is associated with approaches identified as *zhongdao*, the Way of the *zhong*, *zhonghe* (embracing the mean and harmony), or *shizhong* (being timely and correct or appropriate) (Xu, 2012). In the *Doctrine of the Mean* this becomes a creative vision of humans as co-makers of the world in which they live:

> This means that the individual thing or person is only understood and acting in the context of a field and web of forces; in this context one is still capable of making a creative impact, and a contribution to, the formation and transformation of the world (Cheng, 2009: 92).

The *Doctrine of the Mean* states that the 'superior man' (the *junzi*, what we might call 'the cultivated person,' someone fit for office) exemplifies the Mean and 'can maintain it at any time' (Chan, 1963). This has political implications. Exemplary figures such as the Emperors Ku, Yao and Shun in the *Book of Documents* were said to hold fast and rule by *zhong,* as did the Emperor Tang, the founder of the Shang Dynasty (Xu, 2012). Likewise, new bamboo slip sources, the *Baoxun* (probably to be dated no later than the Warring States period) often refer to *zhong* as a means of governance and way to moderating relationships with tribes such as the Youyi in the Yellow River Valley (Xu, 2012). Governance is based on wisdom and knowledge:

> Knowing how to cultivate his personal life, he knows how to govern other men. And knowing how to govern other men, he knows how to govern the empire, its states, and the families (Chan, 1963).

The connection to political justice is spelt out by Xu Keqian, where he explains that the Way of *zhong*:

> ... takes a dialectical relative, and non-antagonistic attitude in handling contradictions and conflicts in society, trying to find and keep a *zhong* between the self and others, right and left, majority and minority, rich and poor, central government and local autonomy, and so on, while advocating the value of equilibrium, harmony, peace, and coexistence. This does not mean that *zhong dao* intends to neglect the contradictions and conflicts or that it tries to eliminate all differences and diversity. It only means that *zhongdao* considers harmony and peaceful coexistence as having a higher priority in society (Xu, 2012, 434).

Therefore using 'the mean' does not rely on strict equality, but suggests a kind of 'differentiated equality' with persons as objects of concern. 'Equality' is a dangerous concept, even in Western political analysis. Equality cannot be guaranteed in all areas, even in the most democratic or communist of societies. Equality of opportunity and political rights have been formulated by different thinkers such as Aristotle (a just *polis* is composed of peers who take turns in holding office), Immanuel Kant (via notions of individual autonomy), J.S. Mill (via a self-regulating liberty that does not impinge on the liberty of others) and John Rawls (seeking to create improved judgements of fairness that help the least well-off) (Dallmyer, 2003). The obvious point is that a numerical notion of equality cannot cover all aspects of an individual's needs and rights. Both a child and an adult have a need for food, but one needs more than another to survive. We often expect those with more power or knowledge to act with greater responsibility and care for those around them. This shows that even 'equality of treatment' is embedded in a set of relational and situational judgements, with needs and context taken into account (this is not the same as mere relativism).

In early Chinese thought there was a strong recognition that social roles and functions were differentiated and that harmony did not rely on equality of knowledge, power or status. Even Mengzi (Mencius), among the most democratic of ancient writers, noted that 'it is the nature of things to be unequal' and accepted the necessary division of labour and governance, though all persons share characteristics that make them human and worthy of esteem (Mencius, 1988). Likewise, Taoist thinkers such as *Zhuangzi* noted that the effort to enforce equality or uniformity destroys natural relationships and undermines proper judgement (Chuang, 1891, 1968). For classical Chinese thinkers, harmony itself relied on numerous roles and differentiation in judgements: harmony among different persons was the basis of a functioning society with all its diverse needs and skills.

HUMAN RELATIONS AS THE MODEL FOR STATE RELATIONS

It can be seen that there is an overlap across family and governmental relations in the Confucian thinking. This has led to the postulation that the state was modelled in part on familial relations, with China being literally a 'family state' (*guojia*) (Kutchner, 2000). This interpretation should not be exaggerated, but is partly true for the imperial period where patterns of loyalty were attached to ruling dynasties: hence the denomination of the Chinese ethnically as the Han, historically linked the formative Han dynasties. There was some tendency to take ethical principles and read them across into political relationships, e.g., the idea found in the *Analects* that a loyal official learns proper behaviour from his role as a devoted son (Confucius, 1979). Likewise, simply being a good son and brother was seen as 'taking part' and 'exerting an influence' on government (Confucius, 1979; Kutchner, 2000).

Certain relationships may be taken as ready metaphors for inter-state relations. Thus Father-Son relations can be seen as a model for superior-to-lesser relations implied in the inter-state 'tribute system' that China developed from the Han period onward (better conceived of a pattern of asymmetric international relations, with more formalized forms being developed in Ming period) (Womack, 2009; 2012; Zhang, 2009, 2010). China was seen as the imperial centre of a family of tributary states whose relations were carefully regulated through court ritual. Even within these tribute relations, there was scope for patterns of trade, accommodation and inter-marriage, allowing for the *heqin* policy of "peaceful and friendly" relations across China's imperial borders (Waldron, 1992). Likewise, the uncle-nephew or patron-priest roles have been used to describe early Tibet-China relations, implying differential roles and levels of authority (VanSchaik, 2012; Snellgrove, 1986; Perelomon and Martynov, 1983). In the modern period, however, such metaphors imply a primacy rejected by modern notions of equal sovereignty and non-interference. Brotherly relations or friendship patterns are the only other two relational metaphors left, since the idea of a 'marriage' would parallel exceptional or problematic cases, e.g., a confederation of separate states as found historically in Czechoslovakia and Yugoslavia, or the often problematic use of dynastic marriages among kingdoms to create patterns of transnational kinship. Likewise, notions of brotherhood and fraternity have at times been invoked in actions of modern socialist solidarity, e.g., support for Cuba and Venezuela by the PRC, but are less commonly mobilized than notions of 'friendship', 'cooperation' and 'strategic partnerships' in the 21st century. Beyond these general categories there are still numerous variations in the way that particular relationships are conducted. It is the *nature* of the relationship, both intrinsically and in its beneficial outcomes, that needs careful analysis. Here the 'mean' becomes a 'dynamic equilibrium' recognizing the individuals involved and the particular nature of the relationship as it evolves (Plaks, 2014).

In China's historical international relations, diverse relational models have been propounded including the 'tribute system' (asymmetrical relations supporting China's primacy), *Tianxia* as an inclusive empire embracing 'all-under heaven' that has cosmopolitan implications for a humane world order today, and the idea of Chinese culture as an attractor and stabilizer (Carlson, 2011; Zhao, 2006; Barabantseva, 2009; Zhang, 1998). There is also another layer of the 'near and far' in Chinese philosophical accounts of international relations, with core areas contrasted to tribal peripheries and the wild domain beyond Chinese influence. The *Doctrine of the Mean* also provides some practical advice on how to deal with 'far' or weaker countries:

> ... this is the way to show tenderness to strangers from far countries. To restore lines of broken succession, to revive states that have been extinguished, to bring order to chaotic states, to support those states that are in danger, to have fixed times for their attendance at court, and to present them with generous gifts while expecting little when they come – this is the way to extend kindly and awesome influence on the feudal lords (Chan, 1963: 106).

Even if couched with the context of Chinese primacy, this short section implies notions of political intervention and a responsibility to sustain the state system, thereby maintaining Chinese influence without direct imperial control or acquisition of territory. This approach has some parallels with modern ideas of humanitarian invention and soft power influence, though focused on states and ruling houses rather than populations and human rights.

For international relations scholars, the implications of Confucian relational thinking are profound. No rigid balance of power can be achieved because inter-state relations are dynamic, changing and evolving. Furthermore, under conditions of regionalization, globalization and complex interdependence, states can only develop themselves through extensive interaction with other states, societies and cultures. However, due to the diversity of these states, their peoples, and interactions with other groups, one set of rigid norms cannot embrace a full and developing relationship. This line of thought provides insights for beneficial and benevolent relations among states, institutions and diverse actors, even when they have unequal power levels and different cultures, e.g., the PRC's relations with smaller states in Central Asia.

Relations in Modern Chinese Foreign Policy

From the early 1950's China's foreign policy moved along two tracks. The first supported communist and revolutionary movements in Asia and elsewhere, the second focused on sovereign control of its territory and inter-state cooperation, especially with developing countries. From the 1980s, as China engaged open-door policies and domestic reform, there was a gradual shift towards multilateralism, multipolarity, and mutual benefit in an evolving international system. Contemporary Chinese foreign policy mobilizes principles that emphasize harmony and cooperation: the Five Principles of Peaceful Coexistence, notions of co-governance (*guojia gongzhi* and *quanqiu gongzhi*), and building communities of 'common destiny', treating countries as equals in the context of cooperative security and mutual learning among civilizations (Kuik, 2005; Chan, Lee, and Chan, 2008; Dellios and Ferguson, 2013). These ideas have had both a philosophical and practical evolution over the last sixty-seven years.

The Five Principles of Peaceful Coexistence have been a cornerstone of PRC's international relations since 1954, with their well-known concepts of "mutual respect for sovereignty and territorial integrity, mutual non-aggression, non-interference in each other's internal affairs, equality and mutual benefit, and peaceful coexistence." Formulated in the context of India-China relations, they were part of wider efforts by China to reach out to developing countries in the 'third world'. Furthermore, the Five Principles expressed in the Pancha Sila channelled the hope that India and China might become comprehensive partners rather than peer competitors, a factor already at play as China moved to reclaim complete control of Tibet through 1950-1959. In spite of the short, sharp and bitter war of 1962, plus ongoing nuclear and border tensions, this hope for cooperation has never been completely lost in the long-term relationship. This idea is found reflected in aspects of the April 2005 'Strategic and Cooperative Partnership for Peace and Prosperity' between the two countries, though this has been hard to sustain in recent years (Kaura, 2015; Wolpert, 2004). Likewise, the recent leadership and cultural diplomacy between PM Modi and President Xi Jinping has sought to emphasise common ground between the two rising powers. Part of the tensions between these two countries, however, lies in different perceptions of the relationship: India tends to benchmark itself against Chinese capacities across the board, whether in nuclear weapons, military capabilities, economic growth, or soft power. In turn, China sees India as only one part of a much wider fabric of relations that it needs to manage, with the US and Russia being of more immediate concern. However, any view of India as a second-tier power or young-brother to a rising China would be totally rejected by India's strategic culture and by its emerging narrative as a modernising cyber-power. It is in this context that India has been critical of China's limited support for its bid to become a permanent member of the UN Security Council and recent objections to its membership in the Nuclear Suppliers Group (Kaura, 2015).

This is where notions of co-governance (*guojia gongzhi* and *quanqiu gongzhi*) could be brought into play, seeing both countries as rising powers that have special but overlapping spheres of interest (Ferguson and Dellios, 2017). Thus, while India might be seen as the natural shaper of Indian Ocean affairs, China's need to trade through this oceanic expanse is well known. In turn, China's strong energy, trade and security engagement with wider Central Asia is well known, but does not preclude India improving its relations with Afghanistan and Tajikistan. It is partly on this set of mutual relations that India was welcomed as a full member of the Shanghai Cooperation Organization, while the PRC has become a dialogue partner to IORA (Indian Ocean Rim Association) and an observer to IONS (Indian Ocean Naval Symposium). Though usually cast in a negative light (due to border disputes, tensions over Pakistan, and ongoing strategic competition), in the long run these two states will need to cooperate more closely if shared problems are to be resolved. This may require, however, a revised conception of balance between these rising powers.

The notion of 'friendship' (between states and peoples) as a meaningful concept in international relations has been resurrected by a number of writers, suggesting an enduring relationship that goes beyond short-term, shared interests (Koschut and Oelsner, 2014; Digeser, 2016). Even past adversaries and enemies sometimes cement treaties of friendship to mark a reversal in relations, e.g., the 1976 Basic Treaty of Friendship and Cooperation between Australia and Japan. This was soon followed by the Treaty of Peace and Friendship between Japan and the People's Republic of China (*Zhonghua Renmin Gongheguo he Ribenguo heping youhao tiaoyue*), finalized in 1978, an important stage of China's opening and normalization of international relations. The embedding of the term 'friendship' in such cases is as much an expectation of an improved future relationship as a statement of current fact. Modern China has invoked the terminology of 'Friendship' or friendly cooperation in at least 17 of its treaties, e.g., The Treaty of Good-Neighbourliness and Friendly Cooperation between the People's Republic of China and the Russian Federation (2001) and the China-Pakistan Treaty of Friendship, Cooperation and Good-Neighbourly Relations (2005). The PRC has such agreements with North Korea, Mongolia, Yemen, Nepal, Afghanistan, the Republic of Guinea, Ghana, Tanzania, Kyrgyz Republic, Uzbekistan, Tajikistan and Kazakhstan, though such terminology is usually reserved for countries in Asia, Africa and Eastern Europe rather than with the West (Devere, 2009; Leallsla, 2009). More generally, Chinese foreign policy has come to focus on qualitative relationships as a mean to promote win-win diplomacy. Increasingly over the last two decades the flexible terminology of 'partnerships' (*Cihai*) has been used, with China having over 50 of these special relationships (Feng and Huang, 2014).

Unfortunately, these formulations do not provide detailed guidelines for positive and nuanced interactions. Modern neo-realist thinkers tend to dismiss this terminology as merely part of the ritual of diplomacy without serious import. This may be unwise given China's distinctive evolution of its strategic and political cultures (Ferguson and Dellios, 2017). We can test this by looking at an 'unequal relationship' between a rising power (China) and a small, rather troubled state - Tajikistan. As we shall see, there are very good reasons for both states to go beyond narrow formulations of gain and benefit in their relations.

DIFFERENTIAL RELATIONS: RESPECT BETWEEN THE BIG AND THE SMALL

As we have seen, relationships in Confucian thinking focus on diversity rather than equality: indeed, difference, rather than uniformity is the basis of harmony in this kind of thinking (Cheng, 2006). Friendship can occur between equals, but also between older and young, someone with lesser or more knowledge, so long as there are shared (good) intentions and a certain level of reciprocity.

This issue is quite acute in the case of China's relations with Tajikistan and Kyrgyzstan, two small, relatively fragile states in Central Asia. Though both states have strong economic and security ties with Russia, the PRC has become an increasingly important partner over the last two decades (Ferguson, 2018). Both abut Chinese borders, have growing trade relations with PRC, are likely to gain from major Belt and Road Initiatives (BRI), and are members of the Shanghai Cooperation Organization. These states are links in China's wider economic and strategic embrace of Greater Central Asia, crucial for China's access to diversified energy sources, new markets, and a 'belt' of potential stabilization (or de-stabilization) across its western borders. This raises the importance of even small states for a China that is seeking a wider footprint of economic interests and geopolitical influence across Eurasia, thus escaping over-reliance on easily interdicted maritime routes through Southeast Asia and the Indian Ocean for trade and energy access (the Malacca Straits dilemma).

We can explore some of these nuances by looking at the relationship with Tajikistan in a little more detail. Tajikistan is a small country with a population of approximately 8.8 million, long borders (including problematic frontiers with Afghanistan), and a procedural democracy dominated by the family and party of President Emomali Rhamon. Although it has some natural resources, including hydro-power, gold, silver, lead, and tungsten, its economic growth operates from a low base line, circa 6.9% GDP growth in 2016 but with GDP per capita of only $2,980 (PPP) per capita (BTI, 2017; Farcky, 2016; BTI, 2016). Still suffering from the after-effects of a civil war in the 1990s and Islamic militancy in recent decades, and it has relied strongly on security support from Russia via the CSTO (Collective Security Treaty Organization) and the presence of several thousand Russian troops to bolster is stability.

However, in recent years the relationship with China has become increasingly important. China engaged in early diplomatic relations with Tajikistan in 1992, soon after it emerged as an independent state after the breakup of the Soviet Union. A Complementary Agreement on China-Tajikistan Boundary was signed in 2002, followed by the Good-Neighbourly Treaty of Friendship and Cooperation between China and Tajikistan in 2007, covering the 'One China' policy and security cooperation (Leallsla, 2009). China's trade with the country increased eight-fold through 2007-2010, reaching $685 million and 17.8% of Tajikistan's trade volume – the PRC is now its' largest trade partner and biggest lender via China's EximBank (Muzalevsky, 2007; BTI, 2014). China will provide credit of $140 million to improve the capacity of the Zarafshon gold mining company and build an oil refinery in the south of Tajikistan, while China National Petroleum Corporation (CNPC) has been involved in oil and gas development within the country from 2012, as well as building new road networks (BTI, 2016; Fazullina, 2017).

This has evolved to the point where China and Tajikistan have signed more than 105 agreements, with this relationship seen as an integral part of the Silk Road Economic Belt. The heightened importance of relations has led to it being described as a Strategic Partnership from 2013 onward. At that time 'President Rahmon and Chairman Xi Jinping signed energy, banking, agriculture, tourism, and other cooperation agreements, and China pledged $300 million for development projects in Tajikistan' (Nichol, 2013; Jones, 2012). This Strategic Partnership is a fascinating case of a very powerful state engaging a weak one in a relationship covering many areas of cooperation and high levels of leadership dialogue.

Part of the reason for this strategic partnership, however, may be due to real issues and tensions between the countries that need a deepened 'friendship' to solve. Tensions have emerged about the level of Chinese influence in the business sector (impacting on small and medium companies), with over the 82,000 Chinese skilled workers involved in projects during 2014, including 1,500 Chinese farmers growing rice in Khatlon province on 2000 hectares of land bought as part of PRC's food security agenda (Reeves 2015; Eurasianet, 2011). Resolution of a past border dispute with PRC led to return of 1,142 square km of mountainous land to China, ending a long term irritant between the two countries, but sparking debate on Chinese influence regionally (Eurasianet, 2011). China has also viewed Tajikistan, with its poorly controlled borders with Afghanistan, as one transnational route for illicit goods into Xinjiang, including militant ideologies, arms and drugs networks. On this basis the PRC has been active in developing a 'Quadrilateral Cooperation and Coordination Mechanism' with Tajikistan, Afghanistan and Pakistan to help contain regional militancy, with high level military meetings in August 2016 (Eurasianet, 2016; Nasar and Hand, 2016).

The China-Tajikistan relationship is also located within regional processes. Tajikistan's engagement in the Shanghai Five Forum emerged out of early confidence building measures and efforts to delineate inner Asian borders from 1997 onwards. Its evolution into the Shanghai Cooperation Organization placed Tajikistan and China's relationship in the midst of a multilateral understanding to improve transnational security. At first focused on the 'three evils' of terrorism, fundamentalism and separatism, the SCO has moved onto a wider dialogue to ensure positive inter-state relations across wider Central Asia and much of Eurasia. Although a soft-balancing mechanism against external powers such as the US, the SCO has also helped small states to balance their relations with stronger powers, especially Tajikistan in relation to Russia, China and Uzbekistan (Rambler News Service, 2012). Tajikistan is an active member of the SCO and has joined in SCO's regional counter-terrorism exercises and Peace Missions in 2003, 2006, 2007, 2009, 2010, 2012, 2014, including bilateral drills with a focus on border security and high level meetings in 2016. A major Peace Mission was held in Tajikistan in 2012, with Tajikistan perhaps hoping this would allow the SCO to balance its negative relations with nearby Uzbekistan (*Tajkistan Monitor*, 2012).

The SCO, however, is much more than a security dialogue. The Shanghai Five was based on the 'Shanghai Spirit': "mutual trust, mutual benefit, equality, consultation, respect for diverse civilizations and pursuit of common development," itself largely structured from China's Five Principles of Peaceful Coexistence (Ferguson, 2018). It seeks to transcend 'the idea of Clash of Civilizations and advocates respect for diversity of civilizations', following elements of China's 'Harmonious World Order' Concept and Russia's 'Sovereign democracy' and civilizational dialogue concepts. It aims 'to promote peace, cooperation, development and win-win progress in the context of independence', as expressed by Zhang Deguang, first Secretary-General of the SCO (Zhang, 2011).

In this content the relationship is part of China's wider effort to ensure Eurasian stability through cooperation with pan-Asian mechanisms such as the Istanbul process (Heart of Asia dialogues), the CICA (Conference on Interaction and Confidence-Building Measures in Asia) initiative, and the Asia Cooperation Dialogue (ACD).The main point is that China's long-term strategic interests in Central Asia go beyond energy and resources:

> China's push into the region is not purely economic. It is an integrated geopolitical approach, combining "*zhoubian zhengce*" (periphery policy), "*mulin zhengce*" (good neighbouring policy), and "*wending zhoubian*" (stabilising the periphery).' China considers the wider region as part of its 'direct sphere of influence or "*dingwei*" (Nopens, 2014).

However, we need to be careful with the meaning of 'sphere of influence', since the idea *dingwei* in China's foreign policy includes "the search for a place, the seeking of a proper role, or the undertaking of a process of negotiation to firm up one's position, thereby enabling one to avoid potential conflicts in the future" (Chan, 2001). Likewise, projects such as BRI have now been framed beyond economics to include civilizational exchanges, recognition of cultural diversity with a focus on inclusiveness, protection of heritage sites and creation of friendly people-to-people exchanges (NDRC, 2015). Although seemingly an 'add-on', it is precisely these bonds that will support long-term mutual benefits in the relationship.

The Tajikistan example shows that the relationship is not only embedded in a wider network of relations, but relies on a deeper pattern of cooperation than immediate economic or security benefits. Here, however, China will need to tread carefully: its influence, whether in environmental or societal terms will, have a huge impact on this small nation in the heart of Eurasia. The 'balance' here is precisely to help and engage this small state without opening up new patterns of fragility in its ecological or political system.

METAPHORS FOR ADAPTIVE INTERNATIONAL RELATIONS

We have to be careful in using the Five Relationships or equilibrium-theory as a strict models for contemporary international relations. Human relations, even when postulated as having universal foundations, do not have the multi-layered, multi-actor aspect of the modern state, with its diverse agencies and multi-track diplomacy across many foreign policy conduits and subnational actors (Kischel, 20000). Taking these parallels too far would expose us to false similarities and category mistakes made by linking across different levels of analysis. Nonetheless, politics is about relationships between actors, agents and identities all the way down to the individual human level. Metaphors can help us probe similarities and differences, explore complex organic and mechanistic relationships, and expose us to the nuances of critical irony in the human condition (Ryle, 2009; White, 1973). Linking the rich relational thought of Chinese philosophy to modern inter-state relations is useful for exploring nuanced relationships that may have been missed in current foreign policy analysis. Friendship-like relations among peoples, collectively, is possible, and core notions of benevolence and humaneness should take their place in international relations analysis, alongside the discussion of norms, institutions and power.

References

Albert, E. 2015. "The Shanghai Cooperation Organization." *Council on Foreign Affairs Backgrounders*. 14 October, http://www.cfr.org/china/shanghai-cooperation-organization/p10883.

Ames, R. and D.L. Hall. 2000. *Focusing the Familiar: A Translation and Philosophical Interpretation of the Zhongyong*. Honolulu: University of Hawaii Press.

An, Y. 2004. "Western 'Sincerity' and Confucian 'Cheng.'" *Asian Philosophy* 14(2): 155-159.

Barabantseva, E. 2009. "Change vs. Order: Shijie Meets Tianxia in China's Interactions with the World." *Alternatives: Global, Local, Political* 34(2): 129-155.

Brant, P. 2015. "One Belt, One Road? China's Community of Common Destiny." *The Interpreter*. 31 March, http://www.lowyinterpreter.org/post/2015/03/31/One-belt-one-road-Chinas-community-of-common-destiny.aspx.

BTI. 2014. *Tajikistan Country Report 2014*. Gütersloh: Bertelsmann Stiftung, 2014 http://www.bti-project.de/uploads/tx_jpdownloads/BTI_2014_Tajikistan.pdf.

BTI. 2016. *Tajikistan Country Report 2016*. Gütersloh: Bertelsmann Stiftung. https://www.bti-project.org/fileadmin/files/BTI/Downloads/Reports/2016/pdf/BTI_2016_Tajikistan.pdf.

BTI. 2017. *Tajikistan Country Report 2017*. Gütersloh: Bertelsmann Stiftung. https://www.bti-project.org/fileadmin/files/BTI/Downloads/Reports/2017/pdf/BTI_2017_Tajikistan.pdf.

BTI. 2018. *Tajikistan Country Report 2018*. Gütersloh: Bertelsmann Stiftung. http://www.bti-project.org/fileadmin/files/BTI/Downloads/Reports/2018/pdf/BTI_2018_Tajikistan.pdf.

Carlson, A. 2011. "Moving Beyond Sovereignty? A Brief Consideration of Recent Changes in China's Approach to International Order and the Emergence of the *Tianxia* Concept." *Journal of Contemporary China* 20(68): 89–102.

Chan, A., K. Chu, and A. Young. 2012. "Confucian Principles of Governance: Paternalistic Order and Relational Obligations without Legal Rules." *Social Science Research Network.* January 17, http://papers.ssrn.com/sol3/papers.cfm?abstract_id=1986716.

Chan, G. 2001. "Power and Responsibility in China's International Relations." pp. 48-68 in Y. Zhang and G. Austin, Eds. *Power and Responsibility in Chinese Foreign Policy*. Canberra: Australian National University E Press.

Chan L.H., P.K. Lee, and G. Chan. 2008. "Rethinking Global Governance: A China Model in the Making?" *Contemporary Politics* 14(1): 3–19.

Chan, W.T. Trans. and Comp. 1963. *A Source Book in Chinese Philosophy*. Princeton: Princeton University Press.

Cheng, C.Y. 2006. "Towards Constructing a Dialectics of Harmonization: Harmony and Conflict in Chinese Philosophy." *Journal of Chinese Philosophy* 33(1): 25-59.

Cheng, C.Y. 2009. "The *Yi-Jing* and the *Yin-Yang* Way of Thinking." pp. 71-106 in B. Mou, Ed. *History of Chinese Philosophy*, vol. 3. London: Routledge History of World Philosophies.

Chuang T. [Zhuangzi]. 1891. *The Writings of Chuang Tzu*. trans. J. Legge, Oxford: Oxford University Press.

Chuang T. [Zhuangzi]. 1968. *The Complete Works of Chuang Tzu*. trans. B. Watson. New York: Columbia University Press, 1968.

Confucius. 1979 *The Analects*. trans. D.C. Lau. Harmondsworth: Penguin.

Confucius. 1993. *The Analects*. trans. R. Dawson. Oxford: Oxford University Press.

Connolly, T. 2012. "Friendship and Filial Piety: Relational Ethics in Aristotle and Early Confucianism." *Journal of Chinese Philosophy* 39(1): 71-88.

Dallmayr, F. 2003. "Confucianism and the Public Sphere: Five Relationships Plus One?" *Dao: A Journal of Comparative Philosophy* 2(2): 193-212.

Dellios, R. and R.J. Ferguson. 2013. *China's Quest for Global Order: From Peaceful Rise to Harmonious World*. Lanham, MD: Lexington Books.

Devere, H. 2014. "Friendship in International Treaties." pp. 182-200 in S. Koschut and A. Oelsner, Eds. *Friendship and International Relations*, Houndmills: Palgrave Macmillan.

Digeser, P.E. 2016. *Friendship Reconsidered: What it Mean and How it Matters to Politics*. New York: Columbia University Press.

Elstein, D. 2012. "Beyond the Five Relationships: Teachers and Worthies in Early Chinese Thought." *Philosophy East & West* 62(3): 375-391.

Eno, R. Trans. 2016. *The Doctrine of the Mean: Translation, Commentary, and Notes*. Version 1.0. June, http://www.indiana.edu/~p374/Daxue-Zhongyong (Eno-2016).pdf.

Eurasianet. 2011. "Tajikistan: China's Advance Causing Increasing Unease Among Tajiks." *Eurasianet.org*. 14 February, http://www.eurasianet.org/node/62894.

Eurasianet. 2016. "Afghanistan, China, Pakistan, Tajikistan Deepen 'Anti-Terror' Ties." *Eurasianet.org*. 4 August, http://www.eurasianet.org/node/80006.

Farchy, J. 2016. "Tajikistan and IMF in Talks Over Bailout," *Financial Times*. 23 February, [http://www.ft.com/intl/cms/s/0/3dd384b0-da48-11e5-98fd-06d75973fe09.html#axzz42Am5V0xv].

Fayzullina, K. 2013. "Does Tajikistan Matter? Political Trends in Modern Tajikistan", *Al Jazeera Reports*, 20 June, [http://studies.aljazeera.net/en/reports/2013/06/201362082342345467.htm].

Feng Z. and J. Huang. 2014. *China's Strategic Partnership Diplomacy: Engaging with a Changing World*. European Strategic Partnerships Observatory, Working Paper 8. June, [http://fride.org/download/WP8_China_strategic_partnership_diplomacy.pdf].

Ferguson, R.J. 2018. *China's Eurasian Dilemmas: Roads and Risks for a Sustainable Global Power*. Cheltenham: Edward Elgar.

Ferguson, R.J. and R. Dellios. 2017. *The Politics and Philosophy of Chinese Power: The Timeless and the Timely*, Lanham: Lexington Books.

Gao, R. 2010. "The Source of the Idea of Equality in Confucian Thought." *Front. Philos. China* 5(4): 486-505.

Huang, M.W. 2007. "Male Friendship and *Jiangxeu* (Philosophical Debates) in Sixteenth-Century China." *Nan Nu* 9: 146-178.

Jones, S.L. 2012. *China's Neighbors: Who Is Influencing China in the New Emerging Asia*. Berlin: Springer.

Kaura, V. 2015. "Chinese Ambivalent on UNSC Seat for India." *The Hans India*. 19 June, http://www.thehansindia.com/posts/index/2015-06-19/Chinese-ambivalent-on-UNSC-seat-for-India-158068.

Kischel, U. 2000. "The State as a Non-Unitary Actor: The Role of the Judicial Branch in International Negotiations." University of Mannheim, *IINS Research Paper No. 5*. [http://www.mzes.uni-mannheim.de/publications/wp/wp-23.pdf].

Koschut, S. and A. Oelsner, Eds. 2014. *Friendship and International Relations*. Houndmills: Palgrave Macmillan.

Kuik, C.C. 2005. "Multilaterialism in China's ASEAN Policy: Its Evolution, Characteristics, and Aspiration." *Contemporary Southeast Asia* 27(1): 102–122.

Kutchner, N. 2000. "The Fifth Relationship: Dangerous Friendships in the Confucian Context." *American Historical Review* 5(5): 1615-1629.

Leallsla, A.L. 2009. *Encyclopedia of Modern* China, Vol. 4, Part 2. 21. New York: Charles Scribner's Sons.

Li, S. 2017. *The Reception of Human Rights in Early Modern China*. Milan: Key Editore.

Lo, A. 2016. "Confucianism and Domestic Violence." *Confucian Weekly Bulletin*. 5 June, [https://confucianweekly.com/2016/06/05/confucianism-and-domestic-violence/].

Mencius. 1988. *Mencius*. trans. D.C. Lau. Harmondsworth: Penguin.

Muzalevsky, R. 2011. "India Fails to Gain Military Foothold in Tajikistan." *Central Asia-Caucasus Institute Analyst*. 2 February, [http://www.cacianalyst.org/?q=node/5485].

Nasar, I. and J. Hand. 2016. "Afghanistan Welcomes Chinese Anti-Terror Proposal." *Voice of America*. 1 March, [http://www.voanews.com/content/afghanistan-welcomes-chinese-anti-terror-proposal/3215160.html].

NDRC. 2015. *Vision and Actions on Jointly Building Silk Road Economic Belt and 21st-Century Maritime Silk Road*. Beijing. National Development and Reform Commission, Ministry of Foreign Affairs, and Ministry of Commerce of the People's Republic of China. [http://en.ndrc.gov.cn/newsrelease/201503/t20150330_669367.html].

Nichol, J. 2013. *Tajikistan: Recent Developments and U.S. Interests*. Washington, DC: Congressional Research Service. 25 September, [http://www.fas.org/sgp/crs/row/98-594.pdf].

Nopens, P. 2014. "The Impact of the Withdrawal from Afghanistan on Russia's Security." *Egmont Institute Security Policy Brief No. 54*. March, [http://www.egmontinstitute.be/wp-content/uploads/2014/03/SPB54.pdf].

Nylan, M. 2001. *The Five 'Confucian' Classics*. New Haven: Yale University Press.

Perelomov, L. and A. Martynov. 1983. *Imperial China: Foreign-Policy Conceptions and Methods*, trans. by V. Schneierson. Moscow: Progress Publishers.

Plaks, A.H. 2014. "The *Daxue* (*Great Learning*) and the Zhongyong (*Doctrine of the Mean*)." pp. 139-152 in V. Shen, Ed. *Dao Companion to Chinese Philosophy* New York: Springer.

Qin, Y.Q. 2000. "Translator's Foreword to the Chinese Edition of Social Theory of International Politics." pp. 1-38 in A. Wendt. *Guoji Zhengzhi de Shehui Lilun* (*Social Theory of International Politics*). Shanghai: Shanghai People's Publishing House.

Qin, Y.Q. 2010. "International Society as a Process: Institutions, Identities, and China's Peaceful Rise." *The Chinese Journal of International Politics* 3(22): 129–153.

Qin Y.Q. 2011. "Development of International Relations Theory in China: Progress Through Debates." *International Relations of the Asia-Pacific* 11(2): 231–257.

Rambler News Service. 2016. "EEU, SCO Preparing 'Most Ambitious Trade Agreement.'" *Russia & India Report* 3. March, [http://in.rbth.com/economics/finance/2016/03/03/eeu-sco-preparing-most-ambitious-trade-agreement_572685].

Reeves, J. 2015. *Chinese Foreign Relations with Weak Peripheral States: Asymmetrical Economic Power and Insecurity*. London: Routledge.

RT. 2015. *Russia, China Agree to Integrate Eurasian Union, Silk Road, Sign Deals*. 10 May, [https://www.rt.com/business/256877-russia-china-deals-cooperation/].

Ryle, G. 2009. *The Concept of Mind*. London: Routledge.

Snellgrove, D.L. 1986. *A Cultural History of Tibet*. Boston: Shambhala.

Spina, N., D.C Shin, and D. Cha. 2011. "Confucianism and Democracy: A Review of Opposing Conceptualizations." *Japanese Journal of Political Science* 12(1): 143-160.

Tajikistan Monitor. 2012. "SCO Peace Mission 2012: Lessons for Tajikistan." *CACI Analyst*. 27 June, [http://tjmonitor.wordpress.com/2012/07/14/sco-peace-mission-2012-lessons-for-tajikistan/].

Van Schaik, S. 2012. *Tibet: A History*. New Haven: Yale University Press.

Waldron, A. 1992. *The Great Wall of China: From History to Myth*. Cambridge: Cambridge University Press.

White, H. 1973. *Metahistory: The Historical Imagination in Nineteenth Century Europe*. Baltimore: John Hopkins University Press.

Wolpert, S. 2004. *A New History of India*, 7th Ed. Oxford: Oxford University Press.

Womack, B. 2009. "Recognition, Deference, and Respect: Generalising the Lessons of an Asymmetric Asian Order." pp. 97-110 in John E. Willis, Ed. *Past and Present in China's Foreign Policy: From "Tribute System" to "Peaceful Rise*." Portland: Merwin Asia.

Womack, B. 2012. "Asymmetry and China's Tribute System." *The Chinese Journal of International Politics* 5: 37-54.

Xu, K.Q. 2012. "A Synthetic Comprehension of the Way of Zhong in Early Confucian Philosophy." *Front. Philos. China* 7(3): 422-438.

Zhang, D. 2005. *Key Concepts in Chinese Philosophy*, trans. E. Ryden. Beijing: Foreign Languages Press.

Zhang, D. 2011. "The 'Shanghai Spirit' and Chinese Diplomacy." *The Chinese People's Institute of Foreign Affairs Quarterly* 101: Autumn, [http://cpifa.org/en/q/listQuarterlyArticle.do?articleId=205].

Zhang, F. 2009. "Rethinking the 'Tribute System': Broadening the Conceptual Horizon of Historical East Asian Politics." *Chinese Journal of International Politics*. 2: 545-574.

Zhang, F. 2010. “The Tianxia System: World Order in a Chinese Utopia.” *China Heritage Quarterly* 21: March.

Zhang, X.D. 1998. “Nationalism, Mass Culture, and Intellectual Strategies in Post-Tiananmen China.” *Social Text* 55(Summer): 109–140.

Zhao, T.Y. 2006. ”Rethinking Empire from a Chinese Concept: ‘All-under-Heaven’ (*Tian-xia*).” *Social Identities* 12(1): 29–41.

In: Political Economy
Editors: Caleb M. Clark et al.
ISBN: 978-1-68507-106-6

Chapter 3

When Geopolitics Meets Development on the Belt and Road: A Confucian Journey

Rosita Dellios
Faculty of Society and Design, Bond University,
Gold Coast, Australia

Abstract

As China's Belt and Road Initiative (BRI) traverses the decade that began with a global pandemic, big infrastructure plans are not enough. The coronavirus pandemic, as in many sectors, has hastened the imperative for adaptive change. Development in its wider sense needs to be rediscovered. This is where Confucian philosophy can help. As with the BRI itself there are in fact many routes and directions to development. In cultivating/developing ourselves and others, Confucius would concur that we can live harmoniously without being the same or privileging a more narrowly economic version of development. This change would amount to a culturally-infused political economy within the BRI, where infrastructures of the mind matter as much as the nuts and bolts of ports and transport links. More specifically, the BRI is well positioned to spread a different ontology of development at a time when a virus had forced the world into re-examining its old assumptions.

Keywords: development, geopolitics, Confucianism, China, BRI

INTRODUCTION

In 2013 the People's Republic of China (PRC, China) announced a grand project that promised to add a new chapter to geopolitical and geo-economic history. Known as the 'Silk Road Economic Belt and the 21st Century Maritime Silk Road Initiative' – abbreviated to 'One Belt, One Road' (OBOR) and later rebranded the 'Belt and Road Initiative' (BRI) – it came to represent a distinctively Chinese approach to transregional development. Western media have tended to downplay the strengths of this approach, including its potential for transformative relations. China has commonly been accused of engaging in 'debt-trap diplomacy' (Lindberg and Lahiri, 2018) for the purpose of taking over resources or strategic assets. Not only do such accounts ignore the agency of developing countries with whom China engages, but also feed into the older 'China threat thesis' narrative that sees China as a malign influence in global affairs and US power, in particular (Dellios and Ferguson, 2013). What if the BRI, on the contrary, turns out to be the bearer of values that are more aligned to a post-COVID world than the great power politics that preceded it? The BRI is, after all, a work-in-progress. There is no philosophical channel running deeply within it. So far, the rhetoric of new 'silk roads' connecting markets and cultures in a peaceful way amounts to heritage claims. Such heritage, derived from traditional China, aligns with the national 'rejuvenation' goal of socialist China under President Xi Jinping.

Whilst Chinese philosophy with strategic applications contains several different schools of thought, including a parallel to classical realism, the pandemic has opened the possibility for a stronger Confucian ethic on the part of China and less concern about strategic grievances towards the US and its allies. Indeed, the whole idea of competing powers in an economic and technological race needs to be reconsidered in view of growing demand for global public goods in the COVID era. This is where Confucian philosophy can be of assistance. As van Norren (2020) observes, ". . . traditional ideas go against the current 'Western' capitalistic paradigm, which is putting economy before society and nature. The COVID-19 pandemic exposed challenges of this current model and an urgent need to transform towards a more sustainable society." So, too, Grünberg and Geddes (2020) have found: "The Covid-19 pandemic and the global climate crisis have not only had a dramatic impact on millions of lives across the globe, they have also put the spotlight on critical national responsibilities and the need for global cooperation."

The Future Meets the Past in the Eurasian Heartland and the Indian Ocean Rimland

The BRI, in its geographic spread, cannot ignore geopolitics – be it in terms of realist calculation or Confucian concern for global public goods. Even to the casual observer, the new 'silk roads' point to a return to the pivotal role of Eurasia and the Indian Ocean rimland geopolitically. The importance of Eurasia may be appreciated in the emergence of three 'resuming' powers – China, India and Russia – as well as regional organisations: notably the Shanghai Cooperation Organisation (SCO) and its complementary counterpart, the Eurasian Economic Union (EEU). As to the maritime importance of the Indian Ocean, this is reflected in the shift in terminology from the 'Asia-Pacific,' a term that takes in the Americas, to the more geopolitically-minded 'Indo-Pacific' that shifts the focus in the other direction – to the Indian subcontinent, eastern Africa and the Middle East. An Indo-Eurasian sphere better expresses the proto BRI map that begins in China, travelling across land and sea until it meets in Europe. This terminus of the two silk roads brings Europe back into centre stage, a position that has for so long been overshadowed or subsumed by the New

World of North American power. The latter however is being re-incorporated through the BRI project as it expands in scope.

Before contemplating the future, however, an excursion into the geopolitical past will help elucidate the significance of change via a recalibrated BRI that finds itself on a post-pandemic trajectory. Geopolitics as understood in the West is normally associated with Political Realism or *Realpolitik* – that is, a calculation of advantage, the use of grand strategies across space to access resources, and a ruthless competition with rival powers. This is quite the opposite end of the spectrum of a Confucian-style geopolitics that is yet to be fully realised, even though the philosophy behind it is two-and-a-half thousand years old.

Classical Geopolitics: Heartland, Rimland and Seapower

The guru of classical geopolitics as articulated in the West is British political geographer Sir Halford Mackinder (1861-1947). He is celebrated as the father of geopolitics, even though he was not the originator of the term. This distinction goes to Swedish political scientist Rudolf Kjellen who introduced the neologism 'geopolitics' in 1899 to express in more 'scientific' terms the relationship between geography and politics. Naturally, this relationship goes back to tribal times, but it took on a special significance after the 'great powers' had colonised much of the globe and were in competition with one another. It was within this congested world of colonial intrigue that Mackinder earned his reputation. He argued that whoever controlled the Eurasia heartland – in Mackinder's phrase, the "geographical pivot of history" (1904) – would control the world as political units grew in size. This became known as the Heartland Theory. It found its laboratory in 'The Great Game' played across Eurasia by the imperial powers (Dellios and Ferguson, 2018).

Britain had much at stake in this game. It invaded Tibet in September 1904 (having begun an expedition there in December 1903 under Sir Francis

E. Younghusband) and imposed the Anglo-Tibetan Treaty that attempted to exclude any other foreign power from political influence in the region. Britain wanted to counter Russia's expansion into Central Asia, create a buffer between British-ruled India and Manchu-ruled China (which exercised suzerainty over Tibet) and to advance its own interests by opening trade routes across India, Tibet and China. This "late Victorian imperialist," as Tristram Hunt described Mackinder, offered a theory of power which spoke directly to British foreign policy aims. In doing so, only the Realist rules of the game were applied: "Global diplomacy was now a zero-sum game, with every national victory won through the crushing of a competitor. As such, all talk of ethics and morality in foreign policy was for the birds . . . The most important landmass – the 'geographical pivot of history' – was central Eurasia, stretching from the edges of Europe across the steppes, desert and grassland of Russia until the Sea of Japan" (Hunt, 2009). He then quotes Mackinder's aphorism: "Who rules East Europe commands the Heartland/Who rules the Heartland commands the World-Island/Who rules the World-Island commands the World" (Mackinder, 1919).

In his famous 'Pivot' paper of January 1904, Mackinder argued that the Age of Exploration, which he termed the Columbian Epoch (starting with Christopher Columbus' 'discovery' of America in 1492) was ending after approximately four centuries. The world was becoming a 'closed system' (Mackinder, 1904). He feared Heartland supremacy would rule over European seapowers like Great Britain. While the Second World War (WW2) did show, as C. Dale Walton observed, "how close Mackinder's fears came to being fulfilled" (Walton, 2007: 1), the great geographer underestimated a singular source of protection afforded to European seapowers. This came from offshore American seapower.

So it was that Rimland Theory emerged as the counter to Heartland Theory. Its originator was Nicholas J. Spykman (1893–1943), an academic at Yale University. Through his writings in *The Geography of the Peace* (1944) Spykman planted "the seeds of the Atlantic Alliance [NATO] and advanced the focus on Russian power as a threat to global security" (Garfinkle, 2003: 266). This, in turn, promoted the strategy of containment. Spykman was interested in Mackinder's geopolitical analysis but inverted it: substituting the periphery for the heartland as the true 'pivot.' What Mackinder termed the "outlying island" of America was of prime concern to Spykman: it would not do for the United States to find the Atlantic dominated by Germany and the Pacific zone coming under Japanese control. With both being allied (the axis powers of WW2), encirclement of the United States would have been the outcome. Understandably, Spykman – like Mackinder – reflected the anxieties of his time.

Where geopolitics initially served empire and later found relevance in Cold War containment thinking, today in the 21st century it has seen a revival under the transformative process of globalization, prompting international relations scholars to redefine its workings and protagonists. Some still speak of "the enduring realities of ocean and earth" (Loosely, 2013, book review of Kaplan, 2012), others are captivated by its new possibilities when information technology overrides geography and war is fought not in physical space but in cyberspace. All of this, however, does not dispel the essence of the geopolitical quest. Is it one of controlling power? Can it remain a hegemonic project of 'ruling the world' or 'controlling its destiny'? Does it still presume an underlying 'us' and 'them,' friend and foe, dichotomy? Or can it be one based on 'common destiny' and 'win-win' theory? 'Critical geopolitics' has attempted to break out of the classical mould by analysing the construction of 'space' and 'identity' as narratives of power. However, it tends to be more reactive to classical geopolitics than proactive in turning the page to the next stage of geopolitical thought.

This is where the rise of China and its Confucian cultural base have a role to play. It is one which is performed with a whole cast of 'rising powers' on a stage where the spotlight has returned to the old silk and spice routes across an Afro-Indo-Eurasia world of trade and civilizational diversity. This has revitalized South-South cooperation, especially in light of strengthening trade and aid from China compared to the developed nations of the 'North.' Beijing speaks of a 'Community of Common Destiny' (see below); and India has entered its Act East phase rather than simply 'looking East.' For example, at the inaugural Indian Ocean Conference 2016 (IOC 2016) held in Singapore in September, India's "peaceful and spiritual connections and intent" with "its eastern neighbours" were highlighted (Cordner, 2016).

Moreover, India's strategic interests of the Act East policy have been presented in the evocative language of culture: SAGAR, the acronym for 'Security and Growth for All in the Region,' is a play on the Sanskrit word for ocean, 'sagar,' and the ocean is the unifying element of this regional embrace (Dellios and Ferguson, 2018).

A Confucian Turn in Geopolitical Thinking

Asia has shed its designation as the Far or Near East of the British colonial imagination. It harbours some of the most dynamic nations in the world. Containment is no longer feasible or desirable in an increasingly multipolar world. The Rimland, like the Cold War, has faded from global imaginings but remains troubled in many sites – especially in the Middle East where the promise of an Arab Spring gave way to the 'Islamic State,' unremitting misery and massive refugee flows. From an amphibious buffer between land and sea power, a contested zone of competing strategic systems, the Rimland is now in a state of 'betwixt and between:' neither frozen in past politics nor born into a new transregional modality. It is in this context of China's plans to build 'silk roads' of development from Asia through to Africa and the Middle East – across the Eurasian heartland and the oceanic rimlands – that a new Confucian-style geopolitics may arise. Being of Confucian civilizational origin, one may expect the restoration of geography to the humanities and not only to a deterministic 'science.' This change has been underway even in the Western formulation of geopolitics. As Garfinkle (2003) noted: "Kjellen sought a *science* of international politics" when he coined the term; today, it has kept its name of geopolitics, "but no one thinks of it a science" (264 & 267).

A Confucian turn in geopolitics would add an Eastern route via 'win-win' dynamics and 'infinite game' assumptions (elaborated below). Such a route could become a primary conduit of development as the process would entail a cultivation of the other as well as the self; a mutuality of environmental care and human endeavour; and of economic benefits in the presence of cultural awareness. The security ensuing from such 'geopolitics' would logically – even if in the non-linear fashion typical of complex systems – lead to a Confucian understanding of the ordering of the world (Dellios and Ferguson, 2013).

WHAT IS WIN-WIN?

The term 'win-win' has become a mainstay of official Chinese discourse to describe a strategy of mutual gain. For example, at the 2015 Boao Forum, President Xi Jinping linked the concept of 'win-win' relations in Asia and beyond to the idea of a 'Community of Common Destiny:'

> "... The interests of Asian countries have become intertwined, and a community of common destiny has increasingly taken shape.
>
> ... To build a community of common destiny, we need to seek win-win cooperation and common development. Our friends in Southeast Asia say that the lotus flowers grow taller as the water rises. Our friends in Africa say that if you want to go fast, walk alone; and if you want to go far, walk together. Our friends in Europe say that a single tree cannot block the chilly wind. And Chinese people say that when big rivers have water, the small ones are filled; and when small rivers have water, the big ones are filled. All these sayings speak to one same truth, that is, only through win-win cooperation can we make big and sustainable achievements that are beneficial to all. The old mindset of zero-sum game should give way to a new approach of win-win and all-win cooperation. The interests of others must be accommodated while pursuing one's own interests, and common development must be promoted while seeking one's own development. The vision of win-win cooperation not only applies to the economic field, but also to the political, security, cultural and many other fields. It not only applies to countries within the region, but also to cooperation with countries from outside the region" (Xi, 2015).

President Xi also applied it to the Belt and Road Initiative in 2019, at a time of heightened criticism that China was exploiting poorer countries (the so-called 'debt-trap diplomacy'), when he said the BRI's aim was "to advance win-win cooperation among countries and build a new platform for international trade, while also creating development opportunities for China" (Reuters, 2019).

'Win-win' can be viewed as a slogan borrowed from game theory to indicate no losers in a relationship – in other words, a non-zero sum game. Xi's Boao Forum speech mentions the opposite, a zero-sum game, which he attributes to the "old mindset" (a reference to another commonly employed phrase, the 'Cold War mentality') in which one party benefits at the other's expense. Power transition theory is not confined to Cold War thinking but is based on a zero-sum calculus and represents a Realist reading of international relations (Mearsheimer, 2001)· Thus, a rising power like China is viewed as a challenge by the existing preeminent power, the United States. In keeping with the use of analogous sayings (above), China and the United States might be likened to the proverb about two tigers that cannot live on the same mountain. However, as Andrew Billo (2012) has pointed out: "While it may be true that 'two tigers cannot share one mountain,' China and America, as the Confucian saying goes, can indeed 'live harmoniously without being the same.'" Potentially, under a less polarized geopolitical environment, this would allow "progress in building a new type of international relations," as President Xi expressed it in his 'Community of Common Destiny' speech (Xi, 2015).

How Does Win-Win Relate to Confucian Interdependence?

The Confucian rendering of interdependence flows from the concept of *ren* (benevolence, humaneness) which comprises the characters: 人 meaning 'person' and 二 meaning 'two'. Humaneness, based on the experience of interacting with other people, requires *li* (rites) as its outer expression. Li articulates proper (considerate) behaviour towards others. Translated to international relations, it speaks to the need to build trust, as in the common diplomatic expression in China of 'mutual respect and mutual benefit.' Derived from the PRC's foundational foreign policy of the Five Principles of Peaceful Coexistence. These are: (1) mutual respect for each other's territorial integrity and sovereignty; (2) mutual non-aggression; (3) mutual non-interference in each other's internal affairs; (4) equality and mutual benefit; and (5) peaceful coexistence.

The criticism that this could amount to little more than 'empty ritual' and mere sloganeering is valid when in the hands of *xiaoren* (petty person) leadership or within the scope of zero-sum strategy. Reports indicating that China has been caught up in zero-sum games on its land and sea borders are common. A couple of examples will suffice. On land there is an echo of Mackinder's world, with India being described as moving "another pawn in its Great Game against China by helping to build an east-west rail link across the Himalayan country of Nepal;" while the *The Annapura Post* of Nepal was cited as saying that China was concerned over "Nepal's tardy progress on its One Belt, One Road initiative" that would see infrastructure and new trade routes developed (Bearup, 2016: 10). By 2019, developments were favouring China: Nepal had chosen a Chinese railway-track gauge for the proposed line, saying it was less expensive, compared to the wider Indian gauge (Sharma, 2019). At sea, not only is China vulnerable to a Rimland Theory of encirclement in the US-friendly island chain that stretches from Japan, Taiwan and the Philippines down to the Malacca Strait (whose significance is discussed below), but its 'fortification' of the South China Sea via 'island-building' has been roundly condemned (Gearney, 2020). Similarly, China's relations with the Philippines have been described as having a deficit of soft power with a "net trust rating of minus 24 per cent" (Hodge, 2016: 10). Despite this, at the government level, economic ties have remained strong. The same applies to Sino-Myanmar relations: "anti-Chinese sentiment" among the population is not reflected at the government level (Hodge, 2021).

Even among countries with Confucian traditions, harmony does not come easily, as shown in habits of distrust within Sino-Japanese, Korean-Japanese or Sino-Vietnamese relations. Compounding historical animosities that continue to fuel threat perceptions is the Westphalian system which privileges national interest. The anarchic international order in which there is no higher authority than the sovereign state can, however, lean to the side of friend rather than foe. This would be legitimized in the interests of mutual survival – especially under the current conditions of globalization where cooperation is needed more than ever. This is not readily found due to an increasingly fraught geopolitics globally (US-China, NATO-Russia) and regionally (such as Iran-Saudi Arabia, India-Pakistan) which the Director of the Stockholm International Peace Research Institute (SIPRI), Dan Smith, described in 2021 as "toxic":

> "That toxin hinders co-operation to end armed conflicts. It is the reason why the global system of conflict management is weaker than at any time since 1990. And it means that the appetite for co-operation is declining at the very moment when the world faces a range of challenges – climate change, pandemics, potential cyber vulnerability – to which responding co-operatively is the realistic way forward." (Smith, 2021)

In light of this crucial time of change that demands cooperation in the face of a trust-deficit, alternative ideas are needed. China, in preparing the ground for the growth of an alternative geopolitics (wittingly or unwittingly, irrespective of motives), has largely opted for an 'anarchy of friends' through its win-win developmental strategy of regional, and eventually global, engagement (Dellios and Ferguson, 2013: Chp. 5). Despite – and because of – the "increasingly toxic" (Smith, 2021) geopolitics of the prevailing period in international relations, the correlative (mutually regarding) promise of the BRI is still worth exploring.

New Silk Roads of Development: From Dream to Reality

The headquarters of the United Nations Educational, Scientific and Cultural Organization (UNESCO) in Paris was chosen for the launch for the current leadership's win-win developmental strategy. There, in March 2014, President Xi Jinping articulated a 'Chinese Dream' that included cultural diversity in the global order (CCTV, 2014). The economic and financial underpinnings of the Chinese Dream had taken the form of the BRI. In addition, to help finance this mega project, the Asian Infrastructure Investment Bank (AIIB) was initiated and began operations from its headquarters in Beijing in 2016. By 2020, membership had grown from 57 to 103 states, and it was capitalized at $100 billion (AIIB. 2021). Another recent multilateral bank available to the BRI is the New Development Bank of the BRICS (an acronym that groups the 'rising powers' of Brazil, Russia, India, China and South Africa). There are also national banks for funding development, such as the China Development Bank and the Export-Import Bank of China. A dedicated fund for the new 'silk roads' project is the $40 billion Silk Road Fund established in 2014. In 2018, the China International Development Cooperation Agency (CIDCA) was established for a number of reasons, most notably, according to Cheng (2019), to:

- "be in charge of the flows that are concessional in nature (or the parts that qualify as ODA), such as grants as well as no-interest and concessional loans;"
- "strive to become a unified actor at the center of China's foreign aid system," which relates to the need to manage; and
- "facilitate BRI projects" because of the multiplicity of players (AIIB, New Development Bank, the Silk Road Fund, and others – see above).

When it comes to development, the BRI may have captured the headlines but it is not outside the scope of Chinese policy in developing poorer regions. This goes back to Chinese diplomacy of the 1960s when mutual benefit and solidarity within the developing world were emphasized. This grew out of the spirit of the 1955 Bandung Conference. Leaders of newly independent nations in Africa and Asia met in the city of Bandung in Indonesia to seek a voice in world politics (leading to the Non-Aligned Movement) and to promote mutual help (becoming South-South cooperation). China played an important role at this conference; it is still commemorated with Xi Jinping calling for the "Bandung spirit' to be carried forward (Ministry of Foreign Affairs, PRC, 2015). By the early 1970s,

China's "foreign aid amounted to 5.9 percent of total government spending . . . peaking at 6.9 percent in 1973" (Cheng, 2019).

In the second decade of the 21st century China had overtaken the World Bank as the biggest source of development loans (Hilpert and Wacker, 2015). China remains the world's largest official lender (via the government and state-owned entities), "with outstanding claims in 2017 surpassing the loan books of the IMF, World Bank and of all other 22 Paris Club governments combined" (Horn, Reinhart, and Trebesch, 2020). The World Bank statistics for the period 2014 to 2018 indicate that China was the leading bilateral official lender for "51 of the 72 low-income countries, and for 32 of the 40 African countries" (Huang and Brautigam, 2020). By comparison, Japan is the leading bilateral lender in seven countries, Saudi Arabia in six, and the United States in one – Somalia (Huang and Brautigam, 2020). The same World Bank dataset projects debt service between 2020 and 2024. It found that China accounted for 20% total public external debt in the 72 countries and that for Africa the figure was 22% (Huang and Brautigam, 2020). When the COVID-19 pandemic prompted concern about debt repayment, G-20 members pledged to suspend debt service between 1 May and 31 December 2020. On 17 June, President Xi Jinping called on Chinese banks to join the G-20 moratorium and "to hold friendly consultations with African countries according to market principles to work out arrangements for commercial loans with sovereign guarantees" (Huang and Brautigam, 2020).

In a study which drew on data from the China Africa Research Initiative (CARI) to understand China's debt cancellation and restructuring in Africa, it was found that between 2000 and 2019 China "restructured or refinanced approximately US$ 15 billion of debt" on the continent (Acker, Brautigam, and Huang, 2020: 5). Moreover, as the authors point out, this was done without seizing assets, enforcing payments through the legal system or applying penalty interest rates. More interesting from the Confucian development perspective is that the project's potential is deemed more compelling than the prevailing limitations–that is, being development rather than debt focused:

> "Chinese lenders have tended to treat restructuring or cancellation loan-by-loan, not on the basis of the entire debt portfolio in that country. This parallels an earlier emphasis on 'development sustainability' (looking at the future contribution of the project) rather than 'debt sustainability' (looking at the current state of the economy) as the basis of project lending decisions." (Acker, Brautigam, and Huang, 2020: 5)

According to China's 2021 foreign aid white paper, *China's International Development Cooperation in the New Era*, the PRC has provided three forms of aid – grants, interest-free loans, and concessional loans – to 20 regional and multilateral organizations and 122 countries in the three-year period 2013-2018 (State Council Information Office, PRC, 2021). Compared to the previous 2014 foreign aid white paper, aid has expanded to new areas such as "Gender Equality" (Section IV.5), "Sustainable and Innovation-Driven Economic Growth" (Section IV.7) and "Improving Governance" (Section V1.1), plus more attention has been directed to humanitarian aid (Section V: "Responding to Global Humanitarian Challenges Together") (State Council Information Office, PRC, 2021; Chao and Yuxuan, 2021). With regard to China's COVID-19 humanitarian efforts, the white paper emphasized the extent of Beijing's aid, doing "all it could to aid and assist more than 150 countries and international organizations . . . This was China's most intensive and largest-scale emergency humanitarian assistance mission since 1949" (State Council Information Office, PRC, 2021: Section V.2). The tone of the white paper is notable in its consistency of themes that draw on Chinese philosophy (especially Confucian values) including the "ideal of universal harmony," "repaying kindness with kindness," "a sense of justice and a feeling of sympathy" (Section 1.1), and the standard bearer of Beijing's slogans – "promoting a global community of shared future" that entails "a new model of international relations based on mutual respect, equity, justice and win-win cooperation" (Section I.2). In this respect the BRI is given extensive treatment (Section III).

In many ways, China sees development as the highest form of security (Cohen, 2014), and this has been expressed in terms of shared national interests. Returning to geopolitics, the Shanghai Cooperation Organisation represents another type of Heartland. Instead of Mackinder's notion of control, development through shared interests has a greater affinity with correlative thinking. This can apply not only internally but also across organisations. Thus far the SCO and the Russian-led Eurasian Economic Union (EEU) have opted to cooperate rather than compete for influence in the region, inclusive of the overland component of BRI.

Thus development can be envisaged as a multi-dimensional win-win game. It is one in which, as the 2021 white paper emphasized, "world stability and prosperity cannot be achieved unless developing countries can progress" (State Council Information Office, PRC, 2021: Section I.2). It stands in contrast to the finiteness of 'The Great Game' in Mackinder's day when colonial powers held sway and promises a new kind of geopolitics – one that is played as an "infinite game" (Carse, 1986) of expanding relations philosophically and structurally (via multilateralism), but with zero-sum games still existing at various nodes of interaction. Some categories of zero-sum games are amenable to change into positive-sum games. They include bilateral relations that still suffer from historical and other animosities, such as those noted above, as well as the wider Non-Traditional Security (NTS) issues that concern the environment and society.

Indeed, for the transition from Chinese Dream to a BRI reality that accords with the dream, care needs to be taken to encourage the cultural traditions that are invoked in current policies and that can help shape its future.

BRI's Dimensions

President Xi Jinping's announcement in 2013 of the land and sea routes comprising the BRI was made in neighbouring capitals that represent large, developing and strategically well-placed countries in Central and Southeast Asia. The 'Belt' he announced in September 2013 at Nazarbayev University in Kazakhstan and the 'Road' a month later before the Indonesian Parliament, during his official visits to these countries. As explained in the government document, *Vision and Actions on Jointly Building Silk Road*

Economic Belt and 21st-Century Maritime Silk Road: "Accelerating the building of the Belt and Road can help promote the economic prosperity of the countries along the Belt and Road and regional economic cooperation, strengthen exchanges and mutual learning between different civilizations, and promote world peace and development" (National Development and Reform Commission, Ministry of Foreign Affairs, and Ministry of Commerce of the PRC, 2015). The Belt and Road traverse three continents, two seas and two oceans. The continents are Asia, Europe and Africa, with the Middle East connecting all three. Their maritime counterparts are the South China Sea, the Mediterranean Sea, the Indian Ocean and the Pacific Ocean's southern sector. As the 'Vision and Actions' document continues:

> ". . . The Silk Road Economic Belt focuses on bringing together China, Central Asia, Russia and Europe (the Baltic); linking China with the Persian Gulf and the Mediterranean Sea through Central Asia and West Asia; and connecting China with Southeast Asia, South Asia and the Indian Ocean. The 21st-Century Maritime Silk Road is designed to go from China's coast to Europe through the South China Sea and the Indian Ocean in one route, and from China's coast through the South China Sea to the South Pacific in the other." (National Development and Reform Commission, Ministry of Foreign Affairs, and Ministry of Commerce of the PRC, 2015)

The BRI is concerned with large infrastructure development projects such as ports and highways, as well as the fundamental idea of connecting: this is facilitated by the physical and digital means available in today's world. The cause of connecting across continents and their cultures for trade (as distinct from conquest) was evident in the historical dimension of BRI. It goes back to the trade routes collectively known as the Silk Road, by which caravans transported Chinese silk and other luxury goods. Products, ideas and religions flowed in both directions. Art and music were also diffused, with Indian, Persian, Chinese, Tibetan and Uighur influences detectable in Central Asian paintings. Silk, though the most valuable of trade items, especially when it reached the West (Rome and Constantinople), was in fact one among many on offer. Gold, textiles, and coral, for example, travelled East, while furs, cinnamon and bronze weapons went West. Eventually, the secret of silk production from silk worms could not be kept within China, though it remained a leading supplier of high quality silk. Explorers along the Silk Road region included Chinese, Indians, and even Europeans whose most famous merchant-explorer, Marco Polo (circa 1254-1324 CE), set forth from Venice.

There was also a maritime Silk Road that conveyed both trade and culture. When the Central Asian trade routes were mired in warfare among rival kingdoms, the Tang dynasty (618-907 CE) compensated by turning to southern maritime routes. Beyond conveying goods for trade, the sea also served as a pilgrimage trail. Both China and Southeast Asia engaged in a vast Buddhist cultural sphere of diplomacy. (Islam was to come later for maritime Southeast Asia.) An important centre of Buddhist studies and worship was Srivijaya (7th to possibly the 13th century) – a predecessor to modern day Indonesia, Malaysia and Singapore which jointly manage the Malacca Strait. Chinese pilgrim-scholars on their way to India would regularly stop in Srivijaya for study. Having borrowed Buddhism from India, China identified as a Buddhist country in addition to a Daoist and Confucian one, having little difficulty blending the three. Such inclusiveness bodes well for the future of Confucian values along the new paths of development in the BRI cultural context.

Besides sharing a common religious culture, Srivijaya (which received tribute from its own region) was a tributary to China, and this gave it prestige as well as special trading rights. Tributary relations were the norm in pre-European international relations. The East Asian world order was hierarchically structured rather than horizontally as in today's Westphalian state system. China saw itself as the political and spiritual centre of 'all-under-Heaven' (*tianxia*), while those polities that sent envoys to China with tribute (gifts) and kowtowed to the emperor as the head of the regional 'family,' were also operating within their own politico-cultural logic (known as 'mandala' polities in Southeast Asia), and showed agency in terms of the pursuit of vital interests. These included trade, regional stability and political kudos within a domestic constituency – interests that are still pertinent in a horizontally structured international system.

Relatedly, as a spiritual centre, imperial China viewed its role as ensuring harmony: the Chinese emperor performed rites to ensure the Middle Kingdom was in a state of equilibrium between potentiality and actuality, between the yang-power of Heaven and the yin-nourishment of Earth. This arrangement was intended to bestow harmony to 'all-under-Heaven.' However, no amount of ritual observance on the part of the emperor could prevent the collapse of the *tianxia* system. It ended in the late 19th century when European imperialism imposed its own international norms.

As discussed above, traditional European geopolitics was based on finite games of maximising power at the expense of others. The maritime geography of trade dictated control of the trading routes. Assertion over both rimland and sea mattered in securing ports and vital 'chokepoints' like the Malacca Strait, the most strategic of commercial waterways and maritime passages in the East-West crossroads. Located between the Indian Ocean and the South China Sea, it prompted the early 16th century Portuguese adventurer Tome Pires to observe: "Whoever is lord of Malacca has his hands on the throat of Venice" (Courtesao, 1944). Prior to the Europeans, however, there was a networked system of political relationships superimposed over a map in which the Malacca Strait under Srivijaya (tributary of China) represented the centre of two of three 'trading circles'. Drawing on documentation of traditional maritime routes, Qin and Xiang have shown these three circles to be "between China and Southeast Asia (mainly Sumatra and Java), between Southeast Asia and Arabia and the Persian Gulf, and between the Arabian area and east Africa . . . Sri Vijaya and Basra were the two key points of trading interchange that connected the three circles" (Qin and Xiang, 2011).

China no longer secures its strategic trade routes via tributary relations. Rather, Beijing's position is that it seeks to establish a common security through cooperative regionalism and BRI falls within the scope. This is the theory. What of the practice? What is there to ensure that this does not become another finite game in which China, like the Portuguese and other European imperialists, simply seeks to control its surrounding geography for strictly personal gain (which equates with what Confucius termed *xiaoren* –

the petty person, as opposed to the morally noble person, *junzi*) rather than liberate it from a winner-takes-all mentality? Already there are signs on land and sea, as noted above, of finite game zones and relationships. Moreover, the pitfalls of corruption and the dangers of building expensive but under-utilized 'white elephant' projects are ever-present.

An area which suggests a propensity for Confucian rather than zero-sum games is the concept of an 'ecological civilization.' Enshrined in the CCP constitution in 2012, 'ecological civilization' has been promoted through both legal and motivational means. President Xi Jinping's 'Beautiful China Initiative' was advanced at the 19th CCP National Congress in 2017, positioning the environment as an intrinsic component of the economy rather than a zero-sum victim of growth. In the 2021 development white paper, China has committed to "thc vision of harmonious coexistence between humanity and nature" and "has shared its experience in green development . . . expanded international cooperation on wildlife protection and desertification control, to join other countries in preserving our beautiful planet" (Section IV.8).

There are many paths to development, depending on individual conditions and culture, but it seems that joint efforts to develop within the wider ecological support system brings back the notion of civilization in the presence of nature – not through its conquest. China is clearly trying to reconnect with its 'roots' in order to flourish (even if only initially at the Chinese Communist Party level) and this entails a philosophy of helping others to realise themselves developmentally. A further philosophical foundation may be found in the quest for equilibrium and cosmic unity among Heaven-Human-Earth. This allows for a deeper appreciation of the environment, human potential, and the expanding circles of relationships from one's family to the planet. To ensure that such cosmic unity and ideas of all-under-Heaven being one are shared by others, multiple modes of thought need to be engaged. This is not merely a matter of tolerance but inter-subjectivity and suggests an interplay between Chinese and other traditions. This is because "*tianxia* does not by itself supply an adequate basis for political pluralism or democratic values such as egalitarianism" (Ferguson and Dellios, 2017: 138); and this affects environmental policy too. However, a future *junzi* of geopolitics cannot be ruled out. It will be recalled that Confucius used the term *junzi* for a morally noble person, in contrast to the self-serving *xiaoren* (petty person). Converting PRC slogans to widely accepted norms would take time, but the groundwork has been prepared for the BRI to be elevated to the field of infinite games. The stimulus of a global pandemic may prove to be critical for this transition. Infrastructures of the mind are as much the purview of a philosophically informed BRI as the physical and economic means of development. China's 2021 white paper on development stated, as noted above, that "world stability and prosperity cannot be achieved unless developing countries can progress." This is where geopolitics meets development.

Conclusion

Whether in their historical or contemporary frames of reference, trade and economic interests on the silk roads are accompanied by cultural interchange. Confucian geopolitics seeks out the cooperative and enabling features of geopolitics which are not only desirable in themselves but also beneficial in a practical sense: security is better served – for China and for others – correlatively. As with interpersonal relationships, so too international relations can be modelled on infinite game engagements, but with a clear awareness of lose-lose possibilities if common problems are not approached cooperatively. Confucianism's focus on relationships is ultimately understood within the cosmic triad of Heaven, Earth, and Human Beings, which form a unity. This is much more significant than a territorial empire, or sphere of influence, suggested by the *xiaoren* rendition of BRI. Indeed, because it is still in its formative stages BRI could be hijacked by *xiaoren* profit-driven governance or fragmented by ignorance and haphazard planning. If this were to occur, an opportunity for win-win development would have been delayed yet again, despite the opportunity for new beginnings in a post-COVID era. As the ancients would lament, Heaven has forsaken us. But in the absence of inevitability, a quality intrinsic to the philosophical roots of Chinese culture, putting the ethical or moral *dao*/way into practice (Confucius, 1979: *Analects* 18.7) should be pursued irrespective of anticipated developmental rewards. Despite its geopolitical twists and turns, this 'way' is a process that can be envisaged as a Confucian journey along the Belt and Road.

References

Acker, K., D. Brautigam, and Y. Huang. 2020. "Debt Relief with Chinese Characteristics." *China Africa Research Initiative (CARI)* 39: June.

AIIB - Asian Infrastructure Investment Bank. 2021. AIIB. https://www.aiib.org/en/index.html.

Bearup, G. 2016. "Nepal on a Track from Xi to Modi." *The Australian*. 16 September.

Billo, A. 2012. "Tiger, Tiger: Can the US and China 'Live Harmoniously'?" *Asia Society* 22: February, http://asiasociety.org/blog/asia/ tiger-tiger-can-us-and-china-live-harmoniously.

Carse, J.P. 1986. *Finite and Infinite Games: A Vision of Life as Play and Possibility*. New York: Ballantine Books.

CCTV. 2014. "Xi Talks about Peace, Diversity, Chinese Dream at UNESCO." *CCTV*. 27 March, http://english.cntv.cn/2014/03/27/VIDE1395931443766683.shtml.

Chao, Z. and T. Yuxuan. 2021. "What Does a New White Paper Tell Us About China's International Aid?" *The Diplomat*. 13 January, https://thediplomat.com/2021/01/what-does-a-new-white-paper-tell-us-about-chinas-international-aid/.

Cheng, C. 2019. *The Logic Behind China's Foreign Aid Agency*. Carnegie Endowment for International Peace. 21 May, https://carnegieendowment.org/2019/05/21/logic-behind-china-s-foreign-aid-agency-pub-79154.

Cohen, D. 2014. "'A Clash of Security Concepts:' China's Effort to Redefine Security.'" *China Brief* 14(11): 4 June.

Confucius. 1979, Trans. D.C. Lau. *The Analects*. Harmondsworth: Penguin.

Cordner, L. 2016. "Indian Ocean Conference 2016 in Singapore: India's Soft Power on Display." *RSIS Commentary* 231/2016: 19 September.

Courtesao, A. Trans. and Ed. 1944. *The Suma Oriental of Tomo Pires.* London: Hakluyt Society.

Dellios, R. and R.J. Ferguson. 2013. *China's Quest for Global Order: From Peaceful Rise to Harmonious World.* Lanham MD: Lexington Books.

Dellios, R. and R.J. Ferguson. 2018 "Geopolitics of Development: Opportunities for China and India." pp. 285-297 in K. Roy and S. Kar, Eds. *Developmental State and Millennium Development Goals: Country Experiences.* Singapore: World Scientific Publishing.

Ferguson, R.J. and R. Dellios. 2017. *The Politics and Philosophy of Chinese Power: The Timeless and the Timely.* Lanham MD: Lexington Books.

Garfinkle, A. 2003. "Geopolitics: Middle Eastern Notes and Anticipations." *Orbis* 47(2): 263-276.

Gearney, D. 2020. "China's Island Fortifications are a Challenge to International Norms." *Defense News.* 17 April, https://www.defensenews.com/opinion/commentary/2020/04/17/chinas-island-fortifications-are-a-challenge-to-international-norms/

Grünberg, N. and T. Geddes. 2020. "Towards a 'Principles First Approach' in Europe's China Policy: Drawing Lessons from the Covid-19 Crisis." *Merics.* 15 September, https://merics.org/en/report/towards-principles-first-approach-europes-china-policy.

Hilpert, H.G. and G. Wacker. 2015. "Geoeconomics Meets Geopolitics: China's New Economic and Foreign Policy Initiatives." *SWP Comments* 33. German Institute for International and Security Affairs, June.

Hodge, A. 2016. "Has Beijing Put the Soft Word on Philippines' Rodrigo Duterte?" *The Australian.* 16 September, https://www.theaustralian.com.au/nation/world/has-beijing-put-the-soft-word-on-philippines-rodrigo-duterte/news-story/50cb527090253fca06a684b51dfc493f.

Hodge, A. 2021. "China Stands Ready to Use Its Muscle." *The Australian.* 3 February, https://www.theaustralian.com.au/world/china-stands-ready-to-use-its-muscle/news-story/ecb9342b2ead2837f9ba386cf7d17db3.

Horn, S., C. Reinhart, and C. Trebesch. 2020. "China's Overseas Lending and the Looming Developing Country Debt Crisis." *VoxEU.org – CEPR*. 4 May, https://voxeu.org/article/china-s-overseas-lending-and-looming-developing-country-debt-crisis.

Huang Y. and D. Brautigam. 2020. "Putting a Dollar Amount on China's Loans to the Developing World." *The Diplomat*. 24 June, https://thediplomat.com/2020/06/putting-a-dollar-amount-on-chinas-loans-to-the-developing-world/.

Hunt, T. 2009. 'A Very Foreign Policy: In Cancelling the European Missile Shield, Obama is Overturning a Century of Foreign Policy Based on a One-hour Lecture by a Victorian Geographer.' *BBC Radio 3*. 25 September.

Kaplan, R.D. 2012 *The Revenge of Geography: What the Map Tells Us About Coming Conflicts and the Battle Against Fate*. New York: Random House.

Lindberg, K. and T. Lahiri. 2018. "From Asia to Africa, China's 'Debt-Trap Diplomacy' was Under Siege in 2018." *Quartz*. 28 December, https://qz.com/1497584/how-chinas-debt-trap-diplomacy-came-under-siege-in-2018/.

Loosely, S. 2013. "The Enduring Importance of Lines Drawn in the Sand." *The Weekend Australian*. 16-17 March.

Mackinder, H.J. 1904. "The Geographical Pivot of History." *The Geographical Journal* 24(4).

Mackinder, H.J. 1919. *Democratic Ideals and Reality: A Study in the Politics of Reconstruction*. New York: Holt.

Mearsheimer, J.J. 2001. *The Tragedy of Great Power Politics*. NY: W.W. Norton.

Ministry of Foreign Affairs, PRC. 2015. *Xi Jinping Attends the Asian-African Summit and Delivers Important Speech, Stressing to Carry Forward Bandung Spirit, Intensify Cooperation Between Asia and Africa, and Promote the Construction of Community of Common Destiny for Mankind.* 22 April, https://www.fmprc.gov.cn/mfa_eng/zxxx_662805/t1258694.shtml.

National Development and Reform Commission, Ministry of Foreign Affairs, and Ministry of Commerce of the PRC, with State Council authorization. 2015. *Vision and Actions on Jointly Building Silk Road Economic Belt and 21st-Century Maritime Silk Road.* March, http://www.fmprc.gov.cn/mfa_eng/topics_665678/xjpcxbayzlt2015nnh/t1249618.shtml.

Qin, D. and K. Xiang. 2011. "Sri Vijaya as the Entrepôt for Circum-Indian Ocean Trade." *Études Océan Indien.* http://oceanindien.revues.org/1379.

Reuters. 2019. "China President Xi says Goal of Belt and Road is Advance 'Win-Win Cooperation'." 26 April, https://www.reuters.com/article/us-china-silkroad-xi-idINKCN1S205Z.

Sharma, G. 2019. "Nepal to use Chinese Gauge for its Railway, Not the One India Uses." *Reuters.* 5 March, https://www.reuters.com/article/us-india-nepal-idUSKCN1QM16Y.

Smith, D. 2021. "War and Peace." *New Internationalist.* 31 January, https://newint.org/features/2020/10/06/war-and-peace-peacekeeping-trends.

Spykman, N.J. 1944. *The Geography of the Peace.* New York: Harcourt, Brace and Co.

State Council Information Office, PRC. 2021. *China's International Development Cooperation in the New Era.* January, http://news.xinhuanet.com/english/china/2014-07/10/c_133474011.htm.

van Norren, D. 2020. "COVID-19: Towards a New Economic Order Inspired by Three visions of the Global South?" *The Broker.* November 2020, https://www.thebrokeronline.eu/covid-19-towards-a-new-economic-order-inspired-by-three-visions-of-the-global-south/

Walton, C.D. 2007. *Geopolitics and the Great Powers in the Twenty-First Century.* London: Routledge.

Xi, J. 2015. "Towards a Community of Common Destiny and A New Future for Asia." *Boao Forum for Asia Annual Conference 2015.* Boao, Hainan Province, China, 28 March, *China.org.cn,* http://www.china.org.cn/business/2015-03/29/content_35185720. htm://www.globaltimes.cn/content/831535.shtml.

In: Political Economy
Editors: Caleb M. Clark et al.
ISBN: 978-1-68507-106-6

Chapter 4

NEW DIRECTIONS IN THEORETICAL DISCUSSIONS, EMPIRICAL RESEARCH AND PRACTICAL COOPERATION FOR CHINA-CEEC COOPERATION IN A GLOBAL FRAMEWORK*

Katarzyna A. Nawrot
Committee for Future Studies, Polish Academy of Sciences,
Warszawa, Poland

ABSTRACT

The dialogue and cooperation between China and the Central and Eastern European countries (CEEC) have evolved significantly since the first China-Central Europe-Poland Economic Forum held in Warsaw on the 26th of April 2012. A decade after the beginning of the 16+1 formula

* This article is the result of the research project "East Asia in Regional Cooperation and Governance" financed by the National Science Centre, Poland (decision no. DEC-2013/09/B/HS4/01147).

of cooperation and of rejuvenation of the Silk Road, it seems crucial to assess the current state of the relations between China and the CEECs, as well as to make an attempt to identify and indicate possible future directions for practical cooperation and to highlight the relevant theoretical discussions and empirical research. First, an overview of the historical background and current directions of the relations between China and the CEECs will be presented. Furthermore, the institutional mechanisms of the bilateral and multilateral relations will be discussed as a crucial setting on which the cooperation is evolving. In particular, the evolution of trade patterns and the investment flows between China and CEECs will be examined in the broader context of the EU and Europe. Finally, the possible new directions, dimensions, and fields of cooperation will be discussed for enhancing the relations between China and the Central and Eastern European countries.

Keywords: China, Central and East European countries, cooperation, trade and investment flows

Introduction

The dialogue and cooperation between China and the Central and Eastern European countries (CEEC) have evolved significantly since the first China-Central Europe-Poland Economic Forum held in Warsaw on the 26th of April 2012 with the presence of the Chinese Prime Minister Wen Jiabao and the heads of states from the region. It marked a breakthrough opening of a new era in both bilateral and multilateral relations between China and the Central and Eastern European countries, underpinned by the announcement of twelve proposals put forward by China to promote cooperation with the 16 countries from the region. The official establishment of the Secretariat for Cooperation for Central and Eastern Europe in Beijing followed the same year in September – being the first on the list – as a platform serving to facilitate the implementation of the proposals.

A decade after the beginning of the 16+1 formula of cooperation and of rejuvenation of the Silk Road, it seems crucial to assess the current state of the relations between China and the CEECs, as well as to make an attempt to identify and indicate possible future directions for practical cooperation and to highlight the relevant theoretical discussions and empirical research, which are the main goals of the present study.

First, an overview of the historical background and current directions of the relations between China and the CEECs will be presented. Furthermore, the institutional mechanisms of the bilateral and multilateral relations will be discussed as a crucial setting on which the cooperation is evolving. In particular, the evolution of trade patterns and the investment flows between China and the CEECs will be examined in the broader context of the EU and Europe. Finally, the possible new directions, dimensions, and fields of cooperation will be discussed for enhancing the relations between China and the Central and Eastern European countries. The chapter will conclude with implications for reviewing the challenges for enhancing the cooperation and bringing it to a higher level.

The Evolution and Current Directions of the Relations between China and the Central and Eastern European Countries

Political and economic relations between China and the CEEC were rather limited during the first decades of their transformation from centrally planned to open market economies of the Central and Eastern European countries compared to the relations with western Europe. They certainly didn't make the highest priority in the foreign policies of these nations, which were mostly concentrated on restructuring their economies and adjusting to their new political systems, while resetting their position in transforming Europe. Consequently, current economic relations don't reflect the potential of Chinese markets and don't make the most of the possibilities offered by the Central and Eastern European economies.

The breakthrough in mutual relations between China and the Central and Eastern European countries – as mentioned in the introduction – were marked by the China-Central Europe-Poland Economic Forum held in Warsaw in April 2012. During the Forum twelve proposals were put forward by Chinese Prime Minister Wen Jiabao to promote cooperation with 16 countries from the region, namely Albania, Bosnia and Herzegovina, Bulgaria, Croatia, the Czech Republic, Estonia, Hungary, Latvia, Lithuania, Macedonia, Montenegro, Poland, Romania, Serbia, Slovakia and Slovenia. The establishment of the common Secretariat was first on the list as a platform to facilitate the implementation of the proposals. The official establishment of the Secretariat for Cooperation for Central and Eastern Europe in Beijing followed the same year in September and was set up by the Chinese Ministry of Foreign Affairs.

Among the twelve proposals, the 10 billion USD credit line for the Central and Eastern European states was set by the Chinese government targeted to boost bilateral business and trade by supporting joint projects mainly in infrastructure, new technologies and green energy. An increase in trade to $100 billion with countries from the region was expected by 2015. The cooperation was further promoted in science, education, culture and tourism.

The undertaken initiatives were a good signs of strengthening the cooperation between China and the Central and Eastern European countries, with Poland, the Czech Republic and Hungary as the biggest markets in the region. The Chinese leaders stressed on several occasions that consolidating cooperation between China and the Central and Eastern European countries was an important component in enhancing China-Europe cooperation which should help China and Europe make joint efforts to tackle challenges of the modern world economy and enhance their comprehensive and strategic partnership to a higher level. Besides, there is still a clear necessity to strengthen common trust and understanding between China and the Central and Eastern European countries. The communications between China and Europe have increased significantly over the last decade, through people-to-people contacts, the flow of tourists, and mostly trade and cross border investments, thus contributing to better understanding between Europe and China. The still existing asymmetry of information flow and knowledge between Europe and Asia is evident. Therefore, the need arises to decrease the existing gap on many levels starting with the bottom-up level and then the governmental one. Especially, the communist burden of most of the

Central and Eastern Europe countries still reflects in some unnecessary scepticism towards collaboration with China in certain groups, which rather should be a common ground of experiences, shared values and understanding upon which the cooperation is consolidating. The undertaken initiatives in the field of culture and people-to-people dialogue do contribute to bringing the nations closer together.

Finally, particular Central and Eastern European countries are part of the European Union market. As such their policy towards China should not be inconsistent with the European Union's policy. The hopes and expectations are prevalent among the countries in Central and Eastern Europe, and it seems that they have emerged significantly over the last few years. It is in the interest and will of all sides that political declarations by the Chinese leaders and the leaders from the CEEC will be transformed into the real economy.

Institutional Mechanisms of Bilateral and Multilateral Relations

The institutional framework of bilateral and multilateral relations consists of several mechanisms including trade, capital flows, summits, consultation mechanisms, AIIB, industry meetings and conferences, fairs, local government partnerships, and special economic zones, among others. This section will briefly outline the two most intensive forms of cooperation, which are trade and investment, followed by the discussion of other forms of institutional mechanisms.

Trade is the most important form of cooperation between China and the Central and Eastern European countries. Among the countries from the Central and Eastern Europe, Poland remains the most important trade partner of China, followed by the Czech Republic and Hungary – see Table 1. All of the countries from the region – no matter what the trade volume – record a trade deficit, which in the majority of cases is constantly growing. Closer cooperation between China and the Central and Eastern European countries should serve as a chance to balance the trade exchange with China, as Chinese exports are dominant in all the countries of the region.

The second most important form of cooperation, which is the flow of capital, has been rather limited not reflecting the existing potential on both sides. Among the CEEC the biggest stock of Chinese FDI is recorded in Hungary, and in 2014 it exceeded 556 ml USD. It was more than double compared to the Czech Republic, Romania, Bulgaria – main destinations for Chinese FDI, next to Poland – see Table 2. The stock of Chinese FDI in Poland was estimated around 329 ml USD.

In Central and Eastern Europe, Chinese investments are made mainly in infrastructure, industry and raw materials. Although industry remains the main sector of foreign investment in Central and Eastern Europe, we should expect increasing interest in the service sector. As declared in Warsaw by Wen Jiabao, creation of a special credit line worth $10 billion for the countries of Central and Eastern Europe to support joint projects in infrastructure, new technologies and renewable energy was created. This demonstrates the attitude and the possibilities of cooperation in high-technology sectors. Joint scientific research projects, cultural intensification of tourist flows and interpersonal dialogue can be expected, which should further strengthen cooperation, especially in business and commerce between China and the CEEC. Unused potential between the CEEC and China also refers to cooperation in infrastructure, science and technology, and research and innovation.

The fact remains, however, that the shares of both Chinese foreign investment in the CEEC and the European Union and European investments in China are still small. At the same time, there are also cases of criticism and scepticism of Chinese investors, resulting more from existing antagonisms or insufficient knowledge of their actual size and character. Therefore, reliable monitoring with the support of government agencies and consistently providing the public with accurate information are extremely important.

Table 1. Foreign Trade between China and Selected CEEC, 2015 (in ml euro)

Country	Exports	Imports	Total trade turnover	Trade balance
1. Poland	1,819.3	13,083.4	14902.7	-11,264.1
2. Czech Republic	1,671.5	10,528.3	12199.8	-88,568.8
3. Hungary	1,262.4	5,150.1	6412.5	-3,887.7
4. Slovakia	1,019.9	2,720.2	3740.1	-1,700.3
5. Romania	525.1	2,887.4	3412.5	-2,362.3
6. Slovenia	294.0	1,458.8	1752.8	-1,164.8
7. Bulgaria	550.7	966.4	1517.1	-415.7
8. Lithuania	102.4	725.3	827.7	-622.9
9 Estonia	135.7	625.2	760.9	-489.5
10. Croatia	70.1	524.7	594.8	-454.6
11. Latvia	108.4	416.5	524.9	-308.1

Source: EuroStat. 2016.

Table 2. China's FDI stock in CEEs in 2007-2015 (in ml USD)

	2007	2008	2009	2010	2011	2012	2013	2014
Total	301.00	348.15	410.6	852.6	1,009.8	1,334.0	1,435.8	1,696.5
Hungary	78.17	88.75	97.41	465.70	475.35	507.41	532.35	556.35
Poland	98.93	109.93	120.30	140,31	201.26	208.11	257.04	329.35
Czech Republic	19.64	32.43	49.34	52.33	66.83	202.45	204.68	242.69
Romania	72.88	85.66	93.34	124.95	125.83	161.09	145.13	191.37
Bulgaria	4.74	4.74	2.31	18.60	72.56	126.74	149.85	170.27
Slovakia	5.10	5.10	9.36	9.82	25.78	86.01	82.77	127.79
Serbia	2.00	2.00	2.68	4.84	5.05	6.47	18.54	29.71
Lithuania	3.93	3.93	3.93	3.93	3.93	6.97	12.48	12.48
Croatia	7.84	7.84	8.10	8.13	8.18	8.63	8.31	11.87
Albania	0.51	0.51	4.35	4.43	4.43	4.43	7.03	7.03
Bosnia and Hercegovina	3.51	3.51	5.92	5.98	6.01	6.07	6.13	6.13
Slovenia	1.40	1.40	5.00	5.00	5.00	5.00	5.00	5.00
Estonia	1.26	1.26	7.50	7.50	7.50	3.50	3.50	3.50
Macedonia	0.20	0.20	0.20	0.20	0.20	0.26	2.09	2.11
Latvia	0.57	0.57	0.54	0.54	0.54	0.54	0.54	0.54
Montenegro	0.32	0.32	0.32	0.32	0,32	0.32	0.32	0.32

Source: EuroStat. 2016.

Evidence of the existing political and economic dialogue confirms the willingness and the declaration to strengthen mutual cooperation between China and the Central and Eastern European countries. One of the significant achievements of the recent years in the relations between the CEEs and China is undoubtedly the increase in mutual understanding resulting largely from the dynamics of foreign trade, investment, and people-to-people dialogue. The rising interdependence of the markets and the huge potential of the Chinese economy underline the importance of ensuring and deepening the existing openness and steps towards further liberalization. This is vital for both the CEEs and China, acting as a catalyst for economic dynamism of the world economy.

The existing chances are enormous through trade and being a part of growing production chains, especially with rising costs in China and expanding production within the Asian division of labour, for enterprises to seek partnership in infrastructure projects, high speed trains, air transport and ships; attracting tourists to the region, exchanging students and academia, creating innovation hubs and technology parks – among many others. This leads us to point out some possible new directions, dimensions, and fields of cooperation in the next part of this chapter.

Possible New Directions, Dimensions, and Fields of Cooperation in Theoretical Discussions, Empirical Research, and Practical Cooperation

Almost ten years after the rejuvenation of the Silk Road and the announcement of the New Silk Road by the Chinese President Xi Jingping in Astana, Kazakhstan (2013), the world economy looks significantly different and so does China, as well as the Central and Eastern European countries. The world is undergoing tremendous changes with accelerated speed. Emerging markets are gaining in importance while integrating within the system of the world economy. Old powers, with a leading role of the USA, are redefining and repositioning their role in the existing world order.

New non-state actors have emerged and are gaining the importance, including civil society, cities and megacities. Moreover, the growing interdependence of markets – which the global pandemic due to COVID-19 strongly underpinned – requires a common and comprehensive response and the responsibility for global issues, including the environment, climate change, inequality, security, resolving existing conflicts, and preventing potential ones.

Thus, in discussing potential new directions in practical cooperation between China and the Central and Eastern European countries in the global framework, the following seem crucial: (i) cooperation with non-state actors; and (ii) cooperation for shared goals, which will be discussed in more detail below. Before the brief elaboration of these two points, it is important to further stress that in parallel to practical cooperation those directions also require deep theoretical discussions and empirical research of both a multidisciplinary and interdisciplinary character across the global society.

Referring first to the issue of non-state actors, particular attention should be put on cities and in particular megacities, defined as urban agglomeration with an excess of 10 million inhabitants. As recognized by Kleer and Nawrot (2018), the rise of megacities represents a new phenomenon of the 21st century, which is occurring on a rapidly growing scale and with growing importance. From the global outlook, as well as standpoint of China and the perspective of China-CEEC cooperation, it is significant for at least four interconnected reasons, namely:

- the growth of the world population,
- the growth of urbanization with the rise of the agglomeration of megacities worldwide,
- the growth of power of megacities,
- the lessons and implications from China's urbanization and China's megacities for the world community.

Discussing the demographic changes in the world economy, it must be indicated first that since 1950 the world population has increased dramatically, from 2.5 to 7.3 billion as of mid-2015, making for an almost threefold rise. According to the median variant of UN predictions, the world population is expected to reach 11.2 billion by 2100, which will mean an increase of an additional 3.9 billion from 2015, or an overall surge of 8.7 billion as compared to 1950 (UNDESA, 2015). The biggest increase in population from 1950 to 2015 was observed in Asia, estimated to account for around 62% of the total world population growth over the period. This surge of approximately 3 billion people in Asia alone mainly came in China, whose population more than doubled to reach 1.4 million in 2017. Thus, China remains the most populous nation in the world. However, according to some estimates, it have been already surpassed by India; and together these two countries account for 36.6% of the world population (UNDESA, 2015).

One of the main characteristics of the ongoing demographic change has been the process of urbanization, occurring irrespective of region or country. The share of the urban population has been constantly growing, but only in the first decade of the 21st century has it reached the share of the rural population, being estimated at around 54% (UNDESA, 2014). In case of China, the level of urban population exceeded rural population in 2011 marking significant moment in Chinese history and had reached 57.4% by the end of 2016 (National Bureau of Statistics of China, 2017). China's urbanization ratio has been constantly increasing, the number of urban residents gradually rising and the number of cities and megacities growing. The number of permanent residents living in urban areas increased between 1978 and 2014 from 170 million to 750 million; the number of cities from 193 to 653, while and the number of megacities reached 6 in 2015 (National New Urbanization Plan, 2014).

As for the rise of megacities worldwide, according to UNDESA (2014) there were 29 megacities in 2015, ranging from Bangalore (10.1 million) and London (10.3 million) to Shanghai (23.7 million), Delhi (25.7 million) and Tokyo (38 million) – the latter remaining the biggest megacity uninterruptedly since 1954. By 2030, the group of megacities is set to increase by another 12 agglomerations including Madras (then with 13.9 million), Lahore (13 million), Hyderabad (12.8 million), Lima (12.2 million), Bogota (12 million), Johannesburg (11.6 million), Bangkok (11.5

million), Dar es Salaam (10.8 million), Ahmadabad (10.5 million), Luanda (10.4 million), Ho Chi Minh City (10.2 million) and Chengdu (10.1 million). The rise of megacities has been particularly visible in Asia, which is currently home to eight out of the world's 10 largest urban agglomerations, according to Demographia (2016). The majority of existing and projected megacities are currently situated in China – see Figure 1, ranging from the population number to the rate of their growth. Nevertheless, it would be incorrect to lump all the Asian megacities together (or, *a fortiori*, to assume that the Asian's megacities are largely alike). This is particularly due to China's megacities with some distinct Chinese characteristics, which will be discussed briefly in next part of this section.

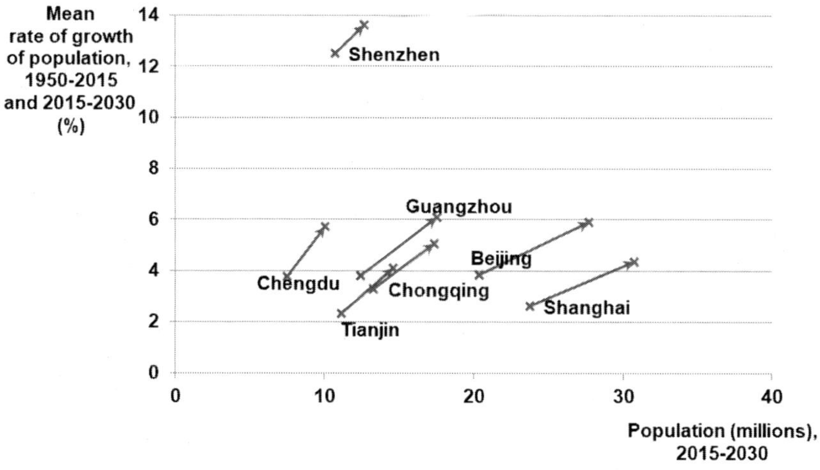

*The starting point of each vector represents the population in 2015 and mean rate of growth of population in 1950-2015, whereas the end marks the population in 2030; and the slope of the vector depicts the mean rate of growth of population in 2015-2030.

Source: UNDESA. 2014.

Figure 1. Chinese Megacities in 2015-2030*.

The distinctiveness of the Chinese megacities is characterized by two unique features. First, their emergence was a top-down process, because the introduction of the market economy in China, which started in the late 1980s, has taken place under the strict control of the state leadership and the power wielded by the Communist Party. Second, the influx of people to major agglomerations, such as Shanghai and Beijing, has been a controlled process as all new arrivals are required to obtain residence permits under the *hukou* system. Despite that, there still are underprivileged inhabitants who are not official residents and, by the same token, cannot avail themselves of many state-provided benefits (Kleer and Nawrot, 2018). The authorities are trying to resolve problems related to the consequences of the *hukou* system, as discussed by Feng (2018). There are, however, plans to still relocate millions of people from rural areas to cities in the coming years, as the largest potential in expanding internal demand in China is considered to be through urbanization, identified by the state as the main contributor to economic growth in the coming decade (Li, 2012; Nawrot, 2012: 18; Liu, 2014: 38; World Bank and DRC, 2014). Thus, we can conclude that there are numerous lessons from China's experiences in urbanization and the governance of megacities, especially for fast growing megacities in developing countries. This very much refers to the fact that China managed to govern fast or even very fast growth of cities with planning and interactions between central and municipal authorities. And in all this – what might be the most important – with decreasing poverty and the absence of slums in cities.

Finally, the observed rise of megacities leaves us without a doubt about their growing potential and power as in some cases they contribute more than one-third of the domestic product of the countries where they are situated and are becoming unique entities in their own right, challenging the developmental policies, governance, and cohesion of states. This requires in depth studies and theoretical consideration in the future.

Another important aspect and perhaps the most significant datum to everything around us is that we live in a civilizational turning point – from an industrial civilisation to a knowledge- based civilisation. Being at this turning point adds to the complexity of challenges the human civilization is facing no matter the geographical location of the country or even context of its economic development. Thus, in all that changes, and to some extend because of them, we can expect a reshaping of the world order and redefinition of existing economic systems. And no matter what shape they end up being, we need to be aware about the future of humanity. As such, we need to find ways and fields of cooperation for the global issues and problems our civilization faces.

The Belt and Road Initiative as a transcontinental framework of cooperation seems to be a suitable platform for collaboration for shared goals. The 16+1 mechanism as a part of that framework should thus extend a focus from the interests of individual sites and two-sided economic benefits of the stakeholders involved to broader and more useful collaboration. Possible fields include international security, environmental issues, urbanisation challenges including energy and transportation, communication, sanitation and water supply. Growing urban inequality, poverty and exclusion in fast growing agglomerations need to be addressed. Better understanding of different cultures, culture systems and multiculturalism also seems crucial. The future of work and AI are other areas for deep discussion and solutions – just to point a few.

It is also worth mentioning that the initiatives of a transcontinental and transcultural character between China and the Central and Eastern European countries have already created existing research and academic networks. One to mention is the "16+1 High level Academic Platform" – the first research network of scientific institutions from Central and Eastern Europe and China established in Warsaw in 2016 and designed to foster cooperation between academic institutions in the framework of a regional cooperation in the formula "16 + 1" (PAP, 2016; UEP, 2016; Polish Science, 2016).

The established research network of scientific institutions from Central and Eastern Europe and from China are the result of long-term efforts and the work of researchers from the partner institutions to provide opportunities for scientific and research cooperation, interdisciplinary projects, and the exchange of scientists and students. In addition, and perhaps more importantly, it is a platform for dialogue and collaboration on global issues and joint research projects in various fields, such as economics, management, medicine, commodity science, construction, geology, electro-mechanics, telecommunication, biology, chemistry, meteorology and many others. This is a first step to establish broader cooperation among universities and academic institutions from China and the Central and

Eastern European countries. Other cooperation between China and the CEEC in academia include The China-CEE Think Tanks Network and The China-CEE Institute, as discussed by Oehler-Sincai (2017).

Academic cooperation is a crucial pillar of the relations between China and the Central and Eastern European countries in the context of One Belt, One Road. There is no better way to build trust and understanding than people-to-people contact. Closer cooperation at the academic level should enable the flow of ideas, values, innovations and innovative thoughts to benefit from synergies, build mutual understanding between nations and to bring regions closer together, concentrating on similarities rather than obstacles and impediments and contributing to the wealth of nations, civilization progress and harmonious global community.

IMPORTANCE, CONCLUSION, AND IMPLICATIONS

The evidence of the existing progress between China and the CEEC over the last few years indicates that it is imperative to deepen the existing cooperation, elaborate on a more comprehensive partnership, and further enhance it. Overcoming existing challenges on both ends cannot be achieved by looking inward but through further global integration. Thus, closer cooperation, securing and deepening existing openness and embarking on further liberalisation of markets for the mutual benefits are recommended for both the CEEC and China. Furthermore, the new dimensions for strengthening ties emerged with the implementation of the 16+1 Dialogue and should be further explored as a mechanism for more effective collaboration between the countries of Central and Eastern Europe and China.

The communications between China and the Central and Eastern European countries, as well as between the Central and Eastern European countries themselves, have increased significantly over the last five years. This was due to numerous political visits at the national, sub regional and the EU levels, common cooperation mechanisms, people-to-people contact, the flow of tourists, exchange of students and scholars and last but not least trade and cross border investments. These contributed enormously to better understanding and building trust among the partners. This is an achievement of great importance. However, there are concerns about the significant asymmetry in bilateral trade for all the CEEC countries, the low level of cross border investments, and the unclear role that the AIIB can play in furthering the process.

For fully benefiting from being 'on the Road,' not only will and strategic geographical position – as is believed among the CEEC – is sufficient, but real action is needed. It requires the coherent and comprehensive cooperation of the Central and Eastern European countries themselves, their governmental resorts and institutions, inter-provincial, city-to-city cooperation, and people-to-people dialogue. What is more, countries from the region of Central and Eastern Europe should elaborate on a common vision, strategies, and concrete infrastructure and investment projects rather than competing to attract Chinese investors to markets not exceeding 38 million people separately. What is more, it should all fit into the broader landscape of Europe – spreading geographically from the Strait of Gibraltar and ending at the Urals. It means developing a long term vision and strategic cooperation not only with CEEC, but also with the UK, France, Germany and other EU and non-EU member states. Last but not least, Russia should not be forgotten in the bigger picture of BRI, since it is the closest neighbour of China and has already declared its support to integrate BRI with Russia-led Eurasian Economic Union.

There are high hopes and expectations in the majority of the Central and Eastern European countries for cooperation to be sustained, strengthened and most of all transformed into the real economy through the New Silk Road idea, which evolved over the years from "One Belt, One Road" concept to "Belt and Road Initiative" (BRI) framework with the AIIB and NSR Fund as its crucial mechanisms. The next step is to move the cooperation to another level through involvement of non-state actors and cooperation for shared goals which should be a focus on the agenda in the years to come.

References

Demographia. 2016. *Demographia World Urban Areas*. 12th Annual Edition, www.demograhia.com.

Eurostat. 2016. *Data*. https//ec.europa.eu.eurostat.

Feng, W.M. 2018. "Rural-Urban Migration, Urbanization, and Megacities in China." pp. 175-201 in J. Kleer and K.A. Nawrot Eds. *The Rise of Megacities. Challanges, Opportunities and Unique Characteristics*. London: World Scientific.

Kleer, J. and K.A. Nawrot, Eds. 2018. *The Rise of Megacities. Challenges, Opportunities and Unique Characteristics*. London: World Scientific.

Li, K.Q. 2012. "The Greatest Potential in Expanding Domestic Demand is Urbanization." *People's Daily*. February 16.

Liu, S. J. 2014. *China's Next Decade: Rebuilding Economic Momentum & Balance*. Hong Kong: CLSA Books.

Nawrot, K.A. 2012. "China at the Crossroads." *Global Asia Magazine* 11-12(28): 14-19.

National Bureau of Statistics of China. 2017. *China Statistical Yearbook.* Beijing: China Statistics Press.

National New Urbanization Plan 2014. *National New Urbanization Plan (2014-2020).* Beijing: People's Publishing House.

Oehler-Sincai, M. 2017. *Budapest, Again the 'Capital' of 16+1.* http://www.themarketforideas.com/budapest-again-the-capital-of-161-a262/.

PAP. 2016. *Powstała Pierwsza Naukowa sieć Badawcza krajów Europy Śr.-Wsch. i Chin.* http://naukawpolsce.pap.pl/aktualnosci/news%2C411711%2Cpowstala-pierwsza-naukowa-siec-badawcza-krajow-europy-sr-wsch-i-chin.html. [*Establishment of the First Scientific Research Network of Eastern and Central European Countries and China.*]

Science in Poland. 2016. *Establishment of the First Scientific Research Network of Eastern and Central European Countries and China.* Science in Poland. Ministry of Science and Higher Education, Republic of Poland. http://scienceinpoland.pap.pl/en/news/news% 2C411766%2

Cestablishment-of-the-first-scientific-research-network-of-eastern-and-central-european-countries.html.

UEP. 2016. *Collaboration between European and Chinese Scientific Institutions.* Poznan University of Economics and Business. http://ue.poznan.pl/en/news,c16/news,c15/collaboration-between-european-and-chinese-scientific,a54088.html.

United Nations, Department of Economic and Social Affairs, Population Division (UNDESA) 2014. *World Urbanization Prospects: The 2014 Revision*, CD-ROM Edition. New York UNDESA.

United Nations, Department of Economic and Social Affairs, Population Division (UNDESA). 2015. *World Population Prospects: The 2015 Revision,* Volume I: Comprehensive Tables. New York. UNDESA.

World Bank and the Development Research Center of the State Council, P. R. China (World Bank and DRC). 2014. *Urban China: Towards Efficient, Inclusive and Sustainable Urbanization*. Washington DC: World Bank.

In: Political Economy
Editors: Caleb M. Clark et al.
ISBN: 978-1-68507-106-6

Chapter 5

Marx's Theory of Value: A Sympathetic Yet Critical Perspective

Miguel D. Ramirez
Department of Economics, Trinity College, Hartford, CT, USA

Abstract

This chapter critically analyzes the important notion of value or exchange-value from a Marxian perspective as opposed to a neoclassical one. It is argued that the value of a commodity is a historically determined social relation between producers, rather than a subjective relation between man and commodities á la Eugen von Böhm-Bawerk and Stanley Jevons. Value, in the Marxian scheme, tends to assume certain specific forms more often than others depending on the particular stage of economic history, reaching its fullest expression under capitalist production—the highest form of commodity production based on private property. In turn, exchange value—a quantitative relation--is the manner in which value expresses its character of being the product of social (abstract) labor. The chapter highlights the classical view of value as expounded by David Ricardo and focuses on how Marx develops and attempts to resolve key problems in Ricardo's labor theory of value. It is argued that Ricardo dealt not only with the problem of relative value but, like Marx, also grappled with the concept of positive (absolute) value. This work also reviews important challenges to Marx's theory of value, ranging from the role of the composition of aggregate demand in determining "socially necessary labor" to the issue of whether the transformation of labor values into prices of production is an unnecessary and irrelevant exercise. Finally, the chapter turns its attention to the economic role of time from a Marxian perspective as it relates to the determination of interest-bearing (loan) capital and Adam Smith's important distinction between productive and unproductive labor—one whose clear comprehension rests on viewing value as a social relation.

Keywords: absolute value, commodity, constant capital, exchange-value, interest-bearing capital, money capital, prices of production, productive and unproductive labor, profit, surplus-value, rate of surplus-value (profit), value, variable capital

INTRODUCTION

In *Lady Windemer's* Fan, Oscar Wilde had Lord Darlington quip that a cynic was "a man who knows the price of everything and the value of nothing." Wilde's saying might just as well apply, doubly, to any contemporary economist or, for that matter, any economist other than those dwindling few who are still interested in the origin and evolution of economic ideas--to which I plead guilty as charged! In this spirit, it may come as a surprise to many, including the present crop of economists, that the debate of what determines the exchangeable value of commodities consumed the profession's interest up until the turn of the 20th century. A debate which pitted followers of the classical school such as Adam Smith, David Ricardo, and Karl Marx against advocates of the, then, rising marginalist school—men like Stanley Jevons, Carl Menger, and Eugen von Böhm-Bawerk—who argued that demand or marginal utility, as opposed to supply or the cost of production, determines the exchangeable value of commodities. Alfred Marshall, one of the most influential economists of the 20th century, along with John B. Clark, the father of the marginal productivity theory of distribution, and Paul Samuelson, the leading American theorist of the post-WWII period, would erect a grand synthesis of both theoretical approaches to the problem of value and distribution which has resulted in the neoclassical approach that pervades and dominates so much of the profession today (Blaug, 1998; Hunt and Lautsenheiser, 2011; Oser and Blanchfield, 1975).

This chapter, contrary to the prevailing neoclassical (and classical) paradigm, treats value or exchange-value as a social construct with specific historical and institutional origins. That is, we shall not view value as being confined in a rigid fashion to any of its various forms, be it its relative, equivalent, general or universal form as money. In fact, by describing and analyzing in which forms it manifests itself, whether it be in a simple commodity or capitalist mode of production, we shall discover, as well as appreciate, its inherent historically determined character. And this, of course, brings us to Marx, for it is thanks to his penetrating analysis of the capitalist mode of production and distribution which enables us today to understand value as a dynamic (multi-dimensional) social concept, or better still, as a process or rule of a socio-historical character. Marx believed that the task of economics as a social science is to systematically uncover and understand the property relations of production and distribution which are the foundation or "essence," if you will, of the market phenomena which "appear" to us in the form of exchange relations and consume our day-to-day activities (McLellan, 1975: 60-61).

From the outset then, it will be expedient to present value or exchange-value as a historically determined concept whose roots lie in the emergence of a world-embracing market in the 16th century. Next, the chapter highlights the classical view of value as expounded by David Ricardo and focuses on how Marx's own theory of value shares important qualities with it, but also differs from it in important respects. In particular, Marx develops and resolves some of the inherent problems in Ricardo's labor theory of value insofar as its applicability to a competitive capitalist economy are concerned. In this section, the paper also discusses important challenges to Marx's (and Ricardo's) theory of value, including the conversion of skilled into unskilled labor, the role of the composition of aggregate demand in determining "socially necessary labor," and the issue of whether the transformation of labor values into prices of production ("natural prices") is an unnecessary and irrelevant economic exercise. This section also discusses David Ricardo's life-long preoccupation with the concept of positive or absolute value and his search for an invariable measure of value that identifies which commodity is responsible for a change in relative value. The penultimate section turns its attention to the economic role of time from a Marxian perspective as it relates to the determination of interest-bearing (loan) capital and Adam Smith's important distinction between productive and unproductive labor—one whose clear comprehension rests on viewing value as a historically determined social construct. The final section summarizes the major arguments presented in this work.

Value as a Historically Determined Process

The conceptualization of value or exchange-value, Marx argues, becomes a reality on any sort of a social scale with "the creation in the 16th century of a world-embracing commerce and a world-embracing market" (*Capital I*, 1967a: 146). With the evolution of money in the form of bullion (gold or silver), direct exchange of one commodity for another (C-C) gives way to simple commodity circulation, i.e., to the exchange of commodities for money (sale or C-M) and, in turn, purchase (M-C). These distinct and independent acts (in time and space) only become a reality when a growing number of articles of utility are regularly produced by independent producers for the sake of exchange in a market; viz, C-M-C, the transformation of commodities (C) into money (M), and the change back into commodities (C). The key point here is that commodity production implies a high degree of specialization and "a person's productive activity has no direct connection to that person's consumption … [and it] has no direct connection to the people who produce the commodities. This social relationship is [just] mediated by the market" (Dobb, 1963; Hunt and Lautzenheiser, 2011: 5; Mandel, 1971: 63-68).

Once capitalism was firmly established in England by the middle of second half of the 18th century, direct producers are separated from their means of production on a massive scale and labor (more correctly, labor-power) becomes a commodity that is routinely bought and sold by capitalists in the labor market. The historical process by which the capitalist mode of production was established in England, from the end of the 15th century to the middle of the 19th century, involved the forcible eviction of peasants from their land via the enclosure movement and the imposition by the state of vagrancy laws, thereby forcing hundreds of thousands of displaced peasants to work long hours in the emerging capitalist manufactures and factories under squalid and miserable conditions (Braverman, 1974: 52-53; Brewer, 1990: 36-40; Hunt and Lautzenheiser, 2011: 17-18; Mandel, 1971: 116-118). In *Capital I*, Marx (1967a) refers to this process as the "primitive accumulation of capital" and writes:

> "In themselves money and commodities are no more capital [value] than are the means of production and of subsistence. They want transforming into capital ... The process that clears the way for the capitalist system, can be none other than the process which takes away from the labourer the possession of his means of production; a process that transforms, on the one hand, the social means of subsistence and of production into capital, on the other, the immediate producers into wage labourers. The so-called primitive accumulation ... is nothing else than the historical process of divorcing the producer from the means of production. It appears primitive, because it forms the pre-historic stage of capital and of the mode of production corresponding with it" (714-715).

It is only when capitalist commodity production is firmly rooted that it is possible to reveal the essence of capitalism, its internal laws and contradictions, because production for the market is in its most developed form. In the words of Harry Braverman (1974),

> "Capitalist production requires exchange relations, commodities, and money, but its *diffentia specifica* is the purchase and sale of labor power. For this purpose, three basic conditions become generalized throughout

society. First, workers are separated from their means of production … Second, workers are freed of legal constraints, such as serfdom or slavery, that prevent them from disposing of their labor-power. Third, the purpose of the employment of the worker becomes the expansion of unit of capital belonging to the employer, who is thus functioning as a capitalist" (52).

With this new stage in the development of commodity producing societies, the circuit of value or money capital takes on a new expanded form, as sketched in Figure 1. In other words, the merchant-capitalist comes to the commodity and labor markets with capital (potential) in the form of money (value in its universal form). Potential money capital with which he intends to purchase a sum of commodities in the form of means of production and labor-power that constitute his productive capital (P). By means of whose social function he expects to obtain commodities which have a greater value than that of its constituent elements (L and MP). These, in turn, the capitalist will exchange for money—the universal equivalent—with which he will be enabled to start the process anew on a larger scale. Incidentally, the dots in the expanded circuit merely indicate that the process of circulation is interrupted with the functioning of productive capital—productive in the sense of generating a surplus-value (M') for capitalists.

$$\mathrm{M} - \mathrm{C} \begin{cases} \mathrm{L} \\ \mathrm{MP} \end{cases} \ldots \mathrm{P} \ldots \mathrm{C'} - \mathrm{M'}, \text{ with } \mathrm{C'} = \mathrm{C} + \Delta C$$

Where L= labor-power (capacity to work); MP = means of production; P = productive capital (value terms); and C' = commodity capital (value terms).

Figure 1. Expanded Circuit of Money Capital.

Thus, the more capital-value takes this expanded form and the less the discontinuities present in the various phases of the circuit, the more developed is the capitalist mode of production, for "the formula of the circuit of money capital, M-C … P …C'-M', is the matter-of-course form of the circuit of capital only on the basis of already developed capitalist production, because it presupposes the existence of wage-labourers on a social scale" (Marx, *Capital II*, 1967b: 32). As a matter of terminology, value or money capital which takes on this expanded form on an ever more frequent basis is dubbed industrial capital by Marx—industrial in the sense that it assumes and discards its various forms in the total circuit of capital. In particular,

> "... it comprises every branch of industry run on a capitalist basis... its existence implies the class antagonism between capitalists and labourers. To the extent that it seizes control of social production, the technique and social organization of the labour-process are revolutionized and with them the economico historical type of society" (Marx, *Capital II*, 1967b: 48 and 55; also see Marx and Engels, 1964: 62-65).

To be sure, the movement of value in the form of money capital is not confined to a single circuit; it is repeatedly being turned over by the capitalist in order to accumulate more surplus-value via the exploitation of wage-labor. In fact, industrial capital is distinguished from earlier forms of capital by its continuous repetition, as summarized in Figure 2.

L L

$M^0 - C^0 \ldots P^0 \ldots C^1(C + \Delta C) - M^{1'} (M + \Delta M) - C^{1'} \ldots P^1 \ldots C^{2''} - M^{2''}$, and so forth.

MP MP

Figure 2. Continuous Circuit of Industrial Capital.

Notice that over time the various individual industrial capitals comprising the total social capital-value of society must constantly go through their various forms, viz., money, productive and commodity, in order to accumulate capital and reproduce it on an extended basis. However, at any given point in time, the individual industrial capitals may exist in all three of them simultaneously. Put differently, at any given point, there may be individual capitals entering their money phase (M...M'), while others are in their productive (P ... P') or commodity (C ... C') forms. Marx's (1967b) incisive (and relatively neglected) analysis in *Capital II*, Chapter IV thus views the reproduction of the total social capital of society as a constantly repeating cycle where every point of departure is also a point of return. For Marx (1967b), "The entire circuit [of capital-value] is thus really a unity of all three forms" (101). To reiterate, only at this stage of development of the productive forces of society (economic resources and technology) is it possible to conceptualize and fully appreciate the social basis of key economic categories such as value, exchange-value, labor-power, surplus-value, and capital-value.

MARX'S THEORY OF VALUE IN LIGHT OF THE CLASSICAL SCHOOL

In the Marxian scheme, a product is said to have value or exchange-value only if it is a use-value (object of utility) of some sort and if a quantum of socially necessary labor time has been expended in its production or acquisition. Like Ricardo before him in *Principles* (1977), Marx includes not only the labor directly applied to the production of commodities but the previous or past labor expended on the "implements, tools and buildings, with which such labor is assisted" (13). For Marx, machines, implements and tools simply transfer their existing value to commodities during the labor process, either gradually in the case of long-lasting fixed capital or wholly in the case of circulating capital in the form of raw materials and fuel (*Capital I,* 1967a: 165-166). Marx defined the part of the capital invested in machinery, raw materials, and fuel as constant capital (c) or a flow variable if we assume, as Marx did, that the whole of the capital stock turns over once a year (Blaug, 1998: 216). As discussed in more detail below, both Ricardo and Marx believed that machines and the forces of nature, such as a waterfall, the wind or the sun, add greatly to value in use (quantity of commodities) but do not create exchangeable value. In this connection, Ricardo observes that "as soon as by the aid of machinery, or by the knowledge of natural philosophy, you oblige natural agents to do the work which was before done by man, the exchangeable value of such work falls accordingly" (Blaug, 1998: 190).

In his analysis of exchange value, Marx, like Ricardo, also excludes from consideration scarce (non-reproducible) goods whose price is determined by scarcity alone, such as "... rare statues and pictures, scare books and coins, and wines of a peculiar quantity ... Their value is wholly independent from the quantity of labour originally necessary to produce them, and varies with the varying wealth and inclinations of those who are desirous to possess them" (Ricardo, 1977: 6; Marx, 1967a: 40). Ricardo argues that for commodities which are scarce or monopolized, "their price has no necessary connection with their natural price [as determined by the cost of production]" and "vary according to the law which Lord Lauderdale has laid down: they fall in proportion as the sellers augment their quantity, and rise in proportion to the eagerness of the buyers to purchase them" (1977: 262). But the prices of commodities which are subject to competition "will ultimately depend, not on the state of demand and supply, but on the increased or diminished cost of their production [in terms of socially necessary labor]" (Ricardo, 1977: 262).

He surmises correctly that in a capitalist economy these products represent a very small part of the mass of commodities exchanged in the market and focuses instead on the production of those commodities whose exchangeable value is determined by the socially necessary labor required to produce them under competitive conditions and constant average costs. Thus, Marx, like the other classical economists, was mainly concerned with the determination of long-run (natural) prices which are primarily determined by current and past labor costs, and not with fluctuations in short-run market prices (around these long-run prices of production) where demand is the main consideration. Apropos, Ricardo (1977) makes the following discerning observation in Chapter XXX of his *Principles* about the role of supply and demand in relation to the natural or long-run price of bread:

> "If the natural price of bread should fall 50 per cent from some great discovery in the science of agriculture, the demand would not greatly

> increase, for no man would desire more than would satisfy his wants, and as the demand would not increase, neither would the supply; for a commodity is not supplied merely because it can be produced, but because there is a demand for it. Here, then ... where the supply and the demand have scarcely varied, or, if they have increased, they have increased in the same proportion; and yet the price of bread will have fallen 50 per cent. at a time, too, when the value of money had continued invariable" (262).

That is, the shorter the period under consideration, the more likely it is that market values or prices are subject to day-to-day fluctuations in supply and demand that cause them to deviate from their long-run equilibrium (natural) prices; but the longer the time period, the more likely it is for these changes in supply and demand, driven primarily by irregular events and passing fads, to cancel each other out, and the greater the importance of the cost of production (as determined by socially necessary labor) in determining the exchange-value of commodities. However, one should be careful in interpreting Marx's statements on supply and demand in present-day terms because, like Ricardo and Smith before him, he did not conceive of demand and supply as schedules but as distinct quantities (Shoul, 1967: 448-460). That is, for him and the classical economists in general, an increase in demand does not refer to an increase in the quantity demanded of the good at all possible prices, but what the purchaser is willing and able to "to buy more of at the current prices" (Marshall, 1997: 97). The conception of supply and demand as schedules where the quantity demanded or supplied varies according to different prices (values) would have to await the seminal contribution of a contemporary of Marx, viz., John Stuart Mill (Oser and Blanchfield, 1975: 36; Marshall, 1997: 95-98).

To recap, the use-value or utility of an object is a necessary but not a sufficient condition for an article to have value or be transformed into a commodity. For these, or any use-values, to have exchange-value it is necessary that they embody "... the expenditure of simple labour-power, i.e., of the labour-power which, on an average apart from any special development, exists in the organism of every ordinary individual" (Oser and Blanchfield, 1975: 44). Labor-power is to be understood as the capacity to work of the laborer; its expenditure over a given period of time is defined as labor. In other words, labor is to a flow what labor-power is to a stock. Marx refers to capital invested for the purchase of labor-power or the wages of production workers as variable capital (v) (for further details, see Marx, 1967a *Capital I*, Chapter VI; Braverman, 1974; Ramirez, 2007: 28-30).

For Marx (1967a), "value is a relation between persons [producers]... expressed as a relation between things [commodities]" (*Capital I*, 74). Exchange-value or the "relation between things" is nothing but the *form* in which value manifests itself and it "presents itself as a quantitative relation, as the proportion in which values in use of one sort are exchanged for those of another sort" (*Capital I*: 36). That is, when commodities with different use values are regularly exchanged in the market, such as a pair of shoes for a pair of pants or a metal plough for 10 bushels of wheat, their different use-values cannot be the basis of the exchange because they cannot be compared—they are qualitatively different. There must be a common property which enables the producers to equate and exchange them and, according to Marx (and Ricardo), this common immaterial property or quality is the social (abstract) labor embodied in a commodity---the latter measured by socially necessary labor-time or in units of average, homogenous, unskilled labor. Value is not a physical property of commodities, but a social property attributed to them under definite historical and institutional conditions, viz., the constant production and reproduction of commodities for sale in the market under the circuit of industrial capital alluded to in the previous section. Apropos, Marx (1967a) remarks that: "Turn and examine a single commodity, by itself, as we will, yet in so far as it remains an object of value, it seems impossible to grasp it. If, however, we bear in mind that the value of commodities has a purely *social reality* [my emphasis], and that they acquire this reality only in so far as they are expressions or embodiments of one identical social substance, viz., human labour" (47). In this Marx follows, to some degree, Ricardo's (1977) lead as evinced by the following passage in the latter's important and relatively neglected chapter on "Value and Riches": "A franc is not a measure of value for anything, but for the quantity of the same metal of which francs are made, unless francs, and the thing to be measured, can be referred to some other measure which is common to both. This, I think, they can be, for they are both the result of labour; and, therefore, labour is a common measure, by which their real [absolute value] as well as their relative value may be estimated" (*Principles*, 189).

Value, for Marx, is, in the words of David Harvey (2018):

> "like gravity, an immaterial but objective force. I cannot dissect a shirt and find atoms of value in it any more than I can dissect a stone and find atoms of gravity. Both are immaterial relations that have objective material consequences ... Historical materialism recognizes the importance of immaterial but objective powers ... such as power, influence, belief, status, loyalty and social solidarity ... Value ... is exactly such a concept" (5).

That is, value is the social content embodied in all commodities that allows them to be equated and exchanged. And because value is the social property of a thing, abstract (social) labor is the source and substance of value which, in turn, is manifested through exchange value. That is, under simple or capitalist commodity production, we disregard the concrete specific human form in which labor is manifested (shoemaking vs. tailoring), and just focus on the expenditure of human labor-power in general. Marx (1967a), like Smith and Ricardo before him, measured this simple (abstract) labor in units of homogeneous unskilled labor and, in his view, it represented the hidden form of social labor "if we leave out of sight its special form, viz., the useful character of the labour, [it] is nothing but the expenditure of human labor power. Tailoring and weaving, though qualitatively different productive activities, are each a productive expenditure of human brains, nerves, and muscles, and in this sense are human labour" (*Capital I*: 51).

For Marx, the general form of value or value-equation tells us that the relative value of a certain commodity is expressed in terms of another; it informs us that a particular commodity assumes the relative form (e.g., a pair of shoes), while another the equivalent form (say, a pair of pants). By entering into this exchange relation (value relation) with another distinct commodity, it is able to manifest its two-fold character, namely, that of being an object of utility as well as the product of social (abstract) human labor (Sowell, 1967: 64-65). This exchange or value process achieves its fullest development when commodities (including labor-power) are no longer exchanged for other commodities, but for one specific commodity that assumes the form of universal equivalent, namely, money or gold in Marx's time—whose value is also determined by the socially necessary labor time required to produce it. In this connection, Harvey (2018) reminds us that "Marx is very careful in his language. He refers to money almost exclusively as the 'form of expression' or the 'representation' of value. He scrupulously avoids the idea that money is value incarnate or that it is an arbitrary symbol imposed by convention on exchange relations" (51). He goes on to add that "Value cannot exist without money as its mode of expression. Conversely, however autonomous it may seem, money cannot cut the umbilical cord that ties it to what it represents" (52). And value, in turn, is nothing but socially necessary labor time or human labor in the abstract that is embodied in commodities "... as crystals of this [immaterial] social substance, common to them all" (Marx, 1967a, *Capital I*: 4).

The simple average labor-power alluded to above, in order to be expended and remain the same under it various modifications, must have attained a certain level of social development. Thus, when Marx speaks of socially necessary labor-time, he means no more time than is needed on an average to produce a given commodity (cars or smart-phones) under the standard technical conditions of production in that particular sphere of production. It should be noted that the labor time spent on the production of a commodity must not be viewed "as the time spent by a particular labourer on that particular commodity: one must not think that the 'lazier or less skilled a man is,' the more valuable will be his product" (Roll, 1992: 238). In Marx's (1967a) words:

> "The introduction of power-looms into England reduced by one-half the labour required to weave a given quantity of yarn into cloth. The hand-loom weavers, as a matter of fact, continued to require the same time as before; but for all that, the product of one hour of the labour represented after the change only a half an hour's social labour, and consequently, fell to one-half its former value" (39).

Ricardo (1977) makes essentially the same argument regarding socially necessary labor in Chapter XX of his *Principles*. He writes:

> "Suppose, with a given capital, the labour of a certain number of men produced 1000 pair of stockings, and that by inventions in machinery the same number of men can produce 2000 pair … then the value of the 2000 pair of stockings … will be neither more nor less than that of the 1000 pair of stockings before the introduction of machinery; for they will be the produce of the *same* quantity of labour. But the value of the general mass of commodities will … be diminished; an effect is also produced on the portion of goods still unconsumed, which were manufactured previously to the improvement; the value of those goods will be reduced … to the level of the goods produced under all advantages of the improvement" (182).

As is evident from the passage above, Marx, like Ricardo, was careful not to equate the mass of use-values or riches with exchange value in the manner of the influential French economist Jean-Baptiste Say, known for popularizing Smith's ideas on the continent (Oser and Blanchfield, 1975: 122; Harvey, 2014: 15). The latter tried to explain the magnitude of a product's value by the extent of its utility and considered value and riches to be synonymous. Ricardo (1977), for example, thought that Say had "been singularly unfortunate in his definition of riches and value" because, if as a result of an increase in the productivity of labor, "Two sacks [of corn] be of the value that one was of before, he evidently obtains the same value and no more—he gets, indeed, double the quantity of riches—double the quantity of utility—double the quantity of value in use, but not double the quantity of value, and therefore Mr. Say cannot be right in considering value, riches, and utility to be synonymous" (*Principles*: 187). Insofar as we focus on the productivity of labor, we are concerned only with the quantity of use-values (riches) that concrete (useful) labor of some kind, such as tailoring or watchmaking, produces in a given unit of time. In turn, the productivity of the worker is determined by a number of factors such as "… the average amount of skill of the workmen, the state of science, and the degree of its practical application, the social organization of production, the extent and capabilities of the means of production, and by physical conditions" (Marx, 1967a, *Capital I*: 47). If, for example, a technological improvement in the production of cars results in the introduction of new machinery in the form of robotic arms, then 100 cars instead of 50 are now produced in, say, 8 hours of necessary labor time. Then, the value of each car is, after the introduction of the new technology, halved in value. Thus, on average, "the less is the labour time required for the production of an article, the less is the amount of labour crystallised in that article, and the less is its value; and *vice versa*, the less the productiveness of labour, the greater the labour-time required for the production an article. The value of a commodity ... varies directly as the quantity, and inversely as the productiveness, of the labour incorporated in it" (Marx, 1967a: 48).

Challenges to the Labor Theory of Value

Of course, this conceptualization of value as determined by the expenditure of average homogeneous units of simple unskilled labor begs the difficult question of how skilled labor (including natural differences, education, and training) is actually converted into unskilled labor by the labor market. For Marx, as well as Ricardo, skilled labor is nothing but multiplied simple labor and he contended that "... a commodity may be the product of the most skilled labor, but its value, by equating it to the product of simple unskilled labour, represents a definite quantity of the latter labour alone ... Experience shows that this reduction is constantly being made ... by a social process that goes on behind the backs of the producers, and ... appears to be fixed by custom" (Marx, 1967a: 44). Compare this with Ricardo's (1977) definition who writes, "The estimation in which different qualities of labour are held comes soon to be adjusted in the market with sufficient precision for all practical purposes ... If a day's labour of a working jeweler be more valuable than a day's labour of a common labourer, it has long been adjusted and placed in its proper position in the scale of value" (*Principles*: 11-12).

Critics argue that Marx, like his classical predecessors, was guilty of circularity in his argument because by appealing to the labor market (and custom) to determine the differences in the values created by the labor of different skills, he has erected another standard for determining the value of commodities (Böhm-Bawerk, 1923; Robinson, 1957: 12-13). That is, by deducing the higher value of the commodity produced by skilled labor, say an expensive watch, from the higher wage paid for the labor (labor-power) of the watchmaker, you are essentially explaining the relative value of x by the relative value of y which itself needs to be determined. However, as Bernice Shoul (1967) points out, this represents a misunderstanding of Marx's conception of the functioning of the labor market because he considers that the latter "... merely *registers* the magnitude of value already created in production rather than in any way *determining* value" (152; see also Howard and King, 1985: 123-124). That is, the wage differential between skilled and unskilled labor is the effect rather than the cause. And, as indicated by Ronald Meek (1975), the explanation for the different wages received by skilled and unskilled labor (and registered by the market) is taken up later in *Capital I* in the chapter on "The buying and Selling of Labour-Power." Marx (1967a), in this important chapter, essentially argues that it is the higher training and education costs that go into the value of skilled labor-power that explain why its expenditure "also creates proportionally higher values than unskilled labour-power" (170). That is, provided that the differences in skilled vs. unskilled labor are, to quote Meek (1975), "entirely due to differences in training costs, there is little difficulty (at least in theory) in reducing skilled to unskilled labour. One may simply calculate the amount of simple labour (including his own) which was expended in training the labourer, and then average this out over the whole of his expected productive life" (172; see also Braverman, 1974).

This historically-determined (social) view of value or exchange value stands in stark contrast to Say's theory of utility alluded to above, and the subjectivist theory of value advanced by Eugen von Böhm-Bawerk, Carl Menger, and Stanley Jevons in the second half of the nineteenth century. For example, Jevons argued that the value of any material product is determined by the "final degree" or marginal (additional) utility of the last unit consumed, and not the total utility of the good consumed. In this view there are no objective historically determined economic laws such as Marx's "labor theory of value," just each individual consumer living in total isolation from the rest of society. For example, Böhm-Bawerk in his illustration of the principle of marginal utility, posits a farmer (isolated "economic man") who has at his disposal five sacks of corn in his farm house. The first sack is needed in order not to starve to death, the second to improve his diet, another to feed his domestic animals, the fourth to make schnapps, and the fifth to feed parrots for amusement. It is this last or marginal sack of corn that determines the value or exchange value of corn. This subjectivist determination of value, based on the principle of diminishing marginal utility, was also used by Jevons to resolve the so-called diamond-water paradox posited by Adam Smith by showing that despite the fact that water's total value (utility) is very high (infinite) because it is both essential for human life and there is so much of it, its great abundance is the very reason that its marginal utility or value is very low and people pay little for it, and vice-versa for diamonds (Hunt and Lautzenheiser, 2011: 250-264; Oser and Blanchfield, 1975: 231-32). More formally, if the ratio of the marginal utilities for the two commodities, diamonds and water exceed the price ratio for the two commodities, that is, if MUd/MUw > Pd/Pw, then our representative individual would gain utility by trading water for diamonds until the ratios are equal, that is, MUd/MUw = Pd/Pw. Of course, if the inequality was reversed, then our individual would exchange diamonds for water until, once again, the last dollar's worth of diamonds or water yielded the same increment to the individual's total utility (Blaug, 1998: 292-294; McConnell, Brue, and Flynn, 2018: 152-156).

In response, a Marxist would argue that the marginal utilities of different commodities (water or diamonds or smart-phones) cannot possibly be compared to one another even for a given individual over time, and certainly not across different individuals because they are the result of different subjective evaluations by different individuals in isolation from one another. Is the marginal utility per dollar spent on a hamburger greater for a poor person than a rich one? It is impossible to say because there is no objective basis for comparing utilities across different individuals—they are *unobservable* variables. Moreover, if we attempt to measure utility indirectly by the amount of money an individual is willing to give, at the margin, for a good or service rather than do without it (marginal utility per dollar spent), one has to assume--as Alfred Marshall recognized, but Jevons did not-- that the marginal utility of money is fixed throughout the period of analysis. This is a tenuous proposition, at best, and only applicable to changes in the price of goods (services) that represent a small portion of an individual's overall expenditures as evidenced by the fact that Marshall used as his example changes in the price of tea because it represented a very small part of a person's total income (Marshall, 1997: 94-97). Otherwise, it is not possible to make a direct link between an individual's marginal utility schedule and his price schedule and, thus, derive an individual's demand curve. The challenge is made even more formidable in the construction of the market demand curve because it involves horizontally summing across many individuals with *different* marginal utility and price schedules. In Marshall's words, "the price will measure the marginal utility of the commodity to each purchaser individually: we cannot speak of price as measuring marginal utility *in general* [my emphasis], because the wants and circumstances of different people are different" (1997: 100). From a Marxian perspective, whatever may be an individual's subjective evaluations of material things, cars and smart-phones (water and diamonds), for example, the car (diamond) will always be more expensive than the smart-phone (water) because more socially necessary labor has been expended in its production (or acquisition) at the margin; that is, the price of production (natural price) which covers the costs of the least efficient producer. In this respect, Marx was simply following the classical view that "... the particular estimates of the [marginal] utility of a commodity made by the individuals who purchase it do not in fact determine its *long-run* equilibrium price, as is sufficiently shown by the fact that a change in the [subjective] estimates made of its utility by the purchases does not normally alter that price" (Meek, 1975: 162).

A useful statement of the classical view was made by Ricardo in a letter to Malthus dated October 9th, 1820 where he comments on Say's notion that a "commodity is valuable in proportion to its utility." Ricardo writes that this would be true if all buyers "would be willing to give a price for things in proportion to the estimation in which they held them, but the fact appears to me to be that buyers have the least in the world to do in regulating price—it is all done by the competition of the sellers, and however the buyers might be really willing to give more for iron, than for gold, they could not, because the supply would be regulated by the cost of production, and therefore gold would be inevitably in the proportion which it is now to iron, although it probably is by all mankind considered as the less useful metal (Sraffa, 2004a. *Letters VIII*: 276-777).

Therefore, in a competitive market economy based on private property and subject to the production of reproducible goods under constant costs, individual commodity producers pursuing their self-interest unwittingly work for each other by exchanging the products of their labor, and the social character of their labor is revealed to them only when these commodities are realized as values in a market. That is, commodities are not produced for personal consumption ("non-use values for their owners") but for other people ("use-values for their non-owners") in the market, and if a commodity cannot find a buyer then it partially or completely loses its social value. The need for commodities to be realized as values before they can be realized as use-values becomes readily apparent on a massive scale during an economic crisis of overproduction, when a mass of use-values is destroyed because there is a lack of effective demand or "social need" on the part of consumers and producers. Marx (1967c) views the lack of effective purchasing power on the part of workers, capitalists, and non-productive classes as one of the factors responsible for economic crises "… as opposed to [just] the drive of capitalist production to develop the productive forces as though only the absolute consuming power of society constituted their limit" (*Capital III*: 484). In fact, he views the process of producing value and surplus-value and realizing it in the marketplace as inherently contradictory in nature because, on the one hand, capitalists want to maximize the production of surplus-value by minimizing the value of labor-power (keeping real wages low), but this threatens the realization of commodities because workers, as consumers, constitute an important component of effective demand in a capitalist economy (Marx, 1967b,

Capital II: 316; Brewer, 1984: 106). David Harvey (2014) captures this idea well and refers to is as "the contradictory unity of production and realization," that is to say, "Capitalism as a social formation is perpetually caught in this contradiction. It can either maximize the conditions for the production of surplus value, and so threaten the capacity to *realise* surplus value in the market, or keep effective demand strong in the market by empowering workers and threaten the ability to create surplus value in production" (81).

Of particular interest to our discussion of how the market realizes the value and use-value of commodities is the role that Marx assigns to "social need" or "use-value on a social scale." Marx (1967c), in *Capital* III, appears to redefine his concept of socially necessary labor time away from the standard technical conditions of production in a particular sphere or branch of production to one determined by the "social needs" of the economy as a whole. He now appears to suggest that the distribution of social labor among the various spheres or branches of production (based on the prevailing division of labor) must be proportional to the existing structure of social needs if the reproduction process is to proceed without difficulty (see Colliot-Thelene, 1979: 406-407; Robinson, 1957: 14). Consider, for example, the following puzzling argument proffered by Marx (1967c):

> "let us assume that proportionately too much cotton goods have been produced, although *only* [my emphasis] the labour-time necessary under the prevailing conditions is incorporated in this total cloth production. But in general too much social labour has been expended in this particular line; in other words, a portion of this product is useless. It is sold … solely as if it had been produced in the necessary proportion … Only so much is required to satisfy social needs. The limitation occurring here is due to use-value. Society can use so much of its total labour-time for this particular kind of product under prevailing conditions of production" (636).

Critics are quick to seize on this point and argue that there is an apparent contradiction between what Marx (1967a) said at the beginning of Vol. I of *Capital* with regard to the socially necessary labor time required to produce a commodity under normal conditions as it applies to a *specific* branch or sphere of production, and his apparent redefinition of the same concept in Vol. III of *Capital* (Marx, 1967c) where that labor time is now recognized as socially necessary only if social need sets the limit to the value (price of production) of individual commodities. That is, if we admit with Marx that use-value on a macro scale is now able to set the limits on what constitutes the amount of socially necessary labor time needed to produce different commodities, independent of their normal technical requirements within each industry or branch, then as Cutler, Hindess, Hirst, and Hussain (1977) correctly observe "the labour theory of value ... must admit the crucial role of demand if it is (as it must be) combined with a notion of a necessary composition of the social product "(93).

Ronald Meek and Bernice Shoul (and Robinson) are also aware of this underlying problem with Marx's theory of value, and they argue that Marx believed that provided that the output of the various branches properly adjusts itself in accordance with "social need" or aggregate demand, then the unit value of a commodity in a given sphere of production would be determined by the socially necessary labor; i.e., by the normal technical requirements of production in that sector (under constant returns to scale). However, this is an empirical matter, and it is equally possible to presume that such an "appropriate adjustment" does not take place in the marketplace, particularly if increasing or decreasing returns to scale are present. If this is the case, then "social need" or effective demand does play a role in determining the exchangeable value of commodities and "we would seem to have no option but to extend the [Marxian] system further in order to include a set of demand equations" (Meek, 1975: 34). Or in the words of Shoul (1967), "demand may act to alter value itself, and not merely to determine prices which deviate from [labor] values" (450). The important point here is that only in the case of constant cost industries is it possible to assume that changes in the structure or *composition* of demand have no direct effect on the technical coefficients of production and the unit value of commodities in each individual branch. Thus, if Marx's (1967c) "law of value" is redefined in the manner of *Volume III* to include "the quota of social labour-time available for the various particular spheres of production," or "use-value on a social scale," then the internal coherence and validity of his theory of value in *Capital* is legitimately brought into question. A similar (but not the same) criticism of the qualifier "socially necessary" is offered by Robert Nozick (1974). He contends that the use of the qualifier renders Marx's theory of value ambiguous at best, because it conceals a subjective evaluation of "necessity" on the part of consumers in the marketplace. For example, Nozick uses the example of a worker who spends his time tying knots in a piece of cord in the most efficient manner possible, yet, from the standpoint of society, it is likely that tying knots in cords is just a waste of labor time. The problem here is that what constitutes "socially necessary labor-time" is made dependent on whether or not there is demand for the finished product, i.e., the knotted cord. In Nozick's view, by introducing the "socially necessary" qualifier into the labor theory of value, it simply converts the theory into a roundabout and imprecise description of supply and demand. Thus, he contends that there is no labor theory of value as such, but rather the notion that both supply and demand determine what makes labor time socially necessary and whether a commodity has exchangeable value or not in the market (260).

Absolute and Relative Value

Marx, more so than Ricardo before him, based his entire investigation upon the concept that it is the quantity of socially necessary labor expended on a commodity that determines both the magnitude of the product's positive or absolute value and, in turn, regulates its relative or exchangeable value which, through distribution, resolves itself into profit, wages, and rent. The relative expression of value between two commodities does not tell us the whole story because *absolute* changes in the value of both commodities may take place while their relative value remains the same; e.g., suppose it takes four hours of socially necessary labor to produce both a pair of shoes and one pair of pants, then one pair of shoes will exchange for one pair of pants. Now suppose that as a result of an improvement in the productivity of labor, it takes only two hours of socially necessary labor to produce each commodity, then, again, one pair of shoes will exchange for one pair of pants even though the value of each commodity in terms of socially necessary labor has decreased by one half. Changes in the relative value of a given commodity can also occur when its absolute value changes in terms of labor-time, while the value of the other commodity remains constant. That is, the relative value of shoes, expressed in terms of pants, rises and falls directly as the value of shoes, *ceteris paribus.* Contrariwise, let the value of a pair of shoes remain constant while the value of a pair of pants, its equivalent in the exchange equation, varies in value. In this case, the relative value of a pair of shoes expressed in terms of a pair of pants, rises and falls inversely as the value of a pair of pants. Finally, the relative value of commodities changes when the labor-time required to produce both commodities varies in the same direction but at unequal rates, or in opposite directions (e.g., one pair of shoes doubles in terms of labor time, while one pair of pants decreases by half in terms of labor time). That is, simultaneous variations in the absolute value of a commodity and its relative value need not correspond in magnitude.

From a practical standpoint, however, the problem is considerably more difficult to resolve than Marx ever imagined as discussed in more detail in the subsection dealing with the so-called "transformation problem." That is, in order to discern which commodity is responsible for the change in relative or exchangeable value, we need an invariable standard of value or a "standard commodity" which will enable us to measure the absolute value of commodities independent of their exchange or relative values. Ricardo (1977), to his credit, even as early as the writing of the first edition of the *Principles*, clearly understood the inherent difficulties involved in finding or constructing an invariable standard of measure as evinced by his remarks in Section VI of his Chapter *On Value,* "Of such a measure it is impossible to be possessed, because there is no commodity which is not itself exposed to the same variations as the things the value of which is to be ascertained; that is, there is none which is not subject to require more or less labour for its production" (27). He proposed using "gold as an approximation to a standard measure of value" because he was of the opinion that this commodity was produced with a proportion of fixed capital to labor which was "nearest to the average quantity employed in the production of most commodities" (29).

As we will discuss below, Ricardo would return to this vexing problem towards the end of his life, but without much success. A partial and original solution to the search for an invariable standard was provided by Marx, but it would have to await the seminal work of Piero Sraffa (1960), more than one hundred years later, for a theoretically rigorous construction of a standard (composite) commodity capable of fulfilling Ricardo's exacting measurement criteria, viz., one which is independent of the changes in the relative prices of the goods that go into the construction of the standard commodity.

Marx praised Ricardo for disposing of Adam Smith's theory of value which suffered from a number of unresolved problems and contradictions, not the least of which is that it made the revenues of workers and capitalists (wages and profit) along with the rent of the landlord determinants of the value of commodities (Smith 1976; Marx, 1967b, *Capital II*: 241-250.) Ricardo, by developing a consistent theory of value based on embodied labor, argued that it is the size of the product's value which is the primary magnitude and it then resolves itself into wages and profit (rent for Ricardo (1977: 37) is not a component part of the value of the product on the least productive or marginal land. For Marx (1967c), the source of rent (and profit) is surplus-labor in the form of surplus-value, while the natural fertility of the soil is one of the conditions determining the productivity of labor in terms of use-values as alluded to above—it is the *basis* but not the source of rent (*Capital III*, 646). That is, although "land" *per se* has no exchange value because it is not the product of socially necessary labor, it has an "irrational price" which, according to Marx, is nothing but the capitalized rent it yields to landowners. For example, suppose that a plot of land yields a rent which amounts to $2,000 per year, and that the average interest rate is 5% per annum, then the price of the plot of land is $40,000, that is the $2,000 represents the annual (simple) interest on a capital of $40,000, no more no less. Landlords are able to demand payment for the use of land (broadly defined) because they have a monopoly in landed property; thus, rent is a socially (historically) determined category (Mandel, 1971: 282-283; Ramirez, 2009: 76-78).

For similar historical reasons, Marx argued that the source of profits and rent is to be found in surplus-value(s) appropriated by capitalists during the labor process. That is, the capitalist, having concentrated the means of production into his own hands, is able to compel the worker, who has neither means of production nor means of existence, to work a substantial part of the day without pay. In *Capital I* Marx (1967a) defines surplus-value in the following terms: "The fact that half a day's labour is necessary to keep the labourer alive during 24 hours, does not in any way prevent him from working the whole day. Therefore, the value of labour-power, and the value which labour-power creates in the labour process, are two entirely different magnitudes; and this difference of the two values was what the capitalist had in view when he was purchasing the labour-power" (193). That is, surplus-value is nothing but the difference between the (lower) value of labor-power and the (higher) value which the use of that labor-power creates during the labor process.

In terms of Marx's notation, the value of a commodity is comprised of the sum of three components denoted by, c + v + s, where c represents constant capital or "dated labor" which merely transfers its value to the commodity without any increase. On the other hand, v + s, represents the flow of newly created value during the labor process for which the worker is compensated for his wages (v) while the capitalist appropriates the extra value, s. Marx further defined the rate of surplus-value as the ratio of surplus-value (s) to variable capital (v), so, if a worker's labor-power (variable capital) is worth $60 per working day but he generates through his labor $30 of surplus-value for the capitalist, then the rate of surplus-value (s'=s/v) is 50 percent. The rate of surplus-value can be increased by lengthening the working day without increasing the daily wage, and Marx called this *increasing* absolute surplus-value. Or it can be raised by increasing the productivity of those industries that produce wage goods, and thus lowering the value of labor-power for a given length of the working day. This is called *increasing* relative surplus-value. The former manner of increasing the rate of surplus-value prevailed during the early stages of capitalist production, culminating in the struggle to shorten the length of the working day first to 12, and then 10 hours by mid-19th century in England.

The latter means of increasing surplus-value emerges later, and it is the hallmark of the fully developed competitive capitalism of England during the second half of the 19th century (Brewer, 1990: 32-33; Howard and King, 1985: 94-97; Mandel, 1971: 135-137).

One should not lose sight of the fact that surplus-value is a historical category inherent to capitalism that results from the development of the productive forces of society, i.e., the capitalist by virtue of his ownership of the means of production, in the form of factory buildings, machinery, and raw materials, is able to appropriate this surplus-labor in the form of surplus-value during the labor process without compensation. That is, Marx's theory of surplus-value or "exploitation" attempts to explain how unearned incomes are received in an economy based on impersonal market forces and formal "equality" before the law rather than social status or custom. In essence, the extraction of surplus-labor (unpaid labor) under capitalism differs from slave-owner and feudal society only in being concealed or masked by the exchange relations of the purchase and sale of labor-power. In the words of Harry Braverman (1974), "The labor process begins with a contract or agreement governing the conditions of the sale of labor power by the worker ... because social conditions leave him or her no other way to gain a livelihood. The employer, on the other hand ... [sets]... in motion the labor process, which, while it is in general a process for creating useful values, has now also become specifically a process for the expansion of capital, the creation of a profit" (52-53). Marx is thus able to derive a theory of distribution from his theory of surplus-value or "exploitation"; that is, he is able to explain, in a more cogent and compelling manner than Ricardo, how the respective shares of the main social classes in the national income of a capitalist economy are determined.

Despite Ricardo's (1977) significant advance over Adam Smith in terms of advancing a more coherent labor theory of value, he was unable to distinguish between the value of labor-power (a stock concept) and labor (a flow concept), and thus confused factors which affect the rate of surplus-value (s/v) with those that determine the rate of profit (s/c + v), viz., the surplus-value on the flow of advanced capital in the form of constant (c) plus variable capital (v). He also erroneously thought that the "law of value" operated directly under capitalism but with important modifications taken up below. Marx, on the other hand, argued that, under capitalism, commodities no longer sold at their simple labor values, but at their prices of production (Ricardo's "natural prices") which differ from labor values both in form and magnitude. Finally, Ricardo (1977), like his contemporaries, confined most of his analysis to the determination of the relative or exchange value of a commodity; that is, he believed that the relative values of different goods are determined almost exclusively by the relative quantities of labor time embodied in them. He emphasizes this point by warning the reader in his section entitled, *On an Invariable Measure of Value* as follows: "I have not said because one commodity has so much labour bestowed upon it as will cost £1000, and another so much as will cost £2000, that therefore one should be of the value of £1000, and the other of the value of £2000; but I have said that their value will be to each other as two to one, and that in those proportions they will be exchanged; it is of no importance to the truth of this doctrine whether one of these commodities sells for £1100 and the other for £2200, or one for £1500 and the other for £3000; into that question I do not at present inquire" (*Principles*: 29). Marx, as discussed above, thought that socially necessary labor time determines the *absolute* value of goods which, in turn, regulates their relative values.

However, towards the end of his life, Ricardo became more interested in the positive (real) or absolute value of commodities, as revealed by the discovery of his unfinished manuscript entitled, "Absolute Value and Exchangeable Value," and a series of letters between him and political economists such as Hutches Trower and Thomas Robert Malthus (Sraffa, 2004c: 398-412). For example, in a letter dated, June 24th, 1821, Trower raises doubts about Ricardo's definition of exchangeable value as being measured by the labor expended upon a commodity and argues that the term value refers only to the relative value of commodities and cannot possibly refer to the positive or absolute value of commodities because, "If there were no exchange of Commodities they would have no *value*. They would, of course, retain their *use*; but they could not be said to possess *value*; which implies the *worth* of one thing estimated in some other things" (Sraffa, 2004c: 394). He goes on to add "… that the labor, which a commodity can *command* is what actually constitutes its *exchangeable* value" (Sraffa, 2004c: 394). To which Ricardo replies in a letter dated July 4th, 1821, the following:

> "I do not, I think, say that the labour expended on a commodity is a measure of its exchangeable value, but of its positive value. I then add that exchangeable value is regulated by positive value, and therefore is regulated by the quantity of labour expended. You say if there were no exchange of commodities they could have not value, but if I am obliged to devote a month's labour to make me a coat, and only one weeks labour to make a hat, although I should never exchange them, the coat would be four times the value of the hat, and if a robber were to break into my house and take part of my property, I would rather that he took 3 hats than one coat. It is in the early stages of society, when few exchanges are made, that the value of commodities is most peculiarly estimated by the quantity of labour necessary to produce them, as stated by Adam Smith" (Sraffa, 2004b: 2).

Ricardo, with his impeccable logic, then proceeds to dispose of Tower's definition of exchangeable value in terms of the labor (labor-power) it can command in the market as follows:

> "I confess I do not rightly understand what meaning you attach to the words "exchangeable value" ... A yard of super-fine cloth we will suppose can command a month's labour of one man, but in the course of a year, from some cause, it commands only a fortnight's labour of one man, you are bound to say that the exchangeable value of cloth has fallen one half. You are bound to say this whether the cloth be produced with a great deal less labour in consequence of the discovery of improved machinery, or the food and of the other necessaries of the labourer be produced with so much difficulty that wages rise and therefore labour [labor-power] rises as compared with cloth and many other things ... Now the difference between you and me is this: in the latter case I should say with you that cloth has fallen to half its former exchangeable value and my proof would be that it would exchange for only half the former quantity of labour and of *all other things* [emphasis in the original], but in the other case I should say that cloth has not altered in exchangeable value because it will exchange for precisely the same quantity of all other things (Sraffa, 2004b: 2-3).

From the above exchange with Trower, as well as numerous others with Robert Malthus, James Mill, and John McCulloch, it is apparent that Ricardo was searching for an invariable standard of value which would enable him to measure the absolute value of commodities independent of their exchange or relative value. He says so as much in a letter to Trower dated, Sept. 3rd, 1823: "To me it appears, that whatever is the measure of absolute value will be the measure of exchangeable value. Labor was originally that measure" (Sraffa, 2004b: 383). Ricardo understood, perhaps more so than Marx, that without a standard of measure which would enable us to identify which commodity is responsible for a change in exchangeable or relative value, the labor theory of value is not empirically verifiable. This is an important point because, despite the fact that the theory is based on a number of unobservable variables, such as "labor values" and "surplus-value"—very much like the role played by "marginal utility" or "total utility" in the marginalist approach—If it is capable of generating refutable hypotheses and predicting economic behavior, then it is scientifically valid in explaining the actual movement of prices. Alas, Ricardo's search would prove ultimately unsuccessful as revealed in a letter written (Sept. 5th, 1823) to James Mill less than a week before his untimely death from an acute ear infection: "I see the same difficulties as before and am more confirmed than ever that strictly speaking there is not in nature any correct measure of value nor can ingenuity suggest one, for what constitutes a correct measure for some things is a reason why it cannot be a correct one for others" (Sraffa, 2004b: 387).

Value and Prices of Production

It should be noted that Ricardo's analysis of the labor theory of value was purely confined to the quantitative dimension of the problem, and he neglected the qualitative or historical nature which so preoccupied Marx's own analysis of what determines the exchangeable value of commodities under capitalism (Marx, 1971: 405-406; Rubin, 1979). Also, as alluded to above, Ricardo (1977), like Smith before him, was also not able to resolve the issue of how is it possible for the labor theory of value to retain its validity when the commodities being exchanged are produced by capitals of unequal organic compositions [constant (c) relative to variable (v) capital or, loosely speaking, different capital-labor ratios], of different durability, and advanced for different periods of time (27). That is, Ricardo's natural (equilibrium) prices were no longer determined by labor values as measured by the necessary labor time required to produce them. This led to the disintegration of the Ricardian School during the 1820 and 1830s. Marx, to his credit, attempted to show how the so-called "transformation problem" could be solved and, in the opinion of noted historian of economic thought, Mark Blaug (1998), "… it marks the first and only attempt in the history of economic thought to carry the labour theory of value to its logical conclusion" (219).

Marx's (1967c) proposed solution to the problem is given in Vol. III of *Capital* and it basically consists of showing that commodities do not sell at their simple labor values, but at their prices of production. The latter are equal to the cost price of production (c + v) plus the average rate of profit [the ratio of the total surplus value (Σs_i) created by the whole working class to the total capital (constant and variable) invested in all industries, or in equation form, $r = \Sigma s_i/\Sigma(c_i + v_i)$]. That is, labor values deviate from prices of production in a systematic fashion, viz., capitals with a higher than average organic composition of capital (c/v) will sell their goods at prices of production that are higher than abstract labor values, and vice-versa. Sweezy (1970) defines the organic composition of capital by the expression c/(c+ v), which moves in the same direction as Marx's c/v but more slowly. The advantage of using this expression is that it can be used to express the rate of profit as a function of the rate of surplus value and the organic composition of capital as follows: $s/(c + v) = s/v\ [1 - c/(c + v)]$. That is, the rate of profit is positively related to the rate of surplus-value or "exploitation," and inversely related to the organic composition of capital. Sweezy's formula is easily derived from Marx's 1967c equivalent formula for the rate of profit (p'), $p' = s/(c + v) = s'v/(c+v)$, where $s' = s/v$ is the rate of surplus-value (*Capital III* 49-51).

This is because more surplus-value is produced than is realized in the form of average profit in those industries with a lower than average organic composition compared with those branches of industry with an above average organic composition of capital. This outcome is brought about by capitalists striving to maximize profits under the relentless pressure of competition. They will invest their new capital in industries with a higher rate of profit and lower organic composition of capital and in the process lower prices (below labor values) via an excess supply of the given commodity while, at the same time, withdrawing capital from industries with a lower rate of profit and higher organic composition of capital and thus driving up prices (above labor values) via a relative decrease in the quantity supplied of the given good. The constant transfer of capital from one industry into another in search of profits results in an equalization of the different rates of profit into an average rate of profit. In other words, the "law of value" maximizes the overall efficiency of the capitalist economy by transferring surplus from technically backward industries to the leading branches of industry. In those industries in which, by accident, the organic composition of capital is equal to the economy-wide average, prices of production or "natural prices" would equal labor values (Blaug, 1998: 219-224; Ekelund, Jr. and Hebert, 2004; Hunt and Lautzenheiser, 2011: 222-231; Meek, 1975: 16-28; Howard and King, 1989: Chapter 3; Seton, 1957: 149-60; Sweezy, 1970: 109-130; Wolfson, 1990: 179-195).

Critics of Marx's "transformation solution," including sympathetic ones such as Ronald Meek, point out that his solution is incomplete because "it does not take into account that the value of elements of inputs as well as those of the output have to be transformed into prices" (Meek, 1975: 194). Marx's (1967c) numerical illustrations in Chapter IX of *Capital III* are clearly incorrect because he left the input prices proportional to labor values in the five spheres of production, and thus, each sphere produced commodities with two different prices, "one as an output and one as an input" (Hunt and Lautzenheiser, 2011: 231). However, Sweezy (1970) and other knowledgeable commentators contend that Marx *deliberately* simplified the calculation in Chapter IX by assuming that the output of the five different spheres does not enter into the production of any of the others"

(190). It is evident from a careful reading of Chapter IX that Marx was well aware of this problem, and it is wrong to suggest that he ignored it as the following passage reveals:

> "We had originally assumed that the cost price [used up c + v] of a commodity equaled the value of the commodities consumed in its production. But for the buyer the price of production of a specific commodity is its cost price, and may pass as cost price into the prices of other commodities. Since the price of production may differ form the value of a commodity, it follows that the cost-price of a commodity containing the price of production of another commodity may also stand above or below that portion of its total value derived from the value of the means of production consumed by it. It is necessary to remember this modified significance of the cost-price, and to bear in mind that there is always the possibility of an *error* if the cost-price of a commodity in any sphere is identified with the value of the means of production consumed by it" (*Capital III*: 164-165).

Yet, although Marx (1967c) recognized the problem, he did not believe it would alter his main results and goes on to write that, "Our present analysis does not necessitate a closer examination of this point" (165). In this he was too quick to minimize the importance of this problem because without a correct solution to it, the three invariance conditions necessary for the transformation of values into prices of production (and surplus-value into profits) cannot be met, viz.: 1) the sum of prices in each sphere equals the sum of labor values; 2) the sum of profits in each sphere equals the total surplus-value; and 3) the average rate of profit is equal to the ratio of total surplus value to total capital. Following the lead of Howard and King (1985), the first condition can be written as:

$$\sum (c + v + s) = \sum (c_p + v_p + \pi) \qquad (1)$$

Where subscripts denote price magnitudes and π represents profits, and all variables are in flow terms, i.e., assuming the stock of capital turns over once in a year (Blaug, 1998). The second condition requires that:

$$\sum s = \sum \pi \tag{2}$$

From which it follows that total capital in value terms is equal to total capital in price terms, since:

$$\sum (c + v) = \sum (c_p + v_p) \tag{3}$$

And it is easy to see that Marx's value rate of profit (r) is equal to his price rate of profit (r_p):

$$r = \sum s / \sum (c + v) = \sum \pi / \sum (c_p + v_p) = r_p \tag{4}$$

A mathematical solution to Marx's transformation problem that fulfilled his invariance conditions had to wait early in the nineteenth century when German economist Ladislaus von Bortkiewicz showed that, "Marx was right in principle, and wrong in detail" (Howard and King, 1985: 138). Bortkiewicz's solution, however, was dependent on the *ad hoc* assumption that one of the three sectors in his system of equations, producing the luxury commodity gold, has an organic composition of capital equal to the average organic composition in the entire system and, as a result, labor values coincide with prices of production. This, as pointed out by Howard and King, "will not be true in any actual capitalist economy, except by chance" (1985: 138). Subsequent more rigorous mathematical solutions, including that by Seton (1957), involving *n* departments and without the assumption of simple reproduction, have shown that Marx's solution to the transformation "problem admits of a uniquely determined solution" that is consistent with "Marx's conception of the transformation process, and the formal inferences he drew from it" (59).

Despite showing that a solution can be found, sympathetic critics of Marx, such as Ronald Meek (1975) and Piero Sraffa (1960), contend that Marx's journey from labor values to prices of production and surplus-value to profits is an unnecessary detour. A "solution" can be found provided that alternative techniques for producing a commodity and joint-production (two or more commodities produced by single industry) are ignored. According to Howard and King (1985), it is extremely challenging to determine how to allocate the total necessary labor and define labor values in cases of joint production, such as the separate values of wool and mutton generated from the raising of sheep. These cases are from a practical standpoint very important, because by-products are common in both agricultural and manufacturing activities (156-161; also see Steedman, 1977; Brewer, 1984: 139).

One could just start with the conditions of production and the distribution of the net income (output) of society between capitalists and workers in terms of a composite commodity and arrive at Marx's prices of production and rate of profit. Neoclassical critics such as Samuelson (1957), on the other hand, go much further and argue that Marx's approach is from a formal (mathematical) standpoint, nonsensical, because one could just as readily start the transformation process in reverse order, starting with prices and profits and working back into values and surplus values. Thus, as Meek (1975) observes, the question arises "whether the really important things that Marx was trying to say in this part of his analysis can in fact be said in a less exceptionable way through the adoption of an alternative approach?" (26).

In this connection, Sraffa (1960) showed, via the construction of a standard (composite) commodity where value and profit rates are equal, that prices and profits can, in fact, be determined with reference to only "technical conditions of production and the distribution of the net product between capitalists and workers" (Howard and King, 1985: 172). In other words, in Sraffa's "neo-Ricardian" model, a composite borderline industry based on different commodities (e.g., iron, coal, and wheat) and labor can be constructed via an input-output system so that it fulfills the same "yardstick role" that Marx ascribed to an industry with an organic composition of capital equal to the average organic composition for the economy as a whole. That is, "the proportions in which the three commodities are produced in the new system (180:270:360) are equal to those in which they enter its aggregate means of production (150:225:300). The composite commodity sought for is ... made up in the proportions, 1t. iron: 11/2 t. coal: 2 qr. wheat" (Sraffa, 1960: 20).

In a highly ingenious and elaborate (mathematical) derivation that is beyond the scope of this essay, Sraffa shows that the net output of this "balanced" industry relative to its means of production in terms of the composite commodity can, in turn, be used to generate a maximum rate of profit denoted by, R, for the borderline industry which is both independent of the actual rate of profit and the changes in the relative prices of the goods that go into the construction of the standard commodity (Howard and King, 1985: 141-42; Sraffa, 1960: 18-23). That is, he is able to show what happens to the actual rate of profits (r) and prices in the standard commodity as the share of wages (w) in the net output goes from 1 (all the net output goes to workers) to 0 (all the net output goes to capitalists) via the following equation:

$$r = R\,(1 - w) \qquad (5)$$

Using Sraffa's numerical example, and assuming that the maximum profit rate (R) in the standard industry is 0.20 and that three-fourths (w) of the standard net product (income) goes to workers and one-fourth (1-w) to capitalists, then the rate of profits would be 5%; if the national income is divided equally between capitalist and workers, then r = (0.20) x (0.5) = 0.10 or 10 percent; and "if the whole went to profits the rate of profits would reach its maximum level of 20% and coincide with the standard ratio. The rate of profits in the Standard system thus appears as a ratio between quantities of commodities irrespective of their prices" (1960: 22).

In so doing, Sraffa is able accomplish what Ricardo strived for his entire life but could not accomplish, viz., generate an invariable measure of value or "balanced commodity" which "is capable of isolating price-movements of any other product so that they could be observed as in a vacuum" (Sraffa, 1960: 18). Moreover, by doing so, he is able to arrive at essentially the same results as Marx in terms of generating prices of production and identifying the origin of profits (and "exploitation") without prior reference to *unobservable* variables such as labor values and surplus-values. In this connection, Howard and King (1985) remark that

> "Sraffa's standard commodity ... provides a general and intuitively appealing characterization of the relationship between the rate of profit and exploitation ... [the] ... standard commodity is a construct which can cut through the distorting appearances inherent in capitalist price relations" (144).

To which Meek (1975) adds,

> "I believe that one should properly start with some *kind* of prior concrete magnitude which limits the levels of class incomes. But ... the prior concrete magnitude may be conceived in commodity terms [wheat and cloth] rather than in value terms; and it is possible to erect on this basis a theoretical system, not *essentially* different from Marx's in which prices and incomes are mutually and simultaneously determined" (29).

Meek's simple algebraic example of a two-sector capitalist economy (wheat and cloth) is similar to Marx's transformation model, but whose "prior magnitude" is a bundle of commodities rather than labor values. The simple model can be represented as follows:

$$10 \text{ wheat} + 20 \text{ cloth} + 50 \text{ labor} \rightarrow 100 \text{ wheat} \tag{6a}$$

$$20 \text{ wheat} + 30 \text{ cloth} + 50 \text{ labor} \rightarrow 100 \text{ cloth} \tag{6b}$$

Using this commodity-based model á la Sraffa (1960) [assuming that the rate of profit (r) is the same in both industries and that the real wage is 0.4 $(p_w + p_c)$], it is evident that capitalists are able to appropriate a surplus of 30 wheat and 10 cloth after deducting the necessary inputs of wheat and cloth for both industries and total real wages of 40 wheat and 40 cloth. We thus arrive at the following price system:

$$[10\, p_w + 20p_c + 50 \times 0.4\, (p_w + p_c)]\, (1 + r) = 100p_w \tag{7a}$$

$$[20\, p_w + 30p_c + 50 \times 0.4\, (p_w + p_c)]\, (1 + r) = 100p_c \tag{7b}$$

Assuming that the price of corn is the numeraire ($p_c = 1$), equations (7a) and (7b) simplify to:

$$(30p_w + 40)(1 + r) = 100p_w \quad (8a)$$

$$(40p_w + 50)(1 + r) = 100 \quad (8b)$$

Setting each equation equal to (1 + r) and solving for p_w generates a quadratic equation whose solution via the quadratic formula yields p_w = .7807 and r=0.231. These values when plugged into equations (8a) and (8b) ensure that everything "adds up" and Marx's major conclusions hold, viz., prices and income (including profits) are determined by the conditions of production, and second, their unique solution "involves the mutual and simultaneous determination of prices and profits in an equational system which expresses these conditions in price form" (Meek, 1975: xxviii; Sraffa, 1960: 18-33).

If, from a quantitative standpoint, Marx's theory of value is not needed to generate a theory of prices and the origin of profit can be readily explained in terms of the standard (composite) commodity, then why not follow the lead of neoclassical economists and analyze market prices and their movements directly; or, better still, follow the lead of sympathetic but forceful critics such as Joan Robinson (1957), and just "expunge value" from his system because "none of the important ideas which he [Marx] expresses in terms of the concept of *value* cannot be better expressed without it"; and its function is … reduced to that of providing 'incantations' which Marx uses … to slay the 'complacent apologists of capitalism'" (17-20). The major disadvantage of doing this in the view of Harvey (2018) is primarily sociological or qualitative in nature, because "If we erase the dialectical relation between prices and values, then there is no standpoint from which to mount a critique of the monetary representation of the social labour that labourers are called upon to do for others in the course of performing wage labour for capital. We will be powerless to explain where the monetary aspects of crises come from and why crises in general are inevitably expressed in money form" (63-64). Meek (1975) also concurs with this general view, and castigates Joan Robinson for forgetting that for Marx "value is a social relation," and that its qualitative task, if you will, "… is to show how relations of exchange were determined by relations of production," and, more importantly, how capitalist relations of production are primarily dependent on the emergence of labor-power as a commodity and the hidden labor-capital relation (24). The basic idea advanced here is that value represents, under capitalism, an unequal "exploitative" relation between capital and labor which expresses itself in the contradictory unity of the production and realization of commodities "pregnant" with surplus-value. The value of commodities is, in turn, expressed in terms of money or prices and, in this "hidden material form," resides the inherent contradiction between use-value and exchange value which, during times of crisis, erupts into a payments crisis and "the use-value of commodities becomes value-less" and only money is a commodity worth having (Harvey, 2014: 27; Nelson, 1999). In Marx's (1967a) colorful language, "As the hart pants after fresh water, so pants his soul after money, the only wealth" (*Capital I*: 236).

Marx (1967a) also believed that by failing to analyze the social dimensions of the value relation, the economists of his day (including David Ricardo) were misled or deluded by "the illusions created by competition" (the realm of exchange relations), and uncritically (and deliberately) adopted erroneous and confused view on key economic concepts such as exchange value or the origin of profits. For example, they considered that part of capital laid out in wages as no different from that spent on raw materials (circulating capital), and only differed formally from that disbursed on fixed capital in terms of whether it transferred its value to the product in one lump sum or piecemeal. In doing so, Political Economy was able to obfuscate and "fetishize" the social process of production into one where the capital advanced (in wages, raw materials, and machinery) merely reappears in the value of the commodity when sold so that the process can start anew. In other words, "the transformation of the capitalist process of production into a complete mystery is happily accomplished and the origin of surplus-value existing in the value of the product is entirely withdrawn from view" (Marx, 1967a: 225).

Marx believed that with the progressive development of the productive forces in capitalism, the dominance of the market over commodity producers and laborers (sellers of labor-power) would increase concomitantly and lead to the further materialization (commodification) of production (social) relations, recurring economic crises of greater intensity and the "fetishism of commodities." In fact, he viewed the capitalist class as "personified capital" whose transitory historical mission was to "ruthlessly force the human race to produce for production's sake ... [and] thus force the development of the productive powers of society, and create those material conditions which alone can form the real basis of a higher form of society, a society in which the full and free development of every individual forms the ruling principle" (Marx, 1967a: 307). In the meantime, however, the process of accumulation of capital reproduces, on an ever-larger scale, the existing coercive and extractive (property) relations of production, and thus reproduces the objective condition not only for the production of commodities and surplus-value, but "it also produces and reproduces the capitalist relation: on the one side the capitalist, and other the wage-labourer" (Marx, 1967a: 293). In the production and reproduction of commodities (including labor-power), the market becomes endowed in the minds of commodity producers and consumers (believers) with almost supernatural powers that begin to penetrate and control every aspect of their daily lives and thus dominate their well-being, will, and consciousness. In Marx's incomparable words, the fetishism that attaches itself to commodities arises when "...a definite social relation between men, that assumes, in their eyes, the fantastic form of a relation between things. In order ... to find an analogy, we must have recourse to the mist-enveloped regions of the religious world. In that world the productions of the human brain appear as independent beings endowed with life, and entering into relation both with one another and the human race. So it is in the world of commodities with the products of men's hands (Marx, 1967a: 72).

By treating the social relations of production (exchange relation between labor-power and capital) as if they were simply material things or technical relations, it was just a simple step for the "vulgar economists"—as opposed to the classical economists--to adopt the so-called "Trinity Formula" whereby capital earns profit, land earns rent, and labor earns wages. In fact, as argued by Howard and King (1985:102), the idea that profits accrue to the total stock of capital advanced (c + v), rather than to the variable component (v), "enshrined 'capital' as the source of profits, as a 'separate factor of production,'" and laid the foundation for a "nascent marginal productivity theory of income distribution" á la John B. Clark (1965).

Marx (1967c) devoted a whole chapter in *Volume III* to refuting this categorization of revenues and their sources by arguing that labor, means of production (not capital), and land are essential factors in the production of use values but not exchange value. Labor creates value but only under certain historical conditions, viz., a class society based on the generalized buying and selling of labor-power; value or capital-value, as we have indicated, is a social relation of production manifested in certain things (machinery, raw materials, etc.) used in the production process; and finally, land, although an agent of production in creating use-values such as wheat or corn, has nothing to do with the production of exchange-value; it is the private ownership of land--a social relation--which enables the landlord class to capture a part of the surplus value materialized in the agricultural product (see Brewer, 1984: 180-183; Ramirez, 2009: 71-91; Roll, 1992: 252-254). Marx viewed the "Trinity Formula" as the complete mystification of the capitalist mode of production, the conversion of social relations into things, and led him to remark mockingly that, "It is an enchanted, perverted, topsy-turvy world, in which Monsieur le Capital and Madame la Terre do their ghost-walking as social characters and at the same time directly as mere things. It is the great merit of classical economy to have destroyed this false appearance and illusion … this personification of things and conversion of production relations into entities, the religion of everyday life" (Marx, 1967a: 830; Marx, 1971: 514-515).

Piketty (2014) is fond of quoting Marx in his seminal work (e.g., 7-13) and argues that his own analysis is in the tradition of the classical economists. However, there is no doubt that Marx would be highly critical of Piketty's definition of capital and his *de facto* "conversion of social relations into things." On the one hand, he ascribes to nonhuman resources (machinery and land) the capacity of producing exchange-value (as opposed to merely transferring their existing value or helping produce use-values); yet, on the other, he excludes labor-power which, in the Marxian paradigm, is the only factor of production capable of producing an exchange-value greater than its own value—the source of profit and the return to capital.

Time, Interest-Bearing Capital, and Productive vs. Unproductive Labor

Before concluding this paper on value, it will expedient to investigate the role of time in Marxian economics and Adam Smith's important distinction between productive and unproductive labor. Turning first to the role of time in the determination of capital-value, it is not infrequent for many economists, most prominently, Böhm Bawerk (1923), who identified capitalist production with roundabout production, to criticize Marx on his relative neglect of time. Interestingly enough, Bohm Bawerk, like Marx, "treated capital as produced means of production that merely transmit value to the product, and argued that 'surplus value' is produced by labour and land alone, but it accrues only after the passage of time" (Blaug, 1998: 232). Böhm Bawerk in his *The Positive Theory of Capital* (1923) argued that any production process that uses tools and intermediate products was a capitalist production process. He states that, "The roundabout ways are fruitful but long…It is only because the labourers cannot wait till the roundaboutness delivers up its products ready for consumption that they become economically dependent on the capitalists" (Hunt and Lautzenheiser, 2011: 312-313). In this regard, Blaug (1998) contends that Böhm Bawerk did not consider "abstinence" as an independent factor of production nor did he believe that "interest owes its existence to the personal activity of capitalists" (232). However, in light of the quotation above, it is hard not to conclude that the accumulation of capital is made possible because capitalists have the "moral character" to wait or abstain while workers want their reward now.

The category of time is an integral component of Marx's development of a theory of value and surplus value. However, it is not time *per se* or the difference in subjective time preferences between workers and capitalists á la Böhm Bawerk which are central, it is the analysis of the socio-economic and technical (objective) factors evolving through time that distinguish the Marxian paradigm from the neoclassical one. That is, in assessing the role of time we must, above all, "...single out the characteristics of economic objects that are examined in their time dimension and the [historical] factors that influence these economic objects in the period under review" (Shemyatenkov, 1981: 117). These economic entities, as we have seen, include commodities with their dual nature of use-value and exchange-value, and the most important factor influencing the latter over time is socially necessary labor time—a manifestation of the time factor in the capitalist mode of production. That is, the focus should be on identifying (and explaining) those key factors which regulate the production of absolute and relative surplus value over time such as the length (and intensity) of the working day, the productivity of labor, and the turnover of capital.

For Marx, the origin of interest-bearing capital can be traced to the inverted form of the simple circulation of commodities C-M-C, namely:

$$M\text{-}C\text{-}M' \text{ with, } M' = M + \Delta M \qquad (9)$$

Where: M= money (gold in value terms); C= commodities in value terms; and ΔM= surplus money (value) realized during the circuit.

In other words, as opposed to simple commodity production based on the personal labor of the producer and his ownership of the means of production, where the aim is to sell in order to buy use-values for ultimate consumption, we have the emergence of a form in which the goal is to buy in order to sell. The aim is not only to sell, but to sell dearer for, according to Marx (1967a): "...the circuit, M-C-M would be absurd and without any meaning if the intention were to exchange by this means two equal sums of money £100 for £100. The miser's plan would be far simpler and surer; he sticks to his £100 instead of exposing it to the dangers of circulation (147).

Money, the representation of (social) value, circulates in this particular manner and, according to Marx, becomes transformed into capital-value. In fact, "as a matter of history, capital, as opposed to landed property invariably takes the form of money; it appears as moneyed wealth, as the capital of the merchant and of the usurer" (Marx, 1967a: 146). And in the case of the usurer or money-lender the circuit of capital is reduced to its two extremes, M-M'. That is to say, money is endowed here apparently with the power to augment its magnitude without being used for the purpose for which it came into existence, viz., the exchange of commodities. In Marx's words, "Interest-bearing capital [M-M'] is the consummate *automatic fetish* [emphasis in the original], the self-expanding value, the money making-money, and in this form it no longer bears any trace of its origins. The social relation is consummated as a relation of things (money, commodities) to themselves" (Marx, 1971: 455 & 462). Marx treats these two forms of capital (merchant's and usurer's capital) as derivative forms which "appear in the course of history before the modern standard of capital (Marx, 1971: 165). This is a crucial observation because, as we alluded to in the first section, the history of capital-value is quite different from the history of the capitalist mode of production, where direct producers are forcibly divorced from their means of production. The former, under the guise of merchant's and usurer's capital is to be found in quite developed form in the ancient world, while the latter is scarcely more than two and one half centuries old. In this connection, Marx (1967c) observes that:

> "The less developed the production, the more wealth in money is concentrated in the hands of merchants [and usurers] or appears in the specific form of merchants' [usurers'] wealth. Within the capitalist mode of production—i.e., as soon as capital has established its sway over production and imparted to it a wholly changed and specific form—merchant's [and usurer's] capital appears as a capital with a *specific function*. In all previous modes of production ... whenever production ministers to the immediate wants of the producer, merchant's [usurer's] capital appears to perform the function *par excellence* of capital" (*Capital III*: 326-327).

Thus, for Marx, interest-bearing capital is not a direct payment for the "burden of abstaining or waiting" by some abstract [universal] "economic agent" á la Nasau Senior or Alfred Marshall, but a transformed part of surplus value (profit), the product of loan capital—a payment for the use of a sum of money to make a profit (Brewer, 1984: 156-190; Robinson, 1957: 54-55; Roll, 1992: 253-254). Under capitalist production it is created by the division of profit (surplus-value) into interest and profit of enterprise. If the capitalist operates entirely with borrowed funds to run his enterprise, then interest takes part of the profit, while "...the remainder, which Marx calls the profit of enterprise, is a return to the active performance of the functions of a capitalist" (Brewer, 1984: 158). In Marx's words: "Interest ...is nothing but a part of the profit (itself nothing but surplus-value, unpaid labour) which the capitalist pays to the owner of the borrowed capital with which he 'works,' either exclusively or partially. Interest is a part of profit—of surplus-value—which instead of being appropriated by the industrial capitalist himself...is deducted by the industrial capitalist from his own revenue and paid to the owner of capital" (Marx, 1971: 470-471; for further details on Marx's theory of interest, see Brewer, 1984:156-160; Fine, 1986: 387-418; Roll, 1992: 253-254). To Marx, in the words of Joan Robinson (1957) "the *desire* [my emphasis] to own capital does not have to be explained, and, so long as any profit is obtainable, the capitalists not only preserve what wealth they have, but accumulate and accumulate" (54). In this connection, Harvey (2018) contends that capitalists have a choice, viz., "They can invest in further production of value [valorization] or they can put the money on the money market to earn interest. To stay in business, industrial capitalists must earn more than the going rate of interest" (42).

Thus, in the Marxian paradigm, the interest rate or the "price paid for the use of money" is determined by the average rate of profit on industrial capital and the supply and demand for loan capital. The average rate of profit can be taken as the upper limit of the rate of interest; and its movement over time is dependent on the different phases of the business (industrial) cycle. During the boom phase, the rate of interest rises significantly and reaches a maximum during the crisis phase, when the demand for liquidity grows to the limit as many firms are threatened with bankruptcy. The minimum rate which, according to Marx, may fall to a level close to zero, is observed during a depression when, after the crisis, production and employment stagnate. On a secular basis, Marx believed that the rate of interest would have a tendency to fall because the average rate of profit has a tendency to fall over time and also because the supply of loan capital would rise relative to its demand due to the development of the credit system which concentrates the "free money resources" of society into the hands of bankers and stock promoters (Brewer, 1984; Mandel 1971: 222-226). Thus, the circulation of interest-bearing capital (M-M') enables capitalists to speed up and intensify the production and accumulation of surplus-value [valorization] while, at the same time, supplying the credit and financing needed to realize the value of the growing mass of commodities brought to the marketplace. In other words, the growing circulation of interest-bearing capital provides a "fluidity into the valorization and realization process," but it docs so in an erratic and contradictory manner over the course of the business cycle. This is just another way of expressing the contradictory unity of exchange and use-value contained in each representative commodity, but now writ large for the economy as a whole and revealed during crises of overproduction when a mass of use-values (and exchange-values) are partially or completely destroyed because of a lack of effective demand.

Put differently, the extent of the postponement of social consumption is determined by both the accumulation and reproduction needs of capitalist production over the course of the industrial cycle and by the secular (long-run) tendencies inherent to the capitalist system, rather than by the thriftiness or "abstinence" of individuals (Shemyatenkov, 1981: 118). It is dictated by the constant need under competitive capitalism to save time in order to "Accumulate, accumulate! That is Moses and the prophets! ...Therefore, save, save, i.e., reconvert the greater possible portion of surplus-value, or surplus-product into capital" (Marx, 1967a: 595). Hence, it is impossible to have an all-encompassing (universal) definition of the economic role of time as the neoclassical economists would have us believe, for it will differ from one historically determined mode of production to another (e.g., capitalism vs. feudalism).

We see then that value (more correctly capital-value) may assume some forms more often than others depending on the particular stage in economic history in which we find ourselves. Thus, during the formative years of the capitalist mode of production it was more apt to assume the form of money (bullion); while in the 18th and 19th centuries it came to be associated more and more (at least in England) with machinery, plant and equipment. But above all, with this particular stage in history, labor-power becomes integrated into the circuit of money capital as productive capital. For only when the production by means of wage labor becomes universal does commodity production attain its most general expression. This, by the way, gives us a clue into the reason the majority of economists identify capital with means of production and labor-power since under this particular organization of production it assumes this social form most frequently.

Productive and Unproductive Labor

Value or capital-value, then, when conceived in this fashion, not only paves the way for resolving present-day controversies but also supplies us with the means to understand more fully certain topics in the history of economic thought. A case in point would be Adam Smith's important distinction between productive and unproductive labor. A distinction, whose clear comprehension rests upon whether the workers exchange the services of their labor-power directly against capital or against the revenue of the capitalist. In the former case, their labor is said to be of a productive nature, while in the latter situation it is deemed unproductive. In Smith's words,

> "There is one sort of labour which adds to the value of the subject upon which it is bestowed: there is another which has no effect. The former, as it produces a value, may be called productive; the latter, unproductive labour. Thus the labour of a manufacture adds, generally, to the value of the materials which he works upon, that of his own maintenance, and *of his master's profit*. The labour of a menial servant, on the contrary, add to the value of nothing. Though the manufacturer has his wages advanced to him by his master, he, in reality costs him no expense, the value of those wages being generally restored, together with a profit …But the employment of a menial servant never is restored" (Smith, 1976: 351).

Smith is here deriving in an embryonic form, nothing but the notion that when the net income of the capitalist is used to buy use-values for ultimate consumption it is not being converted into capital. Consequently, if the services of a menial servant or, for that matter, of both the gravest and most frivolous professions, such as "lawyers, physicians ... [and] players, buffons, musicians" are used for his personal consumption or enjoyment, they are of an unproductive character (Smith, 1976: 352). Quite the contrary is the case if these very same services are used in running his business along capitalist lines; in this activity they are said to be productive. So, those workers whose labor yields a surplus value (M') are called productive, while those whose labor is merely of a useful nature are called unproductive. Though in both cases they be, materially speaking, the very same services performed, the nature of the social relations of production deems them productive of exchange value in one case, and unproductive in the other.

Smith, as Marx clearly recognized, was a pioneer in formulating a nascent theory of capital and revenue, one in which all wage labor, be it in agriculture or industry, is productive when exchanged for money in order to produce surplus-value (profit). In *Theories of Surplus Value I*, Marx (1971) praises him thus,

> "Productive labour is here defined from the standpoint of capitalist production, and Adam Smith here got to the very heart of the matter, hit the nail on the head. This is one of his greatest scientific merits ... that he defines productive labour as labour *which is directly exchanged with capital*" (emphasis in the original; 157).

Unproductive labor, on the other hand, is that which is directly exchanged against the revenues of the capitalist for the latter's own consumption (a maid, a cook, chauffeur, etc.). It is important to note, in passing, that Smith goes beyond the restricted conception of the Physiocrats who, despite having understood that surplus value is created in the process of production, nevertheless identified it solely with rent and thought erroneously that it was only generated by the labor of agricultural workers (Rubin, 1979: 214; Marx, 1971: 162-163).

Still, despite correctly deriving the distinction between productive and unproductive labor on the basis of their different social relations rather than their technical-material properties, he too falls into the trap of conceptualizing social relations as being the inherent properties of things. In the very same passage quoted above, he offers an alternate definition for productive labor based on whether productive labor is embodied in a vendible commodity. He writes:

> "A man grows rich by employing a multitude of manufacturers: he grows poor, by maintaining a multitude of menial servants ... the labour of the manufacturer fixes and realizes itself in some particular vendible commodity, which lasts some time at least after the labour is past ...The labour of the menial servant, on the contrary, does not fix or realize itself in any particular subject or vendible commodity. His services generally perish in the very instant of their performance, and seldom leave any trace or value behind them, for which an equal quantity of service could afterwards be procured" (Marx, 1971: 351-352).

Smith does not realize that whether or not the services of the worker are directly embodied in use-values is immaterial to the distinction between productive and unproductive labor. Indeed, what really matters is whether the services of labor-power are used to produce a value whose magnitude is greater than its own exchange value. That is, in the capitalist mode of production, this surplus-value is usually embodied in commodities should not in any way detract us from the fact that we are dealing with a social process. Apropos, Marx writes:

> "The cook in the hotel produced a commodity for the person who as a capitalist has bought her labour—the hotel proprietor; the consumer of the mutton chops has to pay her for her labour, and this labour replaces for the hotel proprietor (apart from profit) the fund out of which he continues to pay the cook... On the other hand, if I buy the labour of a cook for her to cook meat, etc., for me [to enjoy it] ... then her labour is unproductive, in spite of the fact that this labour fixes itself in a material product" (Marx, 1971: 165).

Marx's distinction between productive and unproductive labor based on whether it produces surplus-value or not is a highly useful and relevant contribution even today as attested by the rapid growth in certain types of labor in advertising, finance, commerce, and banking. It is also relevant when it comes to explaining why domestic work undertaken mainly by women in the household, although highly useful and essential for the reproduction of labor-power, is "not productive" in the sense of not producing surplus-value for capitalists. Still, Marx's definition is unnecessarily restrictive because it contends that wage-labor is productive only if it is exchanged for capital in the sphere of production rather than circulation (Rubin, 1979). Certainly, the line of demarcation between the production and the circulation of commodities is hard to define precisely, and varies from industry to industry and over time. For example, why are the labor services of a truck driver in transporting commodities to their final destination deemed productive by Marx, but not the services of an advertising agent engaged in the sphere of circulation, when without her services the most frivolous commodities cannot be sold in the marketplace? Or for that matter, why are the non-material services of those employed in a bank's research department who generate valuable information that directly contributes to the bank's bottom line not viewed as productive? According to Howard and King (1985), there is a simple solution to this problem which is compatible with Marx's approach, viz., just abandon the distinction between production and circulation and regard "as productive *all* socially necessary wage-labour which is exchanged with capital" in the sense alluded to above (132). In fact, as they rightly observe, proceeding in this manner is more in line with Marx's sociological approach because it emphasizes that "economic phenomena are determined by the historically specific structure of [social] relations which define the mode of production [capitalism] in which they occur" (Howard and King, 1985: 133).

Summary and Conclusion

This chapter analyzed the important notion of value (exchange-value) from a Marxian perspective as opposed to a neoclassical one. It was shown that when value is viewed as a historically determined relation, rather than simply as the relative or exchangeable value of one commodity in terms of another, it refers to a social relation between producers which is represented in the marketplace as a relation between commodities. In the tradition of Aristotle, Hegel and Spinoza, Marx thought that the task of economics as a social science was to penetrate through how things "appeared" on the surface of the market system (exchange relations) in to the underlying social (property) relations of production or "essence" on which the market was based (see McLellan, 1976). For example, when dealing with simple commodity production, value, more often than not, took the form of commodities and money (bullion) in the hands of independent producers, merchants, and usurers. With the advent of modern industry and the widespread buying and selling (commodification) of labor-power and the concentration of the means of production, value (and surplus-value) now expresses a social relation of domination by capitalists over workers; that is, capitalists, by virtue of their ownership and access to the means of production, can extract unpaid or surplus-labor during the labor process from workers who have nothing to sell but their labor-power or capacity to work.

The chapter emphasized that value in the Marxian scheme is not a physical property of commodities, but a common social property attributed to them under definite historical conditions, viz., the constant production and reproduction of commodities (including labor- power) for sale in the marketplace. In this, there are some important parallels, from a quantitative standpoint, between Marx's treatment of the problem and Ricardo's (1977) discussion in the latter's important and relatively neglected chapter on "Value and Riches." It was shown that in the capitalist mode of production, value, in the form of money, labor-power, and means of production, is repeatedly being turned over by the capitalist in its various circuits in order to generate and accumulate surplus-value (profit)—the raison d'être of the capitalist system. At any given point in time, then, value may be in its money, commodity, or productive forms, and any (prolonged) interruption of these circuits over time generates economic crises in terms of the production and/or realization of surplus-value (profit). It was also indicated that the repeated circuits of capital in their customary forms lead economists (and business people) to treat what are essentially social (historical) relations of production as simply material things or technical relations, and thus to the erroneous adoption of the so-called "Trinity Formula" whereby capital earns profit, land earns rent, and labor earns wages—the genesis of the marginal productivity approach to value and distribution.

It is evident then that value in the Marxian scheme is a dynamic, multi-dimensional, and socially-determined concept. By way of an analogy, we may think of value or capital-value as being a rule or function—in the mathematical sense—which ascribes to certain elements (values) in its domain the image (character) of capital values in its range provided that they augment their value via the production of a surplus-value. As exchange-values then, commodities, money (gold), machinery, and labor-power are just the embodiments of so much necessary labor-time; they only differ quantitatively (and therefore the legitimacy of this analogy). While, on the other hand, as use-values, shoes or computers, they matter to us insofar as they are qualitatively different. Admittedly, this is a somewhat abstract way of interpreting the meaning of value of capital-value, but the analogy of a mathematical function or rule is most useful in capturing the multi-dimensional character of capital and value. When viewing it as such, one surely steers away from the misconception that it is the physical property of an object that determines whether it has value or not. The major disadvantage of this analogy, of course, is that one can easily forget that we are dealing with a concept which is firmly rooted in socio-historical phenomena. For, as we mentioned above, the clear and distinct understanding of value and all its ramifications becomes a reality only when the capitalist-laborer exchange relation becomes the predominant (universal) institutional characteristic of the capitalist mode of production.

Although from a qualitative or sociological perspective, the "law of value" has much to commend it in terms of enhancing our understanding of the inherent and hidden connection between the relations of exchange and the unequal (property) relations of production and power in capitalism, it is, admittedly, from a quantitative standpoint found to be wanting. Marx's "law of value" or, for that matter, Ricardo's labor theory of value—however important they may have been in furthering our understanding of exchange-value—both suffer from a number of inherent conceptual and operational problems that undermine both their internal consistency and prevent them from being empirically verifiable or guiding economic policy. For example, Marx's treatment of the problem of identifying the conversion coefficients for skilled into unskilled labor, although suggestive in nature, is incomplete and fragmentary; and he, like Ricardo before him, clearly underestimated the challenge before them; or, consider Marx's (1967c) puzzling (and contradictory) introduction in *Capital III* of the role of "social needs" in the form of the composition of aggregate demand in determining the "limits" of socially necessary labor (and unit value) of commodities, other than those required by the normal technical conditions prevailing in each individual sphere or branch of production (as explained in, Marx, 1967a, *Capital I*). To his credit, Marx's proposed solution to the transformation problem tackled head on what had so preoccupied Ricardo throughout his life, but ultimately eluded his intellectual acumen, viz., how is it possible for the labor theory of value to retain its validity when the commodities being exchanged are produced by capitals of unequal organic compositions (c/v) or, what amounts to essentially the same thing, advanced for different periods of time. Marx's (1967c) proposed "solution" in *Capital III*, although suggestive and ingenious, was clearly incomplete and, in light of Sraffa's seminal contribution, ultimately proved unnecessary in terms of isolating and explaining relative price movements in a competitive capitalist economy. Finally, Marx (and Ricardo), by just confining their attention to commodities produced under constant costs and fixed technical coefficients, were too quick to downplay the important role played by demand in explaining the determination of long-run prices. All of these challenges, just to name a few, rob the theory of its relevance in terms of explaining the actual movement of prices in a competitive capitalist economy and, as indicated by Meek (1975), "the Marxian labour theory of value as such is pushed into the background, in the sense that its specific quantitative propositions, emerge

... only as by-products of the main analysis" (xlii). That is, in his view and that of other scholars in the field, it is possible to erect a theoretical system á la Sraffa in which the "prior concrete magnitudes" are a bundle of commodities instead of labor values and arrive at a system in which prices and incomes (including profits) are simultaneously and uniquely determined.

The final section of the chapter discussed the economic role of time in the Marxian paradigm and how it relates specifically to capital-value in the form of interest-bearing capital. It was argued that the postponement of social consumption by capitalists is determined by the accumulation and reproduction needs of capitalist production over the course of the industrial (business) cycle, rather than by their individual thriftiness or "abstinence." The section also focused on Marx's important and neglected discussion of Adam Smith's valuable, yet incomplete distinction between productive and unproductive labor. Using Marx's conception of value, it argued that a clear understanding of the distinction between the two types of labor is possible if we focus on the different social relations of these workers in the capitalist system, rather than on their technical-material properties. It was noted that Marx's distinction between productive and unproductive labor is unnecessarily restrictive because it only considers wage-workers as "productive" if they produce surplus-value in the sphere of production rather than circulation. This can be simply overcome within the Marxian scheme by considering all wage-workers "productive" as long as they produce surplus-value for capitalists, regardless of whether they do so in the spheres of production or circulation of commodities.

REFERENCES

Blaug, M. 1998. *Economic Theory in Retrospect*, 5th Ed. New York: Cambridge University Press.

Böhm Bawerk, E.v. 1923. *The Positive Theory of Capital*. New York: Stechert.

Braverman, H. 1974. *Labor and Monopoly Capital*. New York: Monthly Review Press.

Brewer, A. 1984. *A Guide to Marx's Capital*. New York: Cambridge University Press.

Brewer, A. 1990. *Marxist Theories of Imperialism: A Critical Survey*, 2nd Ed. New York: Routledge.

Clark, J.B. 1965. *The Distribution of Wealth*. New York: Augustus M. Kelly.

Colliot-Thelene, J.L. 1979. "Afterword," in I.I. Rubin, Ed. *A History of Economic Thought*. New York: Pathfinder Press.

Cutler, A., B. Hindess, P. Hirst, and A. Hussain. 1977. *Marx's Capital and Capitalism Today*, Vol. 1: London: Routledge and Kegan Paul.

Dobb, M. 1939. *Political Economy and Capitalism*. New York: International Publishers [1963].

Ekelund, Jr., R.B. and R.F. Hebert. 2004. *A History of Economic Theory and Method*, 4th Ed. Long Grove, IL: Waveland Press, Inc.

Fine, B. 1986. "Banking Capital and the Theory of Interest." *Science and Society* 44: 387-413.

Harvey, D. 2014. *Seventeen Contradictions and the End of Capitalism*. New York: Oxford University Press.

Harvey, D. 2018. *Marx, Capital, and the Madness of Economic Reason*. New York: Oxford University Press.

Howard, M.C. and J.E. King. 1985. *The Political Economy of Marx*. New York: Longman.

Howard, M.C. and J.E. King. 1989. *A History of Marxian Economics: Volume II, 1929-1990*. Princeton: Princeton University Press.

Hunt, E.K. and M. Lautzenheiser. 2011. *History of Economic Thought: A Critical Perspective*, 3rd Ed. New York: M.E. Sharpe.

Mandel, E. 1968. *Marxist Economic Theory*, Vol 1. New York: Monthly Review Press [1971].

Marshall, A. 1920. *Principles of Economics*, 8th Ed. [abridged]. New York: Prometheus Books [1997].

Marx, K. 1862-1863. *Theories of Surplus Value: Capital, Vol. IV.*, Parts I-III. Moscow: Progress Publishers [1968 & 1971].

Marx, K. 1867. *Capital, Vol. I.* New York: International Publishers [1967a].

Marx, K. 1885. *Capital, Vol. II.* New York: International Publishers [1967b].

Marx, K. 1894. *Capital, Vol. III.* New York: International Publishers [1967c].

Marx, K. and F. Engels. 1848. *The Communist Manifesto.* New York: Simon & Schuster [1964].

McConnell, C.R., S.L. Brue, and S.M. Flynn. 2018. *Economics*, 21st Ed. New York: McGraw Hill Education.

McLellan, D. 1976. *Karl Marx.* New York: Penguin Books.

Meek, R.L. 1975. *Studies in the Labor Theory of Value*, 2nd Ed. New York: Monthly Review Press.

Nelson, A. 1999. *Marx's Concept of Money: The God of Commodities.* London and New York: Routledge.

Nozick, R. 1974. *Anarchy, State, and Utopia.* New York: Basic Books.

Oser, J. and W.C. Blanchfield. 1975. *The Evolution of Economic Thought*, 3rd Ed. New York: Harcourt Brace Jovanovich.

Piketty, T. 2014. *Capital in the Twenty-First Century.* Cambridge: The Belknap of Harvard University Press.

Ramirez, M.D. 2007. "Marx, Wages, and Cyclical Crises: A Critical Interpretation." *Contributions to Political Economy* 26: 27-41.

Ramirez, M.D. 2009. "Marx's Theory of Ground Rent: A Critical Assessment." *Contributions to Political Economy* 28: 71-91.

Ricardo, D. 1817. *Principles of Political Economy and Taxation.* New York: E.P. Dutton. [1977].

Robinson, J. 1942. *An Essay on Marxian Economics.* London: Macmillan [1957].

Roll, E. 1992. *A History of Economic Thought*, 5th Ed. London: Faber and Faber, Ltd.

Rubin, I.I. 1979. *A History of Economic Thought.* New York: Pathfinder Press.

Samuelson, P.A. 1957. "Wages and Interest: A Modern Dissection of Marxian Economic Models." *American Economic Review* 47: *884-912.*

Seton, F. 1957. "The Transformation Problem." *Review of Economic Studies* 24: 149-160.

Shemyatenkov, V. 1981. *The Enigma of Capital: A Marxist Viewpoint*. Moscow: Progress Publishers.

Shoul, B. 1967. "Karl Marx's Solutions to Some Theoretical Problems of Classical Economics." in M.C. Howard and J. E. King, Eds. *The Economics of Marx*. New York. Penguin Books [1976].

Smith, A. 1776. *An Inquiry into the Nature and Causes of the Wealth of Nations, Book II*. Edwin Cannan, Ed. Chicago: The University of Chicago Press [1976].

Sowell, T. 1967. "Marx's Capital after One Hundred Years." in M.C. Howard and J.E. King, Eds. *The Economics of Marx*. New York, Penguin Books [1976].

Sraffa, P. 1960. *Production of Commodities by Means of Commodities*. Cambridge: Cambridge University Press.

Sraffa, P. 2004a. *The Works and Correspondence of David Ricardo: Letters, Vol.* VIII. Indianapolis: Liberty Fund [1951-73].

Sraffa, P. 2004b. *The Works and Correspondence of David Ricardo: Letters, Vol.* IX. Indianapolis: Liberty Fund [1951-73].

Sraffa, P. 2004c]. *The Works and Correspondence of David Ricardo: Pamphlets and Papers*, 1815-1823, *Vol.* IV. Indianapolis: Liberty Fund [1951-73].

Steedman, I. 1977. *Marx after Sraffa*. London: New Left Books.

Sweezy, P.M. 1942. *The Theory of Capitalist Development* New York: Monthly Review Press [1970].

Wolfson, M. 1990. "The Transformation Problem: Exposition and Appraisal." *Journal of the History of Economic Thought* 12: 179-195.

In: Political Economy
Editors: Caleb M. Clark et al.
ISBN: 978-1-68507-106-6

Chapter 6

SOCIAL BASES AND THE POLITICAL ECONOMY OF DEVELOPMENT

Katie Mills[1] and Alexander C. Tan[1,2]
[1]Department of Political Science and International Relations,
University of Canterbury, Canterbury, New Zealand
[2]Taiwan Institute for Governance and Communications,
National Chengchi University, Mucha, Taiwan

ABSTRACT

Much has been said about the relationship between violence, policy, institutions and development. Are there social bases for development? What is the role of social bases for economic and political development? In this essay, we consider how social bases will constrain the ability to consolidate polities as well as to restrict regime choice options that may have implications and consequences for political and economic development. We also consider how ideological and social factors in the developed nation of the United States of America are perhaps changing or no longer serve to maintain the development of the country, threatening to undermine the state's stability and, therefore, economic growth. This underscores the extent to which development is not linear, even for so-called "developed" states. We fundamentally call into question the use of the term "developed" in the discourse for the way in which it suggests the possibility for completing "development."

Keywords: economic development, elites, ideas, political development, rules, social basis for development, the public, United States

INTRODUCTION

Much has been said about the relationship between violence, policy, institutions and development. Are there social bases for development? What is the role of social bases for economic and political development? Many scholars have debated and offered views on the role that people and their social and ideological tendencies contribute to an environment where economic development can occur. The environment for which states, institutions and humans all operate in has been over centuries formed and maintained by people. Therefore, it is implicit that this environment is a symptom of human needs - the need for seeking trust, security and prosperity.

Variance in these environments across countries reflects the variance in powerful political agents and political terrains that make the journey to establish trust, security and prosperity unique to each polity. As humans have unique historical experiences and cultures, each development journey may also be unique making the understanding of the role of the social, cultural and ideological in development challenging. The social, cultural and ideological are also inherently difficult to manufacture or implant via policy measures, yet appear to have huge salience in a state's development pathways. Whilst we are able to compare countries and the relative level of violence they experience or the institutions they house, comparing the social and ideological supports for a polity is far less tangible. Nonetheless, there are ways that we can identify how it underpins the development story. Hopefully, this essay will inspire researchers to find and monitor accurately the more invisible factors in development, as it is changes to these factors that have the potential to predict changes to policy, economic behaviour, institutions and even regimes.

In this essay, we consider how social bases will constrain the ability to consolidate polities as well as to restrict regime choice options that may have implications and consequences for development. We also consider how ideological and social factors in the developed nation of the United States of America are perhaps changing or no longer serve to maintain the development of the country, threatening to undermine the state's stability and therefore economic growth. This underscores the extent to which development is not linear, even for so-called "developed" states. We fundamentally call into question the use of the term "developed" in the discourse for the way in which it suggests the possibility for completing "development."

Additionally, this essay pushes development theory into a contemporary context. Whilst, relying on the history that has informed our understanding of development to date, the essay turns its focus away from "underdeveloped" states and begins to explore the risks faced by "developed states" when faced with new ideas and challenges. Further, it places our understanding of development into the context of a global development agenda, offering a framework to predict how the social bases of the global community may shape the opportunity for greater global coordination on development challenges.

Social Conditions for Development Pathways

Social conditions and ideology have underpinned the possibilities and pathways for development. In regards to democratic transitions and the effective taming of violence, Olson contended that only polities whose citizens have diverse and dispersed interests would find a pathway to power sharing under a democratic regime due to the inability of any single group to command a monopoly over power (1993). Robert Bates spoke of "political terrains" that constrain pathways to development (2017). For example, the strength of regionalism, ethnic and economic divisions when culminating in a set of reinforcing cleavages would gravely impair a state's pathway to consolidation, controlling violence and subsequently democracy (Bates 2017). These two theories may initially seem at odds in regards to the social conditions for a democratic transition. However, assessing them in tandem offers one important insight: the organisation of citizens' differences in a polity affects development pathways. When differences are dispersed, power sharing is possible, even logical. When differences are concentrated and are aligned across a number of dimensions – economic, ethnic, regional – they can become deeply divisive and, therefore, inhibit the power sharing pathway. Therefore, diversity itself can have a range of effects on development depending on how it is configured in society and in turn the propensity for this to translate into a consolidated power.

Somit and Peterson (2005) build on the idea of social constraints to pathways, considering in more detail specifically what conditions enable the development of a democracy. Working from an anthropological perspective, the authors argue that the human species is genetically more inclined towards authoritarianism due to traditionally organising in hierarchical and tribal ways (Somit and Peterson, 2005: 4). This would account for the dominance and stability of various forms of autocracy in the world compared to otherwise rare examples of democracy (Somit and Peterson, 2005: 23). Therefore, Somit and Peterson argue that democracies arise out of deviations against humans' natural inclinations, such as the willingness to use peaceful mechanisms for political debate, compromise and acceptance of defeat (2005: 52). These deviations arise out of ideas and values popularised by humans, overtime often over centuries (Somit and Peterson, 2005: 53). Though not expressly identified by the authors, this analysis leads us to understand that underpinning any development process is not only the struggle for power in a material sense (e.g., the largest and wealthiest group in a society), but also fundamentally a contestation of ideas about what rules and values should govern society and the ability of these ideas to overcome humans' anthropological dispositions.

Needless to state, underpinning this conclusion is the importance of time. Francis Fukuyama notes that it is precisely the values and traditions in a given society that are the most slow changing aspect to social lives (1995:

8). So it is understandable that the deeply historic values and traditions set by religion or ethnicity, for example, do not quickly compromise or give way to new ideas that may seek to organise social life in new ways. If we consider and understand the journey to democracy or even state building as a process of popularising ideas as well as the absence of deeply divisive cleavages, we should not be surprised that new states often grapple with authoritarianism or are shifting between periods of relative autocracy and democracy, as this process is inherently slow moving.

With a tendency for development studies to focus on key performance indicators, such as gross domestic product, per capita income, labor statistics, levels of education, etc., we should not overlook or underestimate that when polities may appear to be stagnating by these measures, they may in fact be undergoing critical periods of idea contestation and socialisation. Furthermore, we should not be lulled to believe that this process is always linear nor ever complete. Even in consolidated democracies we witness the emergence of new ideas with the potential to undermine the status quo. Nonetheless, the process of idea contestation and how this creates new pathways to development is perhaps understudied and yet absolutely critical.

Elite Influence over Ideas and Rules

If we regard development as partly a consequence of the contestation of ideas, it is incumbent for us to briefly examine how ideas become accepted. Whilst other authors have discussed the need for ideas to prevail in society as a whole, Higley and Burton (2012) discuss the importance for elites to find unity in ideas and the rules that should govern a society. For Higley and Burton if elites in society are "disunified" the regime will be difficult to establish and unstable (2012: 246). However, if elites are "consensually unified," a stable regime can be established, and this creates a possibility for democracy (Higley and Burton, 2012: 246). The authors warn that regime changes unaccompanied by a shift to a "consensually unified" elite are likely to be a strong predictor of a weak, fragile transition that may be doomed to regress (Higley and Burton, 2012: 247). This allows elites to conceptualise politics as "bargaining" rather than "zero-sum" by enabling a platform that values consensus building rather than sudden destabilising changes in society (Higley and Burton, 2012: 247).

The transition to unity is difficult as it requires some elites to defect from conflictual political engagement with each other towards peacebuilding (Higley and Burton, 2012: 251). Subsequently, this defection has to be accompanied by popular support amongst the general public in order to achieve legitimacy (Higley and Burton, 2012: 252). Recalling the assertions of Fukuyama, Somit and Peterson argue that the creation of mass support for such a shift would require the success of new ideas and values in a given polity, a process which takes time (1995, 2005). Further to this, Higley and Burton believe a transition from unity to disunity is rare if not entirely unobserved (2012: 252). They argue that to break from the tradition of compromise and reciprocity would accrue unacceptable costs amongst all elites, making this an unfavourable option (Higley and Burton, 2012: 252). Therefore, development pathways, particularly in regards to regime choice and stability, are to some extent dependent on some level of elite agreement regarding the collective value in principles of compromise and the rules that govern a society and, in turn, how these are accepted by the wider public.

As we have suggested, elite values and interactions are important because they are likely to have platforms to influence society. Druckman, Peterson, and Slothuus (2013) study this idea and the impact of elite polarisation on public opinion formation. The authors highlight specifically the extent to which political parties act as heuristics for the public to form opinions without the need to seek extensive information on every political issue (Druckman, Peterson, and Slothuus, 2013: 60). In times of low elite polarisation, public opinion was only influenced by party frames in a small range of situations (Druckman, Peterson, and Slothuus, 2013: 70). However, in times of high elite polarization, public opinion also became highly polarised and was more likely to be formed purely on the basis of party identification (Druckman, Peterson, and Slothuus, 2013: 72). This analysis highlights the role elites and elite organisations play in the contestation of ideas within a society. High elite polarisation influences public polarisation and leads to opinion formation becoming less substantially grounded as well as reducing the likelihood that people will consider “alternative positions” (Druckman, Peterson, and Slothuus, 2013: 74). Therefore, polarisation amongst elites becomes a vicious cycle by influencing the polarisation of the public and, in turn, increasing the social support for polarisation at the elite level which, in democracies, risks undermining political processes that are otherwise reliant on compromise and consensus building.

Ideological Development in a Developed State: The Case of the USA

The theories put forward by the authors discussed so far are mostly based on the implicit assumption that either the social bases of support for a regime will be limited to supporting an authoritarian regime or can develop over time to support a democracy. There is little discussion around how the social bases may decay or disintegrate over time and lead to regime instability or collapse, particularly in the case of a democracy. Higley and Burton argue that the regression of democratic states back towards autocracy is explained by the fact that elites in these states never actually went through a process of unification and therefore the democratic regime was fragile from the outset (2012: 262). Further, they claim that an elite transformation from unity to disunity is unlikely due to the opportunity costs faced by all elites in a unified system (Higley and Burton, 2012: 252). However, while Higley and Burton (2012) aver that transformation from unity to disunity is rare and largely ‘unobserved,’ we suggest that this reversal is not only theoretically plausible but we may be actually witnessing these processes (though glacial) beginning to take root in the United States.

If, according to Higley and Burton (2012), the enabling conditions for democracy are based on elite agreement on how to play the game and that there is opportunity for them to interact, it is not too radical to infer that these conditions are slowly eroding (at best) or no longer present (at worse) in the contemporary United States. Furthermore, if we compound this observed elite disunity with the knowledge that elite polarisation also influences public opinion and polarisation, we can be concerned more broadly that the mass social base for the regime may also be eroding. In other words, social/ideological support for the U.S. regime may be waning at both the elite and public levels. Of course, the argument could also be put forward that as Higley and Burton (2012) hypothesise, the United States *never* experienced an elite transformation towards unity and, therefore, the regime has always been unstable. Yet, the authors themselves specifically argue that because of the American history of "benign colonial tutelage" followed by a large independence movement, an environment of a "consensually unified national elite" was established from the outset (Higley and Burton, 2012: 249). Indeed, one can argue that the United States has enjoyed a long and stable regime with both the presidential system and the constitution surviving for centuries. Therefore, on this basis we are able to infer that America, at least for a large part of its history, has indeed enjoyed regime stability under the influence of consensually unified elites.

Arguably this high degree of consensually unified elites has been gradually declining since the late 1960s, exacerbated by the aftermath of 2008 Global Financial Crisis, the culture wars that led to negative partisanship and political polarization, and then pushed to the edge under the Trump presidency of 2016-2020. In the US today, numerous points of disagreements on the rules of the game are embodied and evidenced by the significant constitutional contestation between the Democrats and Republicans. At least amongst the political elite, the consensually unified elite seems to be slowly becoming a thing of the past.

Using the 2020 presidential term and election as a case in point, it is striking to observe the extent to which interpretations of the constitution have diverged. Further to this, if the Supreme Court is believed to be the gatekeeper of the constitution in the United States, elites also seem to diverge and disagree on how this institution is used. The constitution itself offers little insight into how the Supreme Court should function, other than how judges are to be appointed and its jurisdiction (Greenhouse, 2012: 3). Therefore, the court is a classic example of an institution that is defined less by law and regulation but by the ideas of people who have the power to lead it. One of these ideas underpinning the court has been the "separation of powers" - the idea that the government should have dispersed powers with multiple checks and balances (Greenhouse, 2012: 4). Yet, with trends tending towards partisan appointments of Supreme Court justices, there is an increasing likelihood, or at least perception, that the judges will make rulings along party lines, undermining the ability of the court to serve as a legitimate check on government powers (Epps and Ganesh, 2019: 150-151).

Furthermore, elites have also clashed over how an election should be conducted in the United States with a series of disputes and legal battles over mail-in voting, voter verification rules, poll watching and vote counting beyond election day (Reality Check Team, 2020). At an extreme, one Republican senator Mike Lee has expressed disagreement with the US regime, asserting that it is not a democracy but actually a "constitutional republic" (Thrush, 2020). These are not minor spats amongst political elites over small public policy differences but *major* and fundamental disagreements over how democracy in the United States should operate. On the basis of the Higley and Burton (2012) study, these disagreements on the fundamental rules could be a sign that we are witnessing elite transformation in the United States that, at the very least, may be fuelling regime instability and at the worst lead to a democratic breakdown.

However, there was a second part to the Higley and Burton theory which we wish to briefly address - that elites have frequent interactions within structures that are reliable and accessible (2012: 247). Through the Senate and Congress, political elites have had a reliable and stable platform for interaction in the U.S. Underpinning Higley and Burton's second condition is the way in which these structures and interactions develop behaviours and expectations of compromise and reciprocity amongst opposing elites (2012: 247). Literature on the presidential system has often been critical of the way in which it does not foster cultures of compromise and reciprocity but rather causes *gridlocks* amongst elites and structures of government (Nooruddin, 2011: 56). So whilst the U.S. may have structures that foster reliable interactions amongst elites, they may not be producing the desired outcomes which Higley and Burton (2012) suggested. Therefore, the structural aspect of Higley and Burton's theory (2012) is not entirely absent in the U.S. but may be failing to create the consensus building environment which is important especially in the face of increasing elite disagreements.

These disagreements amongst elites are even more troubling when we think about the wider context of their impact on public unity. Druckman, Peterson, and Slothuus (2013) posit that elite polarisation can increase public polarisation resulting in less informed opinion formation of the public, and there is evidence to suggest that this is also occurring in the U.S. (Druckman, Peterson, and Slothuus, 2013). A study undertaken between 1994 and 2014 of voting age people in America shows that median Republican and Democrats have steadily moved further and further apart over those two decades (Pew Research Center, 2014). In 2014, "92% of Republicans are to the right of the median Democrat, and 94% of Democrats are to the left of the median Republican" (Pew Research Center, 2014: 6).

The source of this polarization is not within the scope of this essay. However, if Druckman, Peterson, and Slothuus (2013) are to be believed, we can infer that this polarisation amongst the people is at least partially driven or reinforced by polarisation amongst the elite discourse. The findings of Hawkins, Yudkin, Juan-Torres, and Dixon (2018) contend that the most concerning part of this polarisation is the role it may be playing in creating a majority of Americans who feel an increasing sense of political apathy, which in turn allows polarised and vocal *minorities* to dominate the political terrain. Should this majority continue to grow, America will have to grapple with not only an elite landscape that does not agree on the regime but also a public that does not believe or support the regime; and, if the literature is to be believed, such a breakdown of belief is precisely the condition which could cause regime instability with obvious negative consequences for economic development.

TIGHT AND LOOSE PATHWAYS

Another possible predictor of development pathways is the concept of "tight" and "loose" cultures." Gelfand, Raver, Nishii, Leslie, Lun, Lim, and Yamaguchi (2011) explore the concept of tight and loose culture, relating to a nation's or a community's propensity to create social rules and to follow them. Tight cultures will have a high number of rules that are strictly adhered to (Gelfand, Raver, Nishii, Leslie, Lun, Lim, and Yamaguchi, 2011: 1100). Loose cultures will have fewer rules and a more relaxed approach to following these rules (Gelfand, Raver, Nishii, Leslie, Lun, Lim, and Yamaguchi, 2011: 1100). Whilst there may be the ability to generally designate a nation as tight or loose, they will rarely be wholly either way. Any nation will have specific domains which are generally more tight or more loose (Gelfand, 2012: 422). Gelfand, Raver, Nishii, Leslie, Lun, Lim, and Yamaguchi (2011: 1102) find that the origins of these cultures lie in their historical experiences with threat. For example, nations that had historically experienced more natural disaster, food and water insecurity and high levels of pathogens were more likely to be "tight" cultures (Gelfand, Raver, Nishii, Leslie, Lun, Lim, and Yamaguchi, 2011: 1102). The authors argue these experiences have created need the within polities for high levels of social coordination and, therefore, have created societies that are highly rule-governed (Gelfand, Raver, Nishii, Leslie, Lun, Lim, and Yamaguchi, 2011: 1101). "Tight" and "loose" cultures have been shown to be related to regime choice with "tight" cultures perceiving greater effectiveness in autonomous leadership whilst viewing innovative, revolutionary, team-orientated leadership as less effective (Aktas, Gelfand, and Hanges, 2016). Gelfand, Raver, Nishii, Leslie, Lun, Lim, and Yamaguchi (2011: 1011) also contend that these cultures are reflected in the institutions they build with tight societies more likely to have harsh criminal justice systems, restricted media and narrow participation in the political arena. Therefore, similarly to the composition of diversity and elite unity, the extent to which societies create informal rules and follow them can be understood to promote and/or maintain a support for regime type and institutional designs.

From this theory, we offer a few observations - the first being that the experiences of "threat" as being unique to single nation states is being challenged in the contemporary environment which may promote more homogeneity amongst these culture types in future. Globalisation and climate change are making many "threats" highly global experiences. In 2020, the entire world experienced the collective threat of COVID-19 pandemic, as well as an increase in natural disasters. Whilst the presence of a "tight" or "loose" culture is surely the product of centuries of shared experience, it is possible to fathom that over time "loose" cultures may become more "tight" as they create a history of social coordination. If there is a shift to greater "tightness," we could also expect to observe changes in regimes and institutions to reflect this. Further, a perceived "absence" of a truly global community could be explained by an absence of history that has required the global community to coordinate around common threats. Therefore, despite attempts to install global institutions in the form of courts, inter-governmental organisations and trade organisations, the global community remains "loose" because socially it lacks widely accepted rules. Nonetheless, the global community too could become "tighter" as it continues to face collective threats.

Conclusion

In this essay, we ask whether there are social bases for development and if so what role can these social bases play? The answer is decidedly, yes. Social cleavages, elites, informal rules and the general public all play a part in the construction of what Robert Bates (2017) calls the "political terrain." In this brief essay, we suggest that elite convergence or divergence on ideas, rules of the game, and institutions can create a 'terrain' that can either be conducive or detrimental to development. And in the course of a nation-state's historical development, how a culture that is developed out of these experiences – whether they are tight or loose – also ultimately contributes to that 'terrain' that can spur or hinder development. Much has been said about the economic factors which can help or hinder development, the same is true about the critical factors of security, stability, and violence. In this essay, we suggest that attention also needs to be given to the role of these social bases of development.

In emphasising the social bases of development, we are offered the beginnings of a predictive framework to apply to contemporary contexts. In the case of so called "developed" states, with established institutions and rule of law, it is by observing the changes to social bases that we can begin to understand the turning of economic fortunes for the U.S. and possibly other states too. The institutions have not changed in the U.S., but the ideas that govern their use have. As it is people and their ideas who ultimately have the power to change institutions and challenge order, closer monitoring and understanding of social bases may enable political scientists to predict potential regime failures and instability.

This has brought into focus the extent to which development is far from being a linear process. New ideas bring challenges to the status quo at any stage of the development process, bringing with them potentially destabilising contests for popularity. To understand this in greater detail will be important to future development studies, especially as debates continue about changes to global power dynamics. As the U.S. faces these social challenges to its development, states like China have produced stunning economic growth over the past few decades; and, indeed, China is poised in the eyes of some academics to become the next global hegemon. However, it remains to be understood whether China has the supportive social base to sustain its regime for the long term. If the pro-democracy protests in Hong Kong are anything to go by, it would suggest there is an increasingly vocal lack of a supportive social base in China. Growth by economic metrics can quickly be constrained by social discontent. Therefore, when predicting global power, political scientists must search deeper than economic and military metrics and aim to understand the social factors that will be able to sustain their long term growth.

Additionally, in a global context, by understanding the social bases of development we predict a trajectory for coordinated, global development. With increasing global crises, causing many states to have a shared experience, this may foster a greater cultural propensity to cooperate as states begin to share greater agreement on policy responses to development challenges, such as pandemics and climate-change related disasters. Whilst it may take many decades to foster a "tighter" global community, this framework offers some hope for the establishment of a much needed global development agenda in the face of evermore connected economies and global threats to development.

References

Aktas, M., M.J. Gelfand, and P.J. Hanges. 2016. "Cultural Tightness–Looseness and Perceptions of Effective Leadership." *Journal of Cross-Cultural Psychology* 47(2): 294-309.

Bates, R.H. 2017. *The Development Dilemma: Security, Prosperity and a Return to History*. Princeton University Press.

Druckman, J., E. Peterson, and R. Slothuus. 2013. "How Elite Partisan Polarization Affects Public Opinion Formation." *American Political Science Review* 107(1): 57-79.

Epps, D. and G. Sitaraman. 2019. "How to Save the Supreme Court." *Yale Law Journal* 129(1): 148-206.

Fukuyama, F. 1995. "Democracy's Future: The Primacy of Culture." *Journal of Democracy* 6(1): 7-14.

Gelfand, M. 2012. "Culture's Constraints: International Differences in the Strength of Social Norms." *Current Directions in Psychological Science* 21(6): 420-424.

Gelfand, M., J. Raver, L. Nishii, L. Leslie, J. Lun, B. Lim, and S. Yamaguchi. 2011. "Differences Between Tight and Lose Cultures: A 33-Nation Study." *Science* 332(6033): 1100-1104.

Greenhouse, L. 2012. *U.S. Supreme Court: A Very Short Introduction*. ProQuest Ebook Central.

Hawkins, S., D. Yudkin, M. Juan-Torres, and T. Dixon. 2018. *Hidden Tribes: A Study of America's Polarized Landscape*. More in Common. https://hiddentribes.us/pdf/hidden_tribes_report.pdf.

Higley, J. and M. Burton. 2012. "The Elite Variable in Democratic Transitions and Breakdowns. *Historical Social Research/Historische Sozialforschung* 37(139): 245-268.

Nooruddin, I. 2011. *Coalition Politics and Economic Development: Credibility and the Strength of Weak Governments*. Cambridge: Cambridge University Press.

Olson, M. 1993. "Dictatorship, Democracy, and Development." *American Political Science Review 87*(3): 567-576.

Pew Research Center. (2014). *Political Polarization in the American Public*. https://www.pewresearch.org/politics/2014/06/12/political-polarization-in-the-american-public/.

Reality Check Team. 2020. "US Election 2020: What Legal Challenges has Trump Launched?" *BBC News*. https://www.bbc.com/news/election-us-2020-54724960.

Somit, A. and S. Peterson. 2005. *The Failure of Democratic Nation Building: Ideology Meets Evolution*. ProQuest Ebook Central.

Thrush, G. 2020. "'We're Not a Democracy,' Says Mike Lee, a Republican Senator. 'That's a Good Thing,' He Adds." *New York Times*. https://www.nytimes.com/2020/10/08/us/elections/mike-lee-democracy.html.

In: Political Economy
Editors: Caleb M. Clark et al.
ISBN: 978-1-68507-106-6

Chapter 7

The Color-Line and the Classroom: Racialized Space and the Making of Neoliberal Schools

Marcus Bell
Department of Sociology, State University of New York,
Oswego, Oswego, NY, USA

Abstract

This study examines the policies of the Brick City School District in Upstate New York. The BCSD has responded to student poverty in a number of ways. Similar to schooling in other neoliberal cities, the BCSD has prioritized elevating standardized test scores and improving skills, as opposed to combating poverty and reducing racial segregation. In recent years—and spanning the tenure of multiple school superintendents—the Brick City School District has begun a "renewed emphasis" on student achievement. The district has adopted what it terms an "all hands on deck" approach to closing the racial *and* economic achievement gaps. This "new" approach includes more money for technology, teachers and staff, corporate and nonprofit partnerships, and an ambiguous "commitment to innovation." Comparatively, there have been few district-wide efforts to combat, or even mitigate, the effects that concentrated poverty has on its student body. What is ignored is the hyper-segregation, concentrated poverty and chronic joblessness that characterized the schools and the communities that housed them. This reflects a firm commitment to neoliberalism, a political and economic regime that elevates individualism, self-help, and market forces as preferable solutions to any number of institutional inequities. Unfortunately, the practice of crafting neoliberal solutions to neoliberal problems has become routine, ensuring that systemic, more comprehensive solutions to the racialization of space, racial segregation, and concentrated poverty are likely to remain elusive.

Keywords: neoliberalism, poverty, public education, racial segregation, racialization of space

INTRODUCTION

"Malcolm X. My Kids loves Malcolm X." Mrs. Martin (all names of teachers and schools are pseudonyms), a veteran teacher of 15 years, sat across from me in her own living room, explaining why her school, as well as her individual classroom, was "decked out in black face." According to her, many of the students at Cass Tech High School were "really into civil rights," and as a result, the school principal had long since decided that civil rights imagery would be prominently featured throughout the building. All teachers, regardless of their preferences or personal politics, were to contribute to the overall black cultural aesthetic of Cass Tech. While Mrs. Martin did see the utility in such a policy, it left her somewhat uncomfortable, specifically the numerous images of Malcolm X that were plastered throughout the school. As she stated during our interview, "here you have a man who was unapologetically racist against whites, you know. He hated white people…it's a known fact that he thought we were devils, and his picture is in the hall right outside my classroom." Although she would never venerate Malcolm X in her personal life, his picture, as well as those of other African American icons, lined the hallways and classroom walls of Cass Tech High School.

Mrs. Martin teaches in the Brick City School District (BSCD). The Brick City School District is a severely impoverished, underperforming, and hyper-segregated district, primarily serving students of color in Upstate New York. The BCSD has a student body that is over 70% nonwhite, with 53% of its students identifying as African American. Also, the pattern of housing segregation in Upstate New York has led to a number of BCSD schools that are predominantly black, predominantly Hispanic, or predominantly white. For example, there are several BCSD schools in which African Americans comprise more than 90 percent of the student population. Other schools, too, have upwards to 60, 70, and 80 percent African American student bodies. While predominantly black student bodies are quite common, there are exactly zero BCSD schools where the majority of the faculty and staff are nonwhite.

Over the course of 19 months, I interviewed 32 white teachers from the Brick City School District. Identified and recruited through a combination of purposeful and snowball sampling, all teachers came from schools with predominantly black student populations. Preceded by detailed email and telephone conversations, the face to face interviews afforded me the opportunity to examine white racial identity and the local effects of racial socialization. In them, I asked teachers about their racial identities in a general or more abstract sense, as well as how they experienced white racial identity within predominantly black schools. We talked about their respective childhoods, their decisions to become educators, their teacher preparatory programs, and the multitude of paths that led them to urban, racially segregated schools. More than anything else, though, we talked about race: the race of the teachers, the race of the students, indeed, the race of the schools, themselves. As I detail throughout this chapter, in the contemporary United States, racially segregated and economically impoverished schools are not a bug, but a feature of the modern era of neoliberal schools.

In this article, I trace the rise of racially and economically segregated schools in the United States, and I detail the ideological regime that justifies, and in many ways, reinforces their existence. I begin by reviewing the racialization of space. The physical structures and spatial surroundings that contextualize and shape our lives, are, just like people, subject to the forces of racialization (Anderson, 2015; Lipsitz, 2007; Mills, 1997). Next, I trace the racialization of urban schools, particularly in the political aftermath of the *Brown v. Board of Education* decision of 1954. Following the formal invalidation of state mandated school segregation, a number of legal processes, social policies, and individual choices all colluded to link urban centers to black and brown bodies (Kruse, 2005). Over time, the association of "inner-city" with blackness has become a social fact, as the two terms are now interchangeable in the national consciousness. Finally, I document the rise of neoliberal policy in schools. Due to the changing political and economic environment throughout the United States as a whole, education policy increasingly adopted the language and logic of the market. All told, Mrs. Martin and countless teachers like her, perhaps without even realizing it, owe their professional experiences to shifting political economies and the epistemological connection of race and space.

THE RACIALIZATION OF SPACE

The importance of space in American society cannot be overstated (Anderson, 2015; Charles, 2003; Hale, 2010; Lipsitz, 2011; Massey and Denton, 1993). Space, particularly in the form of houses, neighborhoods, schools, and public transit, has been racialized for the greater part of American history (Desmond and Emirbayer, 2010; Freund, 2010; Lipsitz, 2007; Meyer, 2001). Beyond racialization, space is also contested. Where one lives, where one works, what schools are available to one's children, indeed, where one is allowed to physically be, have all been, *and are*, sites of racialized conflict (Japsin, 2008; Lowen, 2018; Rothstein, 2017; Wilkerson, 2011). This is particularly true of white space, which, historically and today, is afforded protection from what are often perceived to be outside threats (Anderson, 2015; Trounstine, 2018). Informally, white space, in the form of the white neighborhood, the white school, and even the white body, is protected through physical and symbolic violence; and formally, white space is protected through the force and finality of law (Dray, 2003; Harris, 1993; Lopez, 1997; Rothstein, 2017). All told, the intersection of race and space has a long and fraught history, and numerous scholars have documented the resulting consequences of the racialization of space.

Sociologist George Lipsitz, in detailing the reciprocal history of race and space, writes, "opportunities in this society are both racialized and spatialized." He continues, "the lived experience of race has a spatial dimension, and the lived experience of space has a racial dimension" and that "the interconnections among race, place, and power in the United States have a long history" (Lipsitz, 2007: 12). In this sense, lived experience does not take place within a vacuum, it takes place within a physical space. We live out our day to day lives, not in some abstract, spaceless void, but in actual neighborhoods, actual schools, actual workplaces, actual hospitals, actual prisons, and actual homes. In doing so, the forces of racialization that affect us as individuals and groups, also come to affect the physical dimensions that shape our lives. As a result, the very space that gives context to our lives as people, over time, themselves become racialized (Mills, 1997). Other sociologists, too, have offered a substantive analysis of race and space.

In his seminal article, "The White Space," renowned urban ethnographer Elijah Anderson delineates between various physical spaces that have been systematically racialized over the course of American history (Anderson, 2015). On the one hand, black space, most powerfully symbolized by the *iconic ghetto*, is marked by extreme poverty, rampant drug use, deadly violence, and, according to Anderson, "appears to verge on self-destruction" (Anderson, 2012, 2015: 12). On the other hand, white space, while economically and politically diverse, is chiefly marked by the "overwhelming presence of white people" and the formal and informal "absence of black people" (Anderson, 2015: 13). In the broad spatial imagination, white and black spaces are diametrically opposed. While black spaces are commonly thought of as loud, dangerous, and unruly, white spaces are largely seen as quiet, peaceful, and orderly. In this regard, physical space can be symbolically linked to race in a manner that seems normal, or, as philosopher Charles Mills puts it, "the norming of space is partially done in terms the *racing* of space, the depiction of space as dominated by individuals (whether persons or subpersons) of a certain race."

The *barrio* for brown people and the *ghetto* for black people, for example, both attest to the racialized norming of space, as these terms, alone, often conjure specific and stereotypical racial imagery (Anderson, 2012; Jargowsky, 1997).

Taking a macro view of the racialization of space, sociologists Matthew Desmond and Mustafa Emirbayer observe that "one of the most pernicious images of America is that the country is white" (Desmond and Emirbayer, 2010: 202). Accordingly, a broad swath of Americans view the country as a white country. This is true, not only in an ideological or symbolic sense, but in a physical and numerical sense as well. The United States is, after all, a physical space, a populated land mass encompassed within socially constructed, geo-political borders. As the single largest racial category and the group that wields a disproportionate amount of political influence and economic power, whites in America have come to represent the default American, the standard to which all other racial classifications are compared (Frankenberg, 1993: Kaufman, 2001; Lipsitz, 2006). Taken together, racial power, racial ideology, and racial demography have so thoroughly linked whiteness to the United States that, in the minds of many Americans, the former is now synonymous with the latter (Desmond and Emirbayer, 2010; Mills, 1997). Such a connection has major implications for how we view and understand physical space.

If America is constructed as a white country, then the physical space that comprises America is a white space. Any reference to the country, its history, its social norms, its cultural values, etc., is also an A) implicit reference to the physical dimensions that make up the country and B) unless explicitly associated with people of color, an implicit reference to whiteness (Hill, 2009). Given the racial and ethnic heterogeneity within the United States, however, as well as the historical legacy and contemporary reality of racial segregation, spatial racialization throughout the country is localized (Hartigan, 1999; Lewis, 2003; McKinney and Feagin, 2004; Perry, 2002). That is, while America as a whole may be constructed as a white space, there are a multitude of spatial localities that have and maintain different racial identities. Urban education, both as a social institution and a physical space, is one such locality. I examine the racialization of urban education next.

URBAN EDUCATION: THE MAKING OF A NONWHITE SPACE

Public schools in the United States cannot be separated from the white supremacist context in which they were born (Adams, 1995; Anderson, 1998; Desmond and Emirbayer, 2010; Watkins, 2001). American schools were founded for the enrichment and enlightenment of white males and, as such, were originally conceived as white spaces (Leonardo, 2009). From school teachers to school curriculum, from school policy to actual schools, race was central to the founding of education, and just as was the case throughout the broader society, whites—or a subset of whites—were the primary beneficiaries (Leonardo and Grubb, 2018). As time moved on, the white supremacist roots of education led to over a century of political and legal battles that were fought to determine who should and who should not have access to schools, both in terms of education and the physical spaces themselves (Anderson, 2016; Delmont, 2016; Kozol, 2005; Goldstein, 2015; Lewis and Diamond, 2015; Olgetree, 2004). While progress has been slow and unsteady, the conflict itself has linked race and place to schooling in indelible and seemingly endemic ways.

Today, public schools are increasingly being associated with students of color (Roda and Wells, 2013; Posey-Maddox, 2014). Although 2014 marked the first time in American history that nonwhite children comprised the majority of public school students, the minoritization of urban education has been an ongoing process spanning the last half of the 20th century (Chemerinsky, 2002; Tatum, 2007, 2017; Watson, 2012). Following the landmark *Brown v. Board of Education* decision of 1954, whites began employing a series of tactics that were designed to reinforce the color-line and protect racial segregation in public schools (Fairlie and Resch, 2002; Lassiter and Lewis, 1998; Rossell, 1975). In order to defend public education as a white space, school districts took extraordinary measures, up to and including shelving public schools altogether (Lewis, 2003; Webb, 2005). This, in conjunction with other political and structural changes, led to the famous adage, *chocolate cities and vanilla suburbs*, a succinct, if not simplistic, representation of race and space over the last 60 years (Farley, Schuman, Bianchi, Colasanto, and Hatchett, 1978).

Following an initial period of massive resistance, the late 60's and early 70's saw real progress towards school desegregation (Clotfelter, 2011). As researchers Jennifer Hochschild and Nathan Scovronick note in their study on education policy, school desegregation efforts "started slowly, but eventually transformed education throughout the south and in northern districts" (Hochschild and Scovronick, 2003: 36). Thus, despite a widespread and multifaceted effort to maintain racial segregation—to preserve the white space—eventually the weight of legal challenges, the momentum of the civil rights movement, and to a lesser degree, the liberalization of white racial attitudes, all combined to defeat this effort, leading to real and meaningful school desegregation (Clotfelter, 2011; Firebaugh and Davis, 1988; Hochschild and Scovronick, 2003). As Jim Crow came crashing down, schools all over the country, but especially in the south, saw genuine racial integration. Unfortunately, in decades since, a fierce and sustained backlash emerged, which, to a large extent, led to a pattern of school re-segregation that exists to this very day (Orfield, Frankenberg, and Lee, 2003; Reardon and Owens, 2014).

After several decades of continued progress, school desegregation efforts came under intense scrutiny. For an increasing number of whites, both inside and outside of the Jim Crow south, federally mandated school integration had outgrown its usefulness. What was once hailed as a vital and virtuous fight for the rights of black children was, after decades of struggle, transformed into an unfair and unnecessary infringement upon the rights of white children (Anderson, 2016; Lewis, 2003; Ogletree, 2004; Webb 2005). As a result, scores of white families migrated from diverse central cities to racially segregated suburbs, where they erected a network of private schools that were almost exclusive to white children from middle-class and affluent backgrounds (Clotfelter, 1976; Hochschild and Scovronick, 2003; Reardon and Yun, 2002). What is more, in a number of communities from different parts of the country, white residents took to the streets to vocally—and sometimes, violently—protest the implementation of compulsory busing, which by that point had come to symbolize federal integration efforts as a whole (Bobo, 1983; Delmont, 2016; Lord, 1975; Sears and Kinder, 1985; Tatum, 2007). Contextualizing everything, from successful school integration to backlash and retrenchment, was a conservative turn in American politics (Carter, 2000; Crespino, 2009; Lopez, 2015; McGirr, 2015). With the success of the southern strategy, large swaths of white and formerly democratic voters shifted to the Republican Party, effectively causing the Democratic Party to rethink, and ultimately retreat from, the battle over civil rights (Steinberg, 1995).

Other factors, too, contributed to contemporary school segregation and the social construction of urban schools as nonwhite spaces. Over the last 40-plus years, the United States Supreme Court has issued a number of rulings that inculcated, and according to some analysis, accelerated the re-segregation of public schools (Baugh, 2011; Desmond and Emirbayer, 2010). Two cases stand out. The first, *Milliken v. Bradley* (1974), ruled that compulsory busing across district lines was not permissible if it could not be proven that specific school districts actively engaged in racial segregation. That is, if school segregation within any given district occurred "organically," as a result of neighborhood segregation or the personal preferences of parents and families, then the school district in question *could not* be subjected to mandatory busing or any other federal desegregation efforts. The *Milliken* decision was groundbreaking because, following the collapse of Jim Crow, or *de jure* segregation, it provided legitimacy and constitutional cover for *de facto* segregation, a practice that remains commonplace today (Baugh, 2011; Logan, Minca, and Adar, 2012; Pettigrew, 2004; Sugrue, 2005).

The second case, *Parents Involved in Community Schools v. Seattle School District No. 1* (2007), argued over 30 years after *Milliken,* considered the constitutionality of voluntary desegregation efforts. *Parents Involved* consolidated two cases, one from Louisville, KY and the other from Seattle, WA. At issue in *Parents Involved* was whether or not individual school districts could increase diversity and reduce isolation by voluntarily using racial classification in student assignments. In a rare 4-1-4 decision, the Supreme Court ruled that racial classification could be used in student assignments, but only if it was "narrowly tailored" to "compelling state interests." In this particular case, state interests included increased racial diversity and decreased racial isolation in public schools. Ultimately, the Supreme Court ruled that the voluntarily desegregation plans in Louisville and Seattle were not sufficiently tailored to compelling state interests and were therefore unconstitutional (Clotfelter, 2011). Though not the only Supreme Court decisions to consider the role of racial segregation in education, the *Milliken* and *Parents Involved* decisions, argued over 30 years apart, rejected involuntary *and voluntary* efforts to desegregate our nation's schools.

In contrast, two additional cases, in particular, were instrumental to school desegregation following the in the *Brown* decisions. The first, *Green v. County School Board of New Kent County* (1968), mandated that school boards must formulate actual school desegregation plans in lieu of the often farcical "freedom of choice" plans that were ways to get around or avoid compliance with *Brown*. The second case, *Swann v. Charlotte-Mecklenburg* (1971), held that school busing could be used to achieve racial integration in public schools, even when schools were segregated because of neighborhood proximity, as opposed to racial classification. Collectively, the *Green* and *Swann* decisions made no distinction between *de facto* and *de jure* segregation.

Overall, however, the Court not only legitimated and provided legal standing for *de facto* segregation, but it also set an incredibly high standard for challenging the constitutionality of racially separate schools. Absent evidence of intentional segregation, separate but equal schooling—what was once characterized as inherently unequal—again became the norm, legally protected by the highest court in the land (Kozol, 2005; Orfield, Frankenberg, and Lee, 2003; Reardon and Owens, 2014). Thus, in the contemporary United States, school segregation, no matter how pervasive or how damaging to black and brown children, is legally permissible when it is considered to be the result of naturally occurring phenomena (Browne-Marshall, 2013; Desmond and Emirbayer, 2010).

DEINDUSTRIALIZATION AND THE NEOLIBERAL TURN IN AMERICAN SCHOOLS

Beyond Supreme Court jurisprudence and shifting (white) racial politics, school re-segregation and the ossification of white versus nonwhite racialized space have been exacerbated by economic change. Contextualizing the battle for, and against, school integration, was a deindustrializing and rapidly changing economy (Wilson, 1978, 1987). Good paying factory jobs that were commonplace throughout much of the 20th century disappeared, only to be replaced by service-sector and retail positions that offered only a fraction of the pay and few of the benefits (Jargowsky, 1997; Wilson, 2011). As manufacturing jobs fled, urban centers for newly constructed suburbs, affluent and upwardly mobile African Americans did so as well, combining with white flight to produce a number of racially *and* economically segregated inner-city communities (Charles, 2003; Sharkey, 2013; Sugrue, 2005). As these neighborhoods deteriorated and social dislocations such as poverty, joblessness, and crime rose sharply, a new term—*the urban underclass*—became a fixture in the American lexicon, casting a shadow over education policy that has remained in place for the last 40 years.

Since the late 70's and early 80's, urban schools have developed a negative reputation, stereotyped as drop-out factories teeming with black and brown students who disregard, and even actively resist, educational achievement (Downey, 2008; Fordham and Ogbu, 1986; Fryer, 2006; Harris, 2006; Noguera, 2003). Often immersed within segregated neighborhoods, marked by concentrated poverty, single-parent households, and high levels of violent crime, these schools are seen as both a byproduct and a genesis of the communities they serve. On the one hand, educational failure is viewed as the inevitable result of an unfair and inequitable environment, while, on the other hand, educational failure is regarded as one of the primary causes of disadvantaged or dysfunctional neighborhoods (Desmond and Emirbayer, 2010). No matter the causal direction, "bad neighborhoods" and "bad schools" are now broadly constructed as symbiotic; they are so mutually reinforcing that, for a great number of people, their epistemological opposites—"good neighborhoods" and "good schools"—are automatically assumed to be white (Johnson, 2014). Therefore, questions of how best to fix so-called bad schools and boost black and brown educational achievement have been, and continue to be, of great concern to educators and researchers alike.

In the wake of growing concerns about urban schools, particularly concerns about the lack of achievement, low standards, and future international competitiveness, America turned to the market (Hursh, 2007; Oeur, 2018). A 1983 report commissioned by the Reagan Administration, *A Nation at Risk* (United States National Commission on Excellence in Education, 1983), sounded the alarm about mediocrity in education and, from a policy perspective, ushered in an era of bipartisan neoliberalism (Hursh, 2007). Schools, once seen as a public good, became private commodities, turning students and their families into consumers who had to *compete* with others for the best possible product (Lubienski, 2003). In lieu of segregation and unequal opportunity, government bureaucracy became the new villain, accused of stifling innovation, eschewing teacher accountability, and, in the words of former President George W. Bush, promoting "the soft bigotry of low expectations." While campaigning for the Republican nomination during the 2000 presidential campaign, then candidate and eventual president, George W. Bush, coined the phrase, "the soft bigotry of low expectations." The crux of Bush's position was that not holding disadvantaged students of color to the same academic standards as their more affluent, white peers, was itself, a form of racism. This thinking served as the ideological basis for the No Child Left Behind policy he would sign into law as president.

Therefore, the market, a hallmark of neoliberal economic theory, was posited as the savior of American schools, one that would discard unnecessary regulatory burdens and ineffective teachers, boost pedagogical innovation, increase standardization for all K-12 students, and fortify American competitiveness in the international marketplace (Fabricant and Fine, 2015; Hursh, 2005, 2007; Oeur, 2018). Despite being central to the material outcomes of people and society, neoliberalism transcends schools and other forms of social policy. Across the political spectrum, a significant fraction of the American public now views neoliberalism as a way of life, as it has become a salient feature of their personal and political identities (Camp, 2016; Harvey, 2007; Oeur, 2018). Constructed as a much needed corrective to heavy-handed government regulation and the overly redistributive policies of the Great Society, neoliberalism has merged seamlessly, if not ahistorically, with other pillars of American ideology, namely colorblindness, meritocracy, and equal opportunity. In the decades since the Civil Rights Movement, neoliberalism rose to prominence alongside colorblindness as two dominant ideologies in the United States. Central to both are frames, including the overlapping frames of individualism and meritocracy. Another commonality of these ideologies is the belief that government intervention, or social engineering, is not only unneeded, but actually does harm and may even be its own form of bigotry. Both neoliberalism and colorblindness have become normative throughout the broader United States (Bonilla-Silva, 2006). In addition to justifying the need for neoliberal policy, including privatization, gentrification, and an amplified surveillance state, neoliberal ideology also provides discursive cover for the disparate and seemingly inevitable outcomes that result from their passage. The language of neoliberalism utilizes various discursive frames to rationalize and explain away contradictions, oversights, and contravening evidence to its legitimacy as a political program. For example, white Brick City teachers clung to popular discursive tropes, such as “the race card,” “personal responsibility,” and “reverse discrimination” to justify existing social arrangements and minimize the stories and lived experiences of their black students and parents. All told, as the dominant ideological framework in many American cities, neoliberalism has given rise to a modern, spatialized, and predatory form of capitalism that, under the pretext of “market forces,” leaves millions of people behind (Camp, 2016; Desmond and Emirbayer, 2010; Lipman, 2013; Oeur, 2018). The Brick City School District—and countless others just like it—is no exception.

CONCLUSION: NEOLIBERAL SOLUTIONS TO NEOLIBERAL PROBLEMS

The BCSD is located in one of the poorest cities in the country. For example, since the Great Recession, Brick City has consistently ranked in the top 10 for cities with the highest percentage of residents living below the poverty line. As of this writing, almost a third (31.8%) of Brick City residents live below the federal poverty line. Compounding matters further, due to steady population decline, as well as entrenched layers of racial and economic segregation, Brick City is also home to elevated levels of concentrated poverty. This all but assures that individual families, regardless of their personal socioeconomic standing, are much more likely to live in impoverished communities with impoverished schools, subjecting them to the pervasive and often deleterious consequences of neighborhood effects (Sampson, 2012; Sampson, Morenoff, and Gannon-Rowley, 2002; Sharkey, 2013). For children, research has shown that living in chronically poor neighborhoods can increase criminal delinquency, exposure to environmental toxins, and adverse effects their mental health and physical wellbeing (Elliot, Wilson, Huizinga, Sampson, Elliot, and Rankin, 1996; Evans, 2004; Sampson, 2012; Sharkey, 2013). Unfortunately—but unsurprisingly—the same pattern of racial and economic segregation that characterizes Brick City, generally, is also reflected throughout Brick City Schools.

According to the latest Census data, 44% of Brick City children live below the poverty line, which, though troubling in its own right, is a noticeable improvement from the 50.2% of children who did so at the time of my fieldwork. While the general trend line may be positive, the fact remains that, even today, almost half the children of an entire city are grappling with poverty, being forced to navigate food and housing insecurity, as well as other aspects of the modern neoliberal city, such as joblessness, increased police surveillance, and a gutted social safety net (Camp, 2016; Desmond, 2016; Oeur, 2018; Rios, 2011; Wacquant, 2009; Wilson, 2011). Although the city's child poverty rate is disconcerting, again, owing to segregation, the resulting effects are not evenly dispersed across Brick City Schools. There are multiple schools that, both in terms of student demographics and physical structure, rival those of nearby, affluent suburbs, while many others, often close in geographical proximity, are home to entire student bodies that qualify for free and reduced lunches. Such an imbalance is reminiscent of the city—and the country—as a whole, where race, socioeconomic status, and opportunities for upward social mobility are connected to space (Anderson, 2012, 2015; Jargowski, 1997; Lipsitz, 2011; Wilson, 1987).

For its part, the BCSD has responded to student poverty in a number of ways. Similar to schooling in other neoliberal cities, the BCSD has prioritized elevating standardized test scores and improving skills, as opposed to combating poverty and reducing racial segregation. In recent years—and spanning the tenure of multiple school superintendents—the Brick City School District has begun a "renewed emphasis" on student achievement. The district has adopted what it terms an "all hands on deck" approach to closing the racial *and* economic achievement gaps. This "new" approach includes more money for technology, teachers, and staff, corporate and nonprofit partnerships, and an ambiguous "commitment to innovation." Comparatively, there have been few district-wide efforts to combat, or even mitigate, the effects that concentrated poverty has on its student body.

In 2014, the BCSD identified seven of its lowest performing schools and converted them to *Innovation Areas Schools*. Each of the selected schools received an influx of financial resources and technology, saw its school day extended by 70 minutes, and was granted leeway to design and implement a new and "innovative" curriculum. Another program, *Chasing Higher Education*, is a collaborative partnership between the BCSD and numerous corporate and non-profit organizations. *Chasing Higher Education* provides college scholarships to any BCSD student who A) qualifies academically for participating colleges and B) spent all four years of high school in the district. Other corporate partnerships incentivize student achievement through professional internships, offering five and six year programs that include a high school diploma and vocational training. Still others focus on parents, offering them classes and workshops to learn skills and improve their own job marketability.

Thinking back to my interview with Mrs. Martin, she had a lot to say about numerous topics pertaining to education. She talked about the race and class of her students, wishing they would take full advantage of the resources available to them and chastising them for playing the race card. She talked about school culture, longing for more support from parents, guardians, and school administrators, alike. She even talked about her own racial identity, going into great detail about how it became visibly meaningful to her within the BCSD. What Mrs. Martin did not talk about, what no teacher talked about, was the hyper-segregation, concentrated poverty, and chronic joblessness that characterized their schools and the communities that housed them. The political economy that, in part, creates and maintains schools like the one that employs Mrs. Martin, has become normalized, as both racial segregation and concentrated poverty are now taken as a given. Ideologically, Mrs. Martin and millions of other Americans hold firm to neoliberalism, a political and economic regime that elevates individualism, self-help, and market forces as preferable solutions to any number of institutional inequities. Unfortunately, the practice of crafting neoliberal solutions to neoliberal problems has become routine, ensuring that systemic, more comprehensive solutions to the racialization of space, racial segregation, and concentrated poverty are likely to remain elusive.

References

Adams, D.W. 1995. *Education for Extinction: American Indians and the Boarding School Experience, 1875-1928*. Lawrence: University Press of Kansas.

Anderson, C. 2016. *White Rage: The Unspoken Truth of Our Racial Divide.* New York: Bloomsbury Publishing.

Anderson, E. 2012. "The Iconic Ghetto." *The Annals of the American Academy of Political and Social Science* 642(1): 8–24.

Anderson, E. 2015. "The White Space." *Sociology of Race and Ethnicity* 1(1): 10–21.

Anderson, J.D. 1998. *The Education of Blacks in the South, 1860-1935.* Chapel Hill: University of North Carolina Press.

Baugh, J.A. 2011. *The Detroit School Busing Case: Milliken v. Bradley and the Controversy over Desegregation.* Lawrence: University Press of Kansas.

Bobo, L. 1983. "Whites' Opposition to Busing: Symbolic Racism or Realistic Group Conflict?" *Journal of Personality and Social Psychology* 45(6): 1196-1210.

Bonilla-Silva, E. 2006. *Racism without Racists: Color-Blind Racism and the Persistence of Racial Inequality in the United States.* Lanham: Rowman & Littlefield Publishers.

Browne-Marshall, G.J. 2013. *Race, Law, and American Society: 1607-Present.* New York: Routledge.

Camp, J.T. 2016. *Incarcerating the Crisis: Freedom Struggles and the Rise of the Neoliberal State.* Berkeley: University of California Press.

Carter, D.T. 2000. *The Politics of Rage: George Wallace, the Origins of the New Conservatism, and the Transformation of American Politics.* Baton Rogue: LSU Press.

Charles, C. Z. 2003. "The Dynamics of Racial Residential Segregation." *Annual Review of Sociology* 29(1): 167–207.

Chemerinsky, E. 2002. "The Segregation and Resegregation of American Public Education: The Court's Role," *NCL Review* (81): 1597-1622.

Clotfelter, C.T. 1976. "School Desegregation, 'Tipping,' and Private School Enrollment." *Journal of Human Resources* 11(1): 28–50.

Clotfelter, C.T. 2011. *After Brown: The Rise and Retreat of School Desegregation.* Princeton: Princeton University Press.

Crespino, J. 2009. *In Search of Another Country: Mississippi and the Conservative Counterrevolution.* Princeton: Princeton University Press.

Delmont, M.F. 2016. *Why Busing Failed: Race, Media, and the National Resistance to School Desegregation.* University of California Press.

Desmond, M. 2016. *Evicted: Poverty and Profit in the American City.* New York: Broadway Books.

Desmond, M. and M. Emirbayer. 2010. *Racial Domination, Racial Progress: The Sociology of Race in America*. New York: McGraw-Hill Higher Education.

Downey, D.B. 2008. "Black/White Differences in School Performance: The Oppositional Culture Explanation." *Annual Review of Sociology* (34): 107–126.

Dray, P. 2003. *At the Hands of Persons Unknown: The Lynching of Black America.* New York: Random House.

Elliott, D.S., W.J. Wilson, D. Huizinga, R.J. Sampson, A. Elliott, and B. Rankin. 1996. "The Effects of Neighborhood Disadvantage on Adolescent Development." *Journal of Research in Crime and Delinquency* 33(4): 389–426.

Evans, G.W. 2004. "The Environment of Childhood Poverty." *American Psychologist* 59(2): 77-92.

Fabricant, M. and M. Fine. 2015. *Charter Schools and the Corporate Makeover of Public Education: What's at Stake?* New York: Teachers College Press.

Fairlie, R.W. and A.M. Resch. 2002. "Is There White Flight into Private Schools? Evidence from the National Educational Longitudinal Survey." *Review of Economics and Statistics* 84(1): 21–33.

Farley, R., H. Schuman, S. Bianchi, D. Colasanto, and S. Hatchett. 1978. "'Chocolate City, Vanilla Suburbs': Will the Trend Toward Racially Separate Communities Continue?" *Social Science Research* 7(4): 319–344.

Firebaugh, G. and K.E. Davis. 1988. "Trends in Antiblack Prejudice, 1972-1984: Region and Cohort Effects." *American Journal of Sociology* 94(2): 251–272.

Fordham, S. and J.U. Ogbu. 1986. "Black Students' School Success: Coping with the Burden of Acting White." *The Urban Review* 18(3): 176–206.

Frankenberg, R. 1993. *White Women, Race Matters: The Social Construction of Whiteness*. Minneapolis: University of Minnesota Press.

Fryer, R.G. 2006. "'Acting White': The Social Price Paid by the Best and Brightest Minority Students." *Education Next* 6(1): 52–60.

Goldstein, D. 2015. *The Teacher Wars: A History of America's Most Embattled Profession*. New York: Anchor Books.

Hale, G.E. 2010. *Making Whiteness: The Culture of Segregation in the South, 1890-1940*. New York: Vintage Books.

Harris, A.L. 2006. "I (Don't) Hate School: Revisiting Oppositional Culture Theory of Blacks' Resistance to Schooling." *Social Forces* 85(2): 797–834.

Harris, C.I. 1993. "Whiteness as Property." *Harvard Law Review* 106(8): 1707–1791.

Hartigan, J. 1999. *Racial Situations: Class Predicaments of Whiteness in Detroit*. Princeton: Princeton University Press.

Harvey, D. 2007. *A Brief History of Neoliberalism*. New York: Oxford University Press.

Hill, J.H. 2009. *The Everyday Language of White Racism*. Hoboken: John Wiley & Sons.

Hochschild, J.L. and N. Scovronick. 2003. *The American Dream and the Public Schools*. New York: Oxford University Press.

Hursh, D. 2005. "The Growth of High-stakes Testing in the USA: Accountability, Markets and the Decline in Educational Equality." *British Educational Research Journal* 31(5): 605–622.

Hursh, D. 2007. "Assessing No Child Left Behind and the Rise of Neoliberal Education Policies." *American Educational Research Journal* 44(3): 493–518.

Jargowsky, P.A. 1997. *Poverty and Place: Ghettos, Barrios, and the American City*. New York: Russell Sage Foundation.

Jaspin, E. 2008. *Buried in the Bitter Waters: The Hidden History of Racial Cleansing in America*. New York: Basic Books.

Johnson, H.B. 2014. The *American Dream and the Power of Wealth: Choosing Schools and Inheriting Inequality in the Land of Opportunity*. New York: Routledge.

Kaufman, C. 2001. "A User's Guide to White Privilege." *Radical Philosophy Review* 4(½): 30–38.

Kozol, J. 2005. *The Shame of the Nation: The Restoration of Apartheid Schooling in America*. New York: Broadway Books.

Kruse, K.M. 2005. *White Flight: Atlanta and the Making of Modern Conservatism*. Princeton: Princeton University Press.

Lassiter, M.D. and A.B. Lewis. 1998. *The Moderates' Dilemma: Massive Resistance to School Desegregation in Virginia.* Charlottesville: University of Virginia Press.

Leonardo, Z. 2009. *Race, Whiteness, and Education*. New York: Routledge.

Leonardo, Z. and W.N. Grubb. 2018. *Education and Racism: A Primer on Issues and Dilemmas.* New York: Routledge.

Lewis, A.E. 2003. *Race in the Schoolyard: Negotiating the Color Line in Classrooms and Communities*. New Brunswick: Rutgers University Press.

Lewis, A.E. and J.B. Diamond. 2015. *Despite the Best Intentions: How Racial Inequality Thrives in Good Schools*. New York: Oxford University Press.

Lipman, P. 2013. *The New Political Economy of Urban Education: Neoliberalism, Race, and the Right to the City*. United Kingdom: Taylor & Francis.

Lipsitz, G. 2006. *The Possessive Investment in Whiteness: How White People Profit from Identity Politics*. Philadelphia: Temple University Press.

Lipsitz, G. 2007. "The Racialization of Space and the Spatialization of Race: Theorizing the Hidden Architecture of Landscape." *Landscape Journal* 26(1): 10–23.

Lipsitz, G. 2011. *How Racism Takes Place*. Philadelphia: Temple University Press.

Loewen, J.W. 2018. *Sundown Towns: A Hidden Dimension of American Racism*. New York: The New Press.

Logan, J.R., E. Minca, and S. Adar. 2012. "The Geography of Inequality: Why Separate Means Unequal in American Public Schools." *Sociology of Education* 85(3): 287–301.

Lopez, I.H. 1997. *White by Law: The Legal Construction of Race*. New York: NYU Press.

Lopez, I.H. 2015. *Dog Whistle Politics: How Coded Racial Appeals Have Reinvented Racism and Wrecked the Middle Class*. New York: Oxford University Press.

Lord, J.D. 1975. "School Busing and White Abandonment of Public Schools." *Southeastern Geographer* 15(2): 81–92.

Lubienski, C. 2003. "Innovation in Education Markets: Theory and Evidence on the Impact of Competition and Choice in Charter Schools." *American Educational Research Journal* 40(2): 395–443.

Massey, D.S. and N.A. Denton. 1993. *American Apartheid: Segregation and the Making of the Underclass*. Cambridge: Harvard University Press.

McGirr, L. 2015. *Suburban Warriors: The Origins of the New American Right*. Princeton: Princeton University Press.

McKinney, K.D. and J.R. Feagin. 2004. *Being White: Stories of Race and Racism*. New York: Routledge.

Meyer, S.G. 2001. *As Long as They Don't Move Next Door: Segregation and Racial Conflict in American Neighborhoods*. Lanham: Rowman & Littlefield.

Milliken v. Bradley. 1974. 418 U.S. 717.

Mills, C.W. 1997. *The Racial Contract*. Ithaca: Cornell University Press.

Noguera, P.A. 2003. "The Trouble with Black Boys: The Role and Influence of Environmental and Cultural Factors on the Academic Performance of African American Males." *Urban Education* 38(4): 431–459.

Oeur, F.B. 2018. *Black Boys Apart: Racial Uplift and Respectability in All-Male Public Schools*. Minneapolis: University of Minnesota Press.

Ogletree, C.J. 2004. *All Deliberate Speed: Reflections on the First Half Century of Brown v. Board of Education*. New York: W.W. Norton & Company.

Orfield, G., E.D. Frankenberg, and C. Lee. 2003. "The Resurgence of School Segregation." *Educational Leadership* 60(4): 16–20.

Parents Involved in Community Schools v. Seattle School District No. 1. 2007. 551 U.S. 701.

Perry, P. 2002. *Shades of White: White Kids and Racial Identities in High School*. Durham: Duke University Press.

Pettigrew, T.F. 2004. "Justice Deferred a Half Century after Brown v. Board of Education." *American Psychologist* 59(6): 521-529.

Posey-Maddox, L. 2014. *When Middle-Class Parents Choose Urban Schools: Class, Race, and the Challenge of Equity in Public Education.* Chicago: University of Chicago Press.

Reardon, S.F. and A. Owens. 2014. "60 Years after Brown: Trends and Consequences of School Segregation." *Annual Review of Sociology* 40: 199-218.

Reardon, S.F. and J. T. Yun. 2002. "*Private School Racial Enrollments and Segregation.*" Harvard Civil Rights Project, ERIC.

Rios, V.M. 2011. *Punished: Policing the Lives of Black and Latino Boys.* New York: NYU Press.

Roda, A. and A.S. Wells. 2013. "School Choice Policies and Racial Segregation: Where White Parents' Good Intentions, Anxiety, and Privilege Collide." *American Journal of Education* 119(2): 261–293.

Rossell, C.H. 1975. "School Desegregation and White Flight." *Political Science Quarterly* 90(4): 675–695.

Rothstein, R. 2017. *The Color of Law: A Forgotten History of How Our Government Segregated America.* New York: W.W. Norton and Company.

Sampson, R.J. 2012. *Great American City: Chicago and the Enduring Neighborhood Effect.* Chicago: University of Chicago Press.

Sampson, R.J., J.D. Morenoff, and T. Gannon-Rowley. 2002. "Assessing 'Neighborhood Effects': Social Processes and New Directions in Research." *Annual Review of Sociology* 28(1): 443–478.

Sears, D.O. and D. Kinder. 1985. "Whites' Opposition to Busing: On Conceptualizing and Operationalizing Group Conflict." *Journal of Personality and Social Psychology* 48(5): 1141-1147.

Sharkey, P. 2013. *Stuck in Place: Urban Neighborhoods and the End of Progress Toward Racial Equality.* Chicago: University of Chicago Press.

Steinberg, S. 1995. *Turning Back: The Retreat from Racial Justice in American Thought and Policy.* Boston: Beacon Press.

Sugrue, T.J. 2005. *The Origins of the Urban Crisis: Race and Inequality in Postwar Detroit.* Princeton: Princeton University Press.

Tatum, B.D. 2007. *Can We Talk about Race?: And Other Conversations in an Era of School Resegregation*. Boston: Beacon Press.

Tatum, B.D. 2017. *Why Are All the Black Kids Sitting Together in the Cafeteria?: And Other Conversations about Race.* New York: Basic Books.

Trounstine, J. 2018. *Segregation by Design: Local Politics and Inequality in American Cities.* Cambridge: Cambridge University Press.

United States National Commission on Excellence in Education. *1983. A Nation at Risk: The Imperative for Education Reform.* Washington, DC: The National Commission on Excellence in Education.

Wacquant, L. 2009. *Punishing the Poor: The Neoliberal Government of Social Insecurity.* Durham: Duke University Press.

Watkins, W.H. 2001. *The White Architects of Black Education: Ideology and Power in America, 1865-1954.* New York: Teachers College Press.

Watson, D. 2012. "Norming Suburban: How Teachers Talk about Race without Using Race Words." *Urban Education* 47(5): 983–1004.

Webb, C. 2005. *Massive Resistance: Southern Opposition to the Second Reconstruction*. New York: Oxford University Press.

Wilkerson, I. 2011. *The Warmth of Other Suns: The Epic Story of America's Great Migration*. New York: Vintage.

Wilson, W.J. 1978. *The Declining Significance of Race: Blacks and Changing American Institutions*. Chicago: University of Chicago Press.

Wilson, W.J. 1987. *The Truly Disadvantaged: The Inner City, the Underclass, and Public Policy*. Chicago: University of Chicago Press.

Wilson, W.J. 2011. *When Work Disappears: The World of the New Urban Poor.* New York: Vintage.

In: Political Economy
Editors: Caleb M. Clark et al.
ISBN: 978-1-68507-106-6

Chapter 8

RACE AND INFLUENZA DEATHS IN THE UNITED STATES

Charles E. Menifield[1] and Caleb M. Clark[1,*]
[1]School of Public Affairs and Administration, Rutgers University, Newark, Newark, NJ, USA
[2]Department of Political Science, Auburn University, Auburn, AL, USA

ABSTRACT

In recent months, we have watched COVID-19 spread across the planet like an out-of-control tsunami. As the deaths mount, evidence suggests that minority communities have been hit harder by the virus in every respect. However, influenza type viruses are not new in the United States or other parts of the world. In fact, the Centers for Disease Control and Prevention estimated that influenza caused 34,000 deaths in the U. S. during the 2018-2019 season. While much of the literature examines the incidence of death from influenza from a medical perspective, this research takes a social science perspective with the goal of influencing public policy. The analysis addresses two important questions. Are certain states

[*] Corresponding Author's E-mail: clarkcm@auburn.edu

and regions of the U. S. more prone to deaths from influenza? Are non-whites more likely to die from influenza than whites? Our analysis demonstrates that certain U. S. states, regions, and racial groups are more likely to die from influenza than other groups.

Keywords: influenza, COVID-19, pandemics, disasters

INTRODUCTION

- In the latter months of 2019, an outbreak of a previously unknown virus was reported in Hubei Province in China. By March of 2020, the virus had spread to nearly every country on the planet leaving countless infections and deaths in its wake. In 2009, French and Raymond argued that the likelihood of a worldwide influenza pandemic was a real threat and that government officials should prepare for this eventuality. While we have seen many advances in medicine and a recent history with a pandemic, no one was prepared for the coronavirus as it has had a worldwide impact on education, medicine, public health, and the economy.
- With respect to the impact of the coronavirus, we examine, what could be called the "common flu," and its impact on various regions and populations in the U. S. as the evidence suggests that certain regions are impacted harder than others and that African-Americans were more likely to become infected and die from the virus.

Similar to COVID-19, influenza also causes respiratory disease, which causes a wide range of illnesses. Also, both viruses are transmitted by contact, droplets, and fomites. Hence, public health prevention recommendations should be similar for both viruses. Hence, we pose several important questions with the ultimate goal of informing public policy on the implementation of policies to reduce the overall impact of the influenza virus.

With respect to the many questions about who is affected by the virus, our overall objective is to answer the following questions using 2014-2018 data: Were influenza deaths spread equally across different regions of the United States? Do social and economic factors impact the death rate due to influenza? Finally, did the influenza virus impact certain states and regions more than others?

History of Influenza Pandemics in the U. S.

There have been four major influenza pandemics in the U. S. since 1918. Each of them affected millions of person with many dying. The 1918 Spanish Flu was the deadliest of the group, estimated to have killed some 50 million persons worldwide and 675,000 in the U. S. In mid-February 2021, the number of COVID deaths in the U. S. passed 500,000 and threatened the record set by the Spanish Flu (Worldometer, 2021). The 1957-58 Influenza A (H2N2) is third on the list with 116,00 deaths in the U. S. One of the most interesting findings about these influenza viruses is that they affect a variety of persons in different ways. For example, the Spanish Flu caused more deaths among those younger than five years of age, twenty to forty, and those older than sixty-five. The 1957-58 virus had a disproportionate impact on children and the elderly. The 1968 virus disproportionately killed people who were 65 years of age and older. The 2009 virus primarily affected young children and young middle-aged adults (CDC, 2020).

Literature Review

Oliver, Stukenborg, Wagner, Harrell Jr., Kilbridge, Lyman, Eibinder, and Connors (2004) examined comorbid disease in racial and ethnic minorities discharged patients in California hospitals from 1996-1999. Despite the fact that research has shown disparities in mortality among racial and ethnic minorities for several diseases, they found that in-hospital deaths related to aspirational pneumonia was similar for African-Americans and white patients. Asian and Hispanics patients had a lower death rate.

In a study of the 2009 influenza pandemic, Dee, Bernsyl, Gindler, Truman, Allen, D'Mello, Parker, Kamimoto, Biggerstaff, Blanton, Fowlkes, Glover, Swerdlow, and Finelli (2011) examined hospitalizations and deaths associated with the virus in the U. S. They found, using a random sample of adults and data from the Behavioral Risk Factor Surveillance System data, that influenza-like illness was similar among non-Hispanic whites and blacks, lower among Hispanics, and substantially higher among American Indians and Alaskan Natives. They also noted higher rates of hospitalization for Hispanics and non-Hispanic blacks than for other groups. Furthermore, they noted that a greater proportion of Hispanics and Asian/Pacific Islander children died from influenza when compared to other racial groups.

Hutchins, Fiscella, Levine, Ompad, and McDonald (2009) argued that racial/ethnic minority populations often experience more severe health outcomes than other groups during and after disasters. In addition, they argued that racial/ethnic minorities have higher rates of "injuries, poor health conditions, adverse health outcomes, and lack of access to health care" (S261). Using data from the National Center for Health Statistics, they found that African-Americans had a higher prevalence of asthma, hypertension, diabetes, HIV/AIDS, limited education, poverty, and lack of insurance, and were more likely to not have influenza coverage. The rates for Hispanics were quite similar for many of these diseases and factors as well. In addition, they argued that racial/ethnic minority groups were disproportionately negatively impacted economically during and after pandemics. This was the direct result of job placement. That is, racial minorities often work in the service industry which is likely to be most impacted by an economic downturn facilitated by a pandemic. Hence, they are not likely be in a financial position to hoard food, water, cleaning supplies and other resources needed to sustain their families (see also Aburto, Lopez-Ridaura, Rojas, Lopez-Gatell, Lazcano, Hernandez-Avila, and Harrington, 2010; Bouye, Truman, Hutchins, Brown, Guillory, and Rashid, 2009; Menifield and Clark, 2020). Hence, government and nonprofit organizations should: seek mechanisms to create safety nets; minimize economic burdens by creating social policies that address job loss and subsequently income; and provide access to the basic essentials, such as food, water, and housing.

Bouye, Truman, Hutchins, Brown, Guillory, and Rashid (2009) indicated in their study that low-income people are more likely to go to work during a pandemic out of fear of losing income and losing their job. In addition, many are employed in service-related sectors, hence negating the ability to work from home. They also argued that low-income persons often have a "high prevalence of and excel morbidity from diabetes; chronic diseases of the lung, heart, and kidneys; and acute respiratory infections, including influenza." In order to ameliorate the spread of pandemics, they recommended the following: mobilization, partnerships, and networks. This included forming partnerships with faith-based organizations, community-based organizations, neighborhood planning unites, and key informants who can educate the community. These entities can facilitate and manage mobile clinics and distribution centers; provide culturally and linguistically appropriate educational material; and deliver food, medication, goods and services. They also recommended creating risk-communication plans, appropriate education and training programs, evidence-based measurement and evaluation systems, community partners and advocates for policy change at all level of government (see also, Hillman, 1996).

Miller, Boaz, Rolfs, Brown, Dascomb, Grissom, Friedrichs, Mayer, Hirshberg, Conklin, Paine, and Dean (2010) conducted an observational study of ICU influenza patients in 2009 and found demographic factors were related to critical illness due to influenza A (H1N1). More specifically, they found that nonwhite patients without medical insurance were disproportionately more like to require ICU care than white patients. In addition, Hispanics or Pacific Islanders may be genetically predisposed to a more severe case of A(H1N1) infection. Lastly, they found that "race/ethnicity, lack of medical insurance, and younger age may be related to less access to care, such that socioeconomic factors, rather than genetic predisposition, may be responsible for severe disease due to novel A(H1N1) infection" (p. 756).

Quinn, Parmer, Freimuth, Hilyard, Musa, and Kim (2013) examined disparities in H1N1 exposure in U. S. households using a national survey instrument. They found that the risk of exposure to the virus was significantly related to race and ethnicity. More specifically, they found that

African-Americans had the highest susceptibility index score followed by whites and Hispanics. This finding was exacerbated by access to health care and discrimination in health care against African-American and Hispanics. They recommended that: the CDC include race/ethnicity data when reporting influenza hospitalizations and death; governments and health officials should ensure that information concerning the virus must be culturally appropriate and define the factors that place minorities at greater risk; governments and health organizations should utilize local and national organizations to target minority groups in their communications; and local, state, and federal health departments should partner with community-based providers that service at-risk populations (see also Entress, Tyler, and Sadiq, 2020).

DATA AND METHODS

This analysis extends the previous literature by examining the relationship between several independent variables in a model explaining the number of deaths from influenza for the period 2014-2018 at the state level. We included four explanatory variables - 1) the percentage of Caucasian residents in a state; 2) a regional dummy variable for the South which stands out for having a high percentage of African-Americas and poor health facilities; 3) state poverty rates; and 4) the number of doctors in the state - as well as three control variables in the final analysis - 1) total population; 2) a dummy variable for the year; and 3) a dummy variable for each state since this was a fixed effects model.

Table 1 summarizes the expected or hypothesized relationships. There are four research or explanatory hypotheses, First, the percentage of the Caucasian population should have a negative association with influenza deaths because of the well documented health disadvantages of minority communities in the United States. Second and likewise, the poverty rate should have a positive association with our dependent variable. Third, and following the same logic, the South should have a higher incidence of incidence than other regions. Finally, the number of doctors in a state, as an indicator of the quality and availability of healthcare, should have a negative relationship with the number of influenza deaths. Among the control variables, the total population variable should, for obvious reasons, have a strong positive association with the number of influenza deaths. In contrast, there is no *a priori* reason to predict the direction of the relationships of influenza deaths with the state and year dummies. The important hypotheses, of course, are for the explanatory items.

Table 1. Predicted Model Explaining Number of Influenza Deaths by State and Year (2014-2018)

Type of Independent Variables	Predicted Association with Influenza Deaths
Explanatory Variables	
Per cent Caucasian	Negative
Poverty Rate	Positive
South Dummy	Positive
Number of Doctors	Negative
Control Variables	
Total Population	Positive
Year Dummy	Ambiguous
State Dummy	Ambiguous

Cross sectional data for the 50 states were collected from the March Current Population Study or CPS (U. S. Bureau of Labor Statistics, 2020) and the Center for Medicare and Medicaid Services (2020). We used an Ordinary Least Squares (OLS) regression model to determine how each of these variables affected changes in the rate of influenza deaths:

$$y=b_0+b_1X_1+b_2X_2+b_3X_3+b_4X_4+b_5X_5+b_6X_6+b_7X_7+e \quad (1)$$

where

y = Influenza Death Rate

Independent Variables
X_1 = Percent of Caucasian Population
X_2 = Poverty Rate
X_3 = Dummy for South
X_4 = Number of Doctors
X_5 = Population
X_6 = Year Dummy
X_7 = State Dummy

Table 2. States with the Highest Influenza Death Rates

2014		**2015**		**2016**	
State	Death Rate	State	Death Rate	State	Death Rate
Nevada	23.8	Hawaii	27.4	Hawaii	24.4
Mississippi	23.5	Mississippi	24.0	Mississippi	23.4
Hawaii	22.6	Tennessee	23.3	Tennessee	20.1
Tennessee	22.1	Nevada	21.3	New York	18.3
Kentucky	22.1	West Virginia	21.2	Nevada	18.1
2017		**2018**			
State	Death Rate	State	Death Rate		
Hawaii	29.6	Mississippi	26.1		
Mississippi	23.0	Hawaii	24.5		
Tennessee	21.3	Alabama	21.4		
Alabama	20.2	West Virginia	21.2		
Arkansas	19.8	Tenn./S. Dakota	20.7		

Source: CDC. 2020.

FINDINGS

We posed several questions regarding the prevalence of influenza deaths at the onset of this paper. The findings below provide the results of the analysis for influenza during the period 2014-2018. Tables 2 and 3 list the states with the five highest and five lowest influenza death rates for the five years in the analysis. Almost all the highest states fell in the range of 20-25 per 100,000 population; and the lowest generally ranged from 8 to 10. Hawaii and Mississippi were clearly the worst, ranking either first or second for 2015-2018 and second or third in 2014. Tennessee also stood out for making the highest five list for every year; Nevada was in the top five for three years, and Alabama for two. Thus, the South stands out for its bad record on influenza deaths. In contrast, there is little regional concentration among the lowest states which included Florida (5 years), Oregon (4 years), and Minnesota and Vermont (3 years).

Table 3. States with the Lowest Influenza Death Rates

2014		**2015**		**2016**	
State	Death Rate	State	Death Rate	State	Death Rate
Oregon	9.1	Alaska	8.4	Vermont	7.0
Vermont	9.3	Florida	8.9	Minnesota	7.8
Washington	9.4	Oregon	9.0	Oregon	8.9
Florida	9.6	Arizona	9.5	Florida	9.3
Minnesota	9.8	Vermont	10	Colorado	9.6
2017		**2018**			
State	Death Rate	State	Death Rate		
Florida	9.6	Florida	9.6		
Vermont	9.7	Colorado	9.7		
Minnesota	9.9	Vermont	9.8		
Arizona	10.1	Minnesota	10.1		
Colorado	10.1	Oregon	10.2		

Source: CDC. 2020.

The results for our influenza regression model are presented in Table 8.4. The top part of the table includes the statistics for the overall equation. In combination, the independent variables have a moderate impact on influenza death rate as indicated by an Adjusted R^2 of .21 that is statistically significant at the .0004 level. That is, the probability that these results occurred by random chance, rather than reflecting a substantive relationship, is 0.04% less. In addition, the Variance Inflation Factors (VIF) for the independent variables range from 1.17 to 1.93, which are considerably below the scores of 4 or 5 which indicate that multicollinearity may be a problem.

Table 4. Regression Results for Model Explaining Number of Influenza Deaths by State and Year (2014-2018)

Adjusted R^2	.21				
F	10.55				
Significance	.0004				
A	285.64				
N	249				
Variables	b	Standard Error	t	Sig	Beta
Controls					
Total Population	-0.00000011	0.00000035	-3.10	.002	-.21
Year Dummy	-0.133	0.159	-0.84	.402	-.05
State Dummy	0.029	0.016	1.84	.067	.11
Explanatory Factors					
Percent White	-0.067	0.016	-4.13	.0004	-.28
Poverty Rate	0.350	0.095	3.68	.0004	.29
South Dummy	1.95	0.689	2.83	.005	.21
Number of Doctors	-0.12	0.006	-2.09	.038	-.15

The effects of the individual independent variables are reported in the bottom portion of the table. There are two estimates of their indictor impact on influenza death rate once the effects of the other predictor items are statistically controlled: 1) b (the unstandardized regression coefficient) and its statistical significance and 2) beta (the standardized regression coefficient) which estimates the comparative strength of each independent variable's impact on influenza deaths.

The research hypotheses about the four explanatory variables are all supported by our statistical analysis. Poverty rate and percent Caucasian are the two most influential independent variables as indicated by their b's in the predicted direction (positive and negative) respectively that are statistically significant at the .0004 level and by their betas of .28 and -.27, which are the two highest in the regression results. The South also stands out for having a higher death rate than other regions with a b that is significant at the .005 level and a beta of .21. Finally, the number of doctors has a somewhat weaker effect with a negative b that is significant at the .038 level and a beta of -.15. In contrast, the three hypotheses about the control variables are all disconfirmed. The dummies for state and year are not statistically significant; and the negative impact of total population is in the wrong direction.

Discussion and Conclusion

The results of our final model are summarized in Table 8.5. A high degree of racial inequality exists, as influenza deaths are considerably lower in states with a proportionately high white population. A high poverty level and location in the South also are very significantly associated with more influenza deaths per capita. While the results from this analysis are somewhat startling with respect to the impact of influenza on minority groups, they are consistent with previous research indicating the African-Americans are most likely to be adversely impacted by pandemics. There are several theories as to why disparities in health care exist. Dee, Bernsyl, Gindler, Truman, Allen, D'Mello, Parker, Kamimoto, Biggerstaff, Blanton, Fowlkes, Glover, Swerdlow, and Finelli (2011) posit that underlying health conditions, such as asthma, diabetes and other chronic conditions are more prevalent among minority groups. In addition, they also argue that "differences in clinical management of self-care of underlying health conditions and reduced access to health care services have been reported by others" (p. 627). However, other research Miller, Boaz, Rolfs, Brown, Dascomb, Grissom, Friedrichs, Mayer, Hirshberg, Conklin, Paine, and Dean (2010) argues that other socioeconomic factors are critical in explaining disparities in health care.

Table 5. Results of Regression Model Explaining Number of Influenza Deaths by State and Year (2014-2018)

Independent Variables	Predicted Association	Result
Explanatory		
Percent Caucasian	Negative	Confirmed
Poverty Rate	Positive	Confirmed
South Dummy	Positive	Confirmed
Number of Doctors	Negative	Confirmed
Control		
Total Population	Positive	Disconfirmed: Wrong Direction
Year Dummy	Ambiguous	Disconfirmed: No Relationship
State Dummy	Ambiguous	Disconfirmed: No Relationship

Other research indicates that African-Americans and other minority groups are less likely to be insured. A 2012 study by Clemans-Cope, Kenney, Buttgens, Carroll, and Blavin (920) indicates that "uninsurance rates among the nonelderly were 2.6 and 1.8 times higher for Hispanics and African-Americans, respectively, than for non-Hispanic whites." Further research indicates that African-Americans are less likely to attend a university and graduate, followed by Hispanics (Banks and Dohy, 2109). Furthermore, African-Americans are predisposed to having a high incidence of diabetes and any number of other chronic diseases (Menifield and Fletcher, 2008; Hales, Carroll, Fryar, and Ogden, 2020); the least likely of the four major racial groups in the U. S. to own a home (Goodman and Mayer, 2018); and less likely to accumulate wealth (Thomas, Herring, Horton, Semyonov, Henderson, and Mason, 2019). These findings are particularly important as the U. S. population becomes more and more diverse (Banks and Dohy, 2019).

Two broader factors exacerbate the health threat facing African-Americans and other minorities in the United States. First, most state and local governments are facing huge budget disasters from their expenditures to fight the COVID pandemic. The Democratic House of Representatives passed legislation providing support to state and local governments, but the Republican President and Senate did not show much support for this initiative (Greenblatt, 2020; Wilkie 2020). The implosion of state and local budgets would, among many other things, greatly increase the barriers to health care faced by marginalized members of American society. Second, the Trump administration fully backed a legal challenge that has reached the Supreme Court which could strike down all of the Affordable Care Act (ACA or Obamacare), thereby ending the opportunity for health insurance for many vulnerable Americans (Luthi, 2020). Individually and especially in combination, these two possibilities have truly devastating consequences. As of late February 2021, it was too soon to know what would happen in these two issue areas.

These findings have important public policy ramifications as they reinforce and highlight previous research which concluded that African-Americans and Hispanics lack many of the economic and social resources and other assets that would afford them an equal footing with the white population. Other countries are not immune to these disparities. Moon (2020) argues that government officials and scholars should revisit policy instrument given the broad impact that pandemics have on the population.

In addition to the above items, we posit that equity also has to be a priority in policy making moving forward as the literature is replete with examples of risk associated with race in America. We realize that it is not easy to modify some of the variables that drive exposure and susceptibility in health care, but we can act with urgency and ensure that those experiencing disparities know their level of risk. Data collection, identifying hotspots, creating pandemic plans, and creating safety nets for the most vulnerable populations, must be a top priority for government officials and health care providers as they create policy objectives (Hollingsworth, Klinkenberg, Hesterbeck, and Anderson, 2011; Teasdale and Yardley, 2011).

Finally, underserved communities should be assured that drugs will be affordable and available. Governments must increase funding for public health agencies and provide safety-nets for those who have the greatest risk.

Finally, more attention has to be paid to examining the social determinants of health. Housing insecurity, food deserts, employment discrimination, access to transportation and many other variables are inextricably connected to disparities in health care.

REFERENCES

Aburto, N.J., E. Pevzner, R. Lopez-Ridaura, R. Rojas, H. Lopez-Gatell, E. Lazcano, M. Hernandez-Avila, and T A. Harrington. 2010. "Knowledge and Adoption of Community Mitigation Efforts in Mexico during the 2009 H1N1 Pandemic." *American Journal of Preventive Medicine* 39(5): 395-402.

Banks, T. and J. Dohy. 2019. "Mitigating Barriers to Persistence: A Review of Efforts to Improve Retention and Graduation Rates for Students of Color in Higher Education." *Higher Education Studies* 9(1): 118-131.

Bouye, K., B.I. Truman, S. Hutchins, R. Richard, C. Brown, J.T. Guillory, and J. Rashid. 2009. "Pandemic Influenza Preparedness and Response among Public-Housing Residents, Single-Parent Families, and Low-Income Populations." *American Journal of Public Health* 99(S2): S287-S293.

Centers for Disease Control and Prevention. 2020. *Data*. Atlanta: CDC, https://www.cdc.gov/nchs/pressroom/sosmap/flu_pneumonia_mortality/flu_pneumonia.htm.

Centers for Medicare and Medicaid Services. 2020. *Data*. Washington DC: Centers for Medicare and Medicaid Service. www.usa.gov/ centers-for-medicare-and-medicaid-services.

Clemans-Cope, L., G.M. Kenney, M. Buettgens, C. Carroll, and F. Blavin. 2012. "The Affordable Care Act's Coverage Expansions will Reduce Difference in Uninsurance Rates by Race and Ethnicity." *Health Affairs* 31(5): 920-930.

Dee, D. L. D. M. Bensyl, J. Gindler, B.I. Truman, B.G. Allen, T. D'Mello, A. Perez, L. Kamimoto, M. Biggerstaff, L. Blanton, A. Fowlkes, M.J. Glover, L. Swerdlow, and L. Finelli. 2011. "Racial and Ethnic

Disparities in Hospitalizations and Deaths Associated with 2009 Pandemic Influenza A (H1N1) Virus Infections in the United States." *AEP* 21(8), 623-630.

Entress, R., J. Tyler, and A.A. Sadiq. "2020. Managing Mass Fatalities during COVID-19: Lessons for Promoting Community Resilience during Global Pandemics." *Public Administration Review*. https://doi.org/10.1111/puar.13232.

French, P.E. and E.S. Raymond. 2009. "Pandemic Influenza Planning: An Extraordinary Ethical Dilemma for Local Government Officials." *Public Administration Review* 69: 823-830.

Goodman, L.S. and C. Mayer. 2018. "Homeownership and the American Dream." *Journal of Economic Perspectives* 32(1): 31-58.

Greenblatt, A. 2020. "Absent State Help, State Budgets Will be the Worst in Decades." *Governing*. April 27, https://www.governing. com/finance/Absent-Fed-Help-State-Budgets-Will-Be-the-Worst-in-Decades.html.

Hales, C.M., M D. Carroll, C D. Fryar, and C.L. Ogden. 2020. "Prevalence of Obesity and Severe Obesity among Adults: United States 2017-2018." *NCHS Data Brief* 360: 1-8.

Hillman, M. R. 1996. "Cooperation between Government and Industry in Combating a Perceived Emerging Pandemic: The 1976 Swine Influenza Vaccination Program." *JAMA* 275(3): 241-243.

Hollingsworth, T.D., D. Klinkenberg, H. Heesterbeek, and R.M. Anderson. 2011. "Mitigation Strategies for Pandemic Influenza A: Balancing Conflicting Policy Objectives." *PLoS Comput. Biol.* 7(2): 1-11.

Hutchins, S.S., K. Fiscella, R.S. Levine, D.C. Ompad, and M. McDonald. 2009. "Protection of Racial/Ethnic Minority Populations during and Influenza Pandemic." *American Journal of Public Health* 99(S2): S261-270.

Luthi, S. 2020. "Trump Will Urge Supreme Court to Strike Down Obamacare." *Politico*. May 6, https://www.politico.com/news/2020/05/06/trump-supreme-court-obamacare-240366.

Menifield, C.E. and C. Clark. 2020. "Pandemic Planning in the U. S.: An Examination of COVID-19 Data." *Public Administration Review*. http://doi.org/10.1111/puar.13326.

Menifield, C. E. and A. Fletcher. 2008. "Obesity in America." *The ABNF Journal* 19: 83-88.

Miller, III, R.R., A. Boaz, R.T. Rolfs, S.M. Brown, K.K. Dascomb, C.K. Grissom, M.D. Friedrichs, J. Mayer, E.L. Hirshberg, J. Conklin, R. Paine, and N.C. Dean. 2010. "Clinical Findings and Demographic Factors Associated with ICU Admission in Utah Due to Novel 2009 Influenza A (H1N1) Infection." *Chest* 137(4): 752-758.

Moon, M. J. 2020. "Fighting COVID-19 with Agility, Transparency, and Participation: Wicked Policy Problems and New Governance Challenges." *Public Administration Review*. https://doi.org/10.1111/puar.13214.

Oliver, M.N., G.J. Stukenborg, D.P. Wagner, F E. Harrell, Jr., K.L. Kilbridge, J.A. Lyman, J. Eibinder, and A.F. Connors. 2004. "Comorbid Disease and the Effect of Race and Ethnicity on In-Hospital Mortality from Aspiration Pneumonia." *Journal of the National Medical Association* 96(11): 1462-1469.

Quinn, S.C., J. Parmer, V.S. Freimuth, K.M. Hilyard, D. Musa, and K.H. Kim. 2013. "Exploring Communications, Trust in Government, and Vaccination Intention Later in the 2009 H1Ni Pandemic: Results of a National Survey." *Biosecurity and Bioterrorism: Biodefense Strategy, Practice, and Science* 11(2): 96-106.

Teasdale, E. and L. Yardley. 2011. "Understanding Responses to Government Health Recommendations: Public Perceptions of Government Advice for Managing the H1Ni (swine flu) Influenza Pandemic." *Parent Education and Counseling* 85 (3): 413-418.

Thomas, M., C. Herring, H.D. Horton, M. Semyonov, L. Henderson, and P.L. Mason. 2019. "Race and the Accumulation of Wealth: Racial Differences in Net Worth over the Life Course, 1989-2009." *Social Problems* 67: 20-39.

U. S. Bureau of Labor Statistics. 2020. *March Current Population Study*. Washington, DC: U. S. Bureau of Labor Statistics. www.bls. gov.

Worldometer. 2021. "United States Coronavirus: 28,431,595 Cases and 501,711 Deaths." *Worldometer*. February 17, www. worldometers. info/coronaviruis/country/us/.

In: Political Economy
Editors: Caleb M. Clark et al.
ISBN: 978-1-68507-106-6

Chapter 9

A Derivative-Based Model of U.S. Presidential Elections: 1880-2020

***Alfred G. Cuzán*[1] *and Richard J. Heggen*[2]**
[1]Department of Government, University of West Florida, Pensacola, FL, USA
[2]Department of Civil Engineering, University of New Mexico, Albuquerque, NM, USA

Abstract

This chapter presents a fiscal model of presidential elections in the United States, which explains electoral outcomes by whether government spending increased or decreased during the previous four-year administration. In particular, as a hike in the price of any good reduces the quantity purchased, we conjecture that as spending increases support for the incumbent party falls at the ballot box, thereby reducing its chances of re-election. A variety of analyses over the past forty years have strongly supported this hypothesis. In this chapter, we describe the core model, its variations, uses, and results and then return to the original model to compare the effect of fiscal policy on American presidential elections between two periods, 1880-1980 and 1880-2020.

Keywords: Democrats, fiscal policies, presidential elections, Republicans, United States

Almost four decades ago, we published "A Fiscal Model of Presidential Elections in the United States" (Cuzán and Heggen, 1984). In that article, fiscal policy accounted for 80% of presidential elections outcomes, i.e., re-election or defeat of the party in the White House, the incumbents or in-party. Application of the model to the United Kingdom yielded a similar pattern: fiscal policy accounted for 73% of parliamentary election results between 1935 and 1979 (Cuzán and Heggen, 1985). Following those publications, variables reflecting economic conditions, political party, war, and incumbency were included into multivariate versions of the fiscal model (Cuzán and Bundrick, 1992, 1996, 1999, 2000, 2005, 2008, 2009; Cuzán, Heggen, and Bundrick, 2009; Tankersley and Cuzán, 2010). In this chapter, we describe the core model, its variations, uses, and results, and then return to the original model to compare the effect of fiscal policy on American presidential elections between two periods, 1880-1980, analyzed in the 1984 article, and 1880-2020. Although the data sources and the coding rules are different, the results are virtually the same as those obtained in the earlier article.

Table 9.1 displays the model's primary components, the concepts and their symbols, their operationalization into variables, and their corresponding descriptive statistics over 1880-1980 and 1880-2020. Note that the statistics are similar between the two. The biggest difference is in F, the ratio of GDP spent by the federal government (henceforth, all references to federal expenditures, spending, or the budget are in this relative sense). In the longer period, the mean is 20% higher, and the median more than two times larger. All other variables experience little or no change. Over the 1880-2020 (1880-1980) period, F', the rate of growth of federal expenditures as a share of GDP, averages 0.19 (0.24) per year, or approximately 0.80 (1.0) every four-year presidential term. That the mean value of F" is zero indicates that the rate of growth in spending is a constant—neither accelerating nor decelerating. F' and F" can be thought of respectively as the first and second derivatives of F with respect to time: F' is the relative change in F and F'' is the change in F'. Fiscal policy, measured with FISCAL, a composite variable made up of combinations of F' and F", describes "expansion" or "cutback" in spending. Cutback describes a reduction in either F or F', which is to say a negative F' or F". This is shown by the 2-by-2 matrix within Table 1.

Table 1. Definitions and measurements, 1880-1980 (*N* = 26) and 1880-2020 (*N* = 36)

Symbol	**Concept**	**Variable measurement**	**Statistics Mean [Median] (SD) 1880-1980**	**Statistics Mean [Median] (SD) 1880-2020**
F	Federal spending	Federal expenditures/GDP	0.11 [0.07] (0.09)	0.13 [0.17] (0.09)
F'	Relative change in federal spending	F'=(Ft - F t-1)/Ft-1, where t is the current presidential election year and t-1 is the previous election year.	0.25 [0.00] (0.89)	0.19 [0.03] (0.77)
F''	Arithmetic change in F'	F''=F't-F't-1,where t is the current presidential election year and t-1 is the previous election year.	0.00 [-0.02] (1.43)	0.01 [-0.01] (1.22)
FISCAL	Fiscal policy, expansionary or cutback	F' (columns: ≤0, >0); F" (rows): ≤0: Cutback, Cutback >0: Cutback, Expansion FISCAL = 0 if cutback FISCAL = 1 if expansion	0.38 [0.0] (0.49)	0.39 [0.0] (0.49)
V1	Incumbent party share of total vote	V1=Vn/T where Vn is the number of votes going to the incumbents and T is the total votes cast	49.1 [49.4] (8.47)	49.1 [49.3] (7.71)
V2	Incumbent party share of two-party vote	V2 = Vn/(Vn + Vo), where Vo is the vote of the challengers, Republican or Democrat, depending on which of the two is the incumbent party	51.7 [50.9] (7.44)	51.6 [51.2] (6.63)

Table 1. (Continued)

Symbol	Concept	Variable measurement	Statistics Mean [Median] (SD) 1880-1980	Statistics Mean [Median] (SD) 1880-2020
Election Outcome	Election outcome for incumbents	E = Win (1 or +) if V2>50% E = Loss (0 or -) if V2<50%	0.58 [1.0] (0.49)	0.61 [1.0] (0.49)
Party	Party of the incumbents	Party = D (or 1) if Democrat Party = R (or 0) if Republican	0.46 [0.0] (0.49)	0.44 [0.0] (0.49)

[a] Election outcome has to do with the share of the two-party vote going to the incumbents, not with the count in the Electoral College. Three times in the series (1888, 2000, and 2016), the winner of the popular vote (a Democrat) fell short in the latter.

Data sources:

Fiscal policy: https://www.usgovernmentspending.com/

Elections: Dave Leip's Atlas of US Presidential Elections, https://uselectionatlas.org/.

Turning to the electoral variables of the model, observe that on average the incumbent share of the total vote is a shade short of 50%. As a proportion of the two party vote for president, the combined total of the votes cast for the Democrat and Republican tickets, it is 52%. On average, the incumbent party has won the popular vote 60% of the time. This is consistent with re-election rates across the developed democracies (Cuzán, 2019, 2022). In both 1880-1980 and 1880-2020, Republicans occupied the presidency more than half the time. We emphasize that our model predicts the popular vote. However, in the United States the election outcome is not decided by the national popular vote, but in the Electoral College, whose members are separately elected by each of the 50 states (plus the District of Columbia). In 1888, 2000, and 2016, the winner of the popular vote (in all three, a Democrat) failed to secure a majority in the Electoral College. This discrepancy is similar to what can happen in a parliamentary system, where the winner of the popular vote may fall short of a legislative majority and fail to forge a coalition with smaller parties to form a government.

Presently we shall examine the relation between fiscal policy by party and by relative success at the polls. Suffice to say at this point that the intuition that informs our model is that fiscal policy as we have defined and measured is akin to a "fee" that the federal government charges the economy for its services As far as we know, only Niskanen (1979) and Peltzman (1992) examined the effect of fiscal policy on presidential elections. Both measured it in per capita terms). As a hike in the price of any good reduces the quantity purchased, we conjecture that as F increases support for the incumbent party falls at the ballot box, reducing their chances of re-election.

As noted at the outset, additional variables have been incorporated into the basic model for different purposes. In one study (Tankersley and Cuzán, 2010), variables measuring economic growth borrowed from Fair (1996), incumbency and party were added in order to estimate the relative efficiency of incumbents in converting these 'inputs" into votes. All presidents elected between 1880 to 2008 received a Data Envelopment Analysis score and ranking. Nine presidents scored a perfect 1.0: seven Republicans (including, surprisingly, Herbert Hoover) and two Democrats (one being Franklin D. Roosevelt in 1936—no surprise there). At the opposite end, there was no difference by party: of the 10 presidents with the lowest rankings (DEA < 0.90), Republicans and Democrats were equally represented (Tankersley and Cuzán, 2010: 151-152).

However, the primary use of an expanded, five-variable fiscal model, with minor variations, was to go beyond accounting for the win-loss outcome for the incumbents to estimate their share of the two-party vote. It was found that a switch in FISCAL from cutback to expansion lowers V2 anywhere from 1.3 to 3.2 percentage points (Cuzán and Bundrick, 1992, 1995, 2000; Cuzán, Heggen, and Bundrick, 2009). Also, estimated over a series starting in 1916, the five-variable model accurately forecast V2 in real time, ahead of the 2004 and 2008 elections (Cuzán and Bundrick, 2005, 2008). However, the model fell wide of the mark in 2012 (Cuzán, 2013), missing President Obama's re-election. In 2016, it wrongly forecast that the Republicans would retake the White House by winning the popular vote, which they did not (Cuzán, 2021).

In sum, as a tool for forecasting the two-party vote in real time, the five-variable fiscal model has had a mixed record. It did well in 2004 and 2008, but not in 2012 or 2016. No forecast was issued with it in 2020. Models by Abramowitz (2016) and Erikson and Wlezien (2016, 2021) have chalked up a good track record at forecasting the popular vote (Cuzán 2021). Also very accurate is the approach used to calculate the PollyVote, an aggregation of multiple sources of information including models, polls, prediction markets, and expert judgments (Graefe, Armstrong, Jones, Jr., and Cuzan, 2014).

The strength of the original fiscal model, the one introduced in our 1984 article, lies in its accounting for a simple win or loss for the incumbents in the popular vote over a long series, and with a single variable that measures policy, something that is missing in every other presidential election forecasting model except that of Lichtman (2020). Thus, it is to the original model that we now return.

Figure 9.1 tracks the behavior of F since 1880, the last of six consecutive elections won by Republicans during the years spanning the Civil War and Reconstruction. Expenditures have grown seven-fold since the 1920s. For half a century prior to that, federal expenditures relative to GDP were stable, ranging between 0.02 and 0.03. Then, in fits and starts, it grew six-fold, to 0.18 by the mid-1960s. First, it spiked during World War I, marked by the 1920 presidential election. Spending subsided for two consecutive administrations until the onset of the Great Depression, when it tripled under two administrations, one Republican, Herbert Hoover's, (contrary to popular opinion, Herbert Hoover was no "laissez faire" president (Horwitz, (n.d.)), the other Democrat (Franklin D. Roosevelt's). It rose to unprecedented levels during World War II, reaching 0.45, only to fall precipitously after the conclusion of that conflict. It jumped yet again during the Korean War, subsiding substantially after that. The conclusion of the Korean War marked the end of a period with by major wars and economic depression spanning 11 presidential terms. Figure 9.2 focuses, as if with a magnifying glass, on that era, omitting the 1944 WWII outlier. On average, spending rose by about 0.015 points per presidential term. Another half a century of stability followed. From the 1960s through all but the last year of the second decade of this century, spending bobbed up and down within a relatively narrow range, from a low 0.18 to a high of 0.21. That ended in 2020 when, in an effort to make up for the economic downturn due to the COVID-19 threat, spending recorded the fifth largest relative increase since 1880.

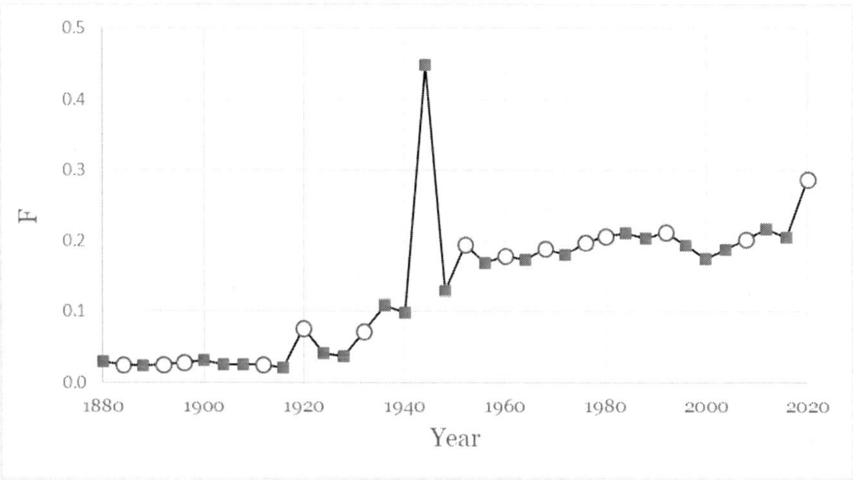

Figure 1. F by Presidential Election Year, 1880-2020.

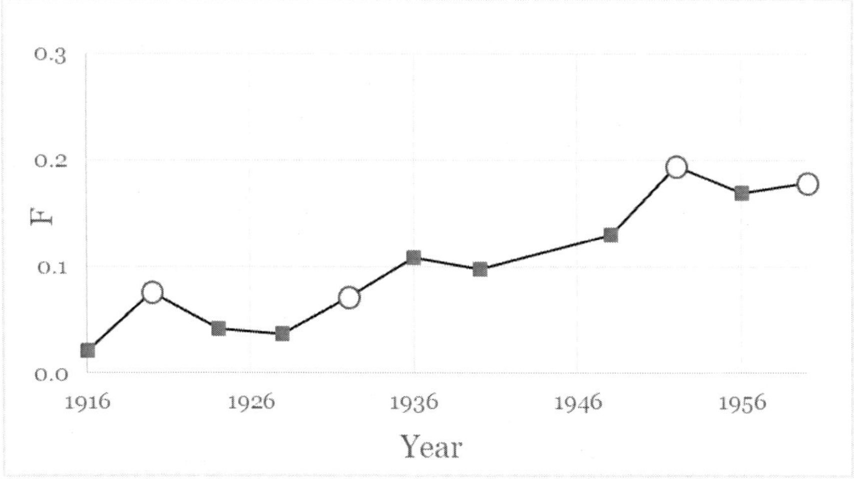

Figure 2. F by Presidential Election Year, 196-1960.

The path of F in Figure 1 appears to indicate something of a "ratcheting" effect, wherein expenditures rise or even explode during a crisis, but the crisis being surpassed it subsequently recedes without, however, returning to their previous level, an interpretation suggested as long as six decades ago by Peacock and Wiseman (1961). This likely portends an eventual reduction of spending below its 2020 high, but to a level somewhere above what it was before the appearance of the virus in these shores.

Figures 3 and 4 exhibit the paths of F' and F", respectively. Recall, from Table 1, that the former measures the relative change in F from one presidential election year to the next, and F" the change in F' between election years. Observe that, as one would expect, the large swings in both plots occur in the same year, upwards in 1920, 1932, 1944, 1952, and 2020, and downwards in 1924, 1936-1940, 1948, and 1956. Note, also, that both plots are trendless. F' (which is to say, the growth of F) has been approximately constant, with decelerations offsetting accelerations throughout the series.

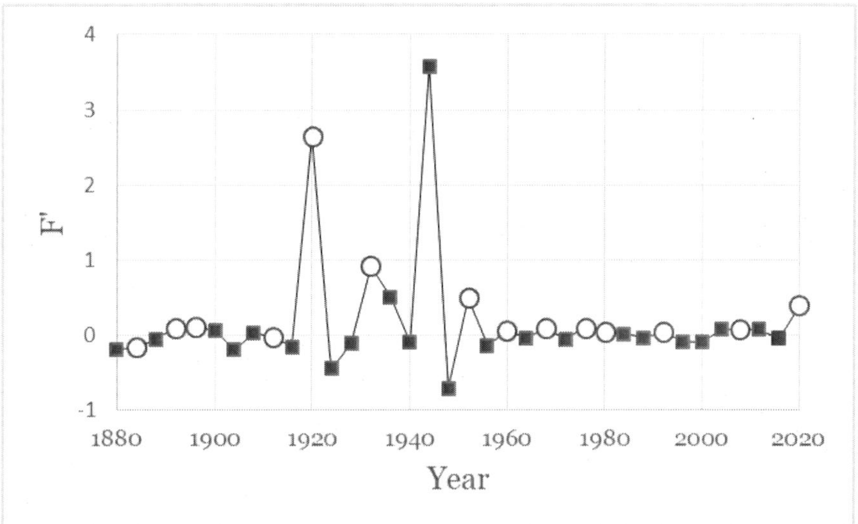

Figure 3. F' by Presidential Election Year, 1880-2020.

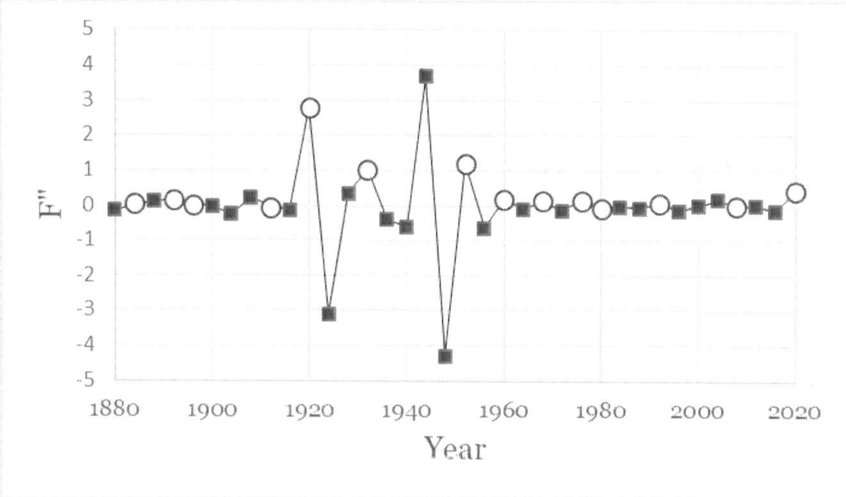

Figure 4. F" by Presidential Election Year, 1880-2020.

Having discussed the behavior of spending since 1880, we now turn to its relation to election outcomes. Figures 1-4 include solid and blank dots, one per election. A solid dot signifies re-election, a blank one, defeat. Absent a crisis, such as war or depression, administrations that increase spending (indicated by an uptick or upsurge in the plot) tend to be ousted, and those that reduce it or its rate of growth (a downward tick or plunge) tend to be re-elected. Table 2 displays this relationship. It arranges all 36 presidencies by fiscal policy, party, and year. Each cell is populated with election years conforming to their respective values on F' and F", along with the party of the incumbents (D or R), a sign indicating whether the election yielded a win (+) or a loss (-) for them, and an asterisk (*) signifying that the result was correctly predicted by the model.

The distribution of the cases shows the following: In 13 out of 14 elections (93%) in which both F' and F" are negative, the incumbents were re-elected. F' and F" are negative in 17 and 19 instances, respectively, and their corresponding re-election rates are virtually the same, 88% and 89%. Thus, the electorate appears to reward both policies equally. By contrast, only 3 out of 14 elections (21%) in which both F' and F" are positive had the same result.

Table 2. F', F'', and Win (+) or Loss (-) of popular vote of incumbents, 1880-2020 R=Republican, D=Democrat

F''	**F'**		**Re-election/ Rate**
	F' ≤ 0	F'> 0	
F'' ≤ 0	1880 R +*	1900 R +*	
	1904 R +*	1936 D +*	
	1912 R[a] -	1980 D -	
	1916 D +*	1984 R +*	
	1924 R +*	2012 D +*	
	1940 D +*		
	1948 D +*		
	1956 R +*		
	1964 D +*		
	1972 R +*		
	1988 R +*		
	1996 D +*		
	2000 D[b]+*		
	2016 D[b]+*		
Re-election rate	13/14	4/5	17/19
F''> 0	1884 R -	1892 R -*	
	1888 D[b]+*	1896 D -*	
	1928 R +*	1908 R +	
		1920 D -*	
		1932 R -*	
		1944 D[c]+	
		1952 D[c]-*	
		1960 R -*	
		1968 D -*	
		1976 R -*	
		1992 R -*	
		2004 R[c]+	
		2008 R -*	
		2020 R –*	
Reelection Rate	2/3	3/14	5/17
Re-election Rate Rate	15/17	7/19	22/36
Correctly Predicted	15	15	30/36

Notes: * Correctly predicted.

[a] Party scission—T. D. Roosevelt, the previous Republican president, bolted to run as the Bull Moose or Progressive Party candidate, placing second.

[b] Incumbent lost in the Electoral College.

[c] War year.

Now consider cases where the variables take the opposite sign. In 4 out of 5 instances or (80%) in which F' is positive but F" negative, indicating that spending grew, but at a slower rate than in the previous administration, the incumbents won another term. Also, in 2 out 3 occasions (67%) in which F' is negative but F" positive, signifying that spending was reduced, but at a slower rate than in the previous term, the party in the White House was re-elected. All 22 of these cases represent administrations that implemented a cutback policy, and 19 of them (86%) resulted in re-election. Altogether, then, 30 out of 36 election outcomes (19 cases of cutback policy, plus 11 of expansionary policy), or 83%, are consistent with our expectations. Also, these results are highly significant as indicated by a Chi-Square test of election outcome by FISCAL: Chi. Sq. = 15.18, df = 1, p-value < 0.00001 (since the data come from a population, not a sample, statistical significance is not relevant, but it is often reported in political science research (Clark, 2013)).

These ratios are comparable to those reported in Table 1 of our original article (Cuzán and Heggen, 1984: 103, 108). A few differences need pointing out. In the earlier paper we included a third possibility for F' and F": a steady-state policy, where the value of either variable was between -0.02 and 0.02 in our current scale. That condition described six elections. Four, two for each party, those of 1900 R+, 1964 D+, 1972 R+, and 1980 D-, were steady-state on F' but negative on F", and two were positive on F' but steady-state on F", 1892 R- and 1896 D-. This time, with a different data series, we made both variables binary, depending simply on their signs without taking into the account their respective values. As a result, from steady-state on F', 1964 and 1972 shifted to the left, or cutback column, 1900 and 1980 moved to the right, or expansionary column, and 1892 and 1896 fell from steady-state on F" to the bottom, expansionary row. Additionally, on account of a different data series, 1888, 1916 and 1940 shifted from right to left on F'. Finally, in the earlier paper, the 1888 election was called a defeat for the Democrats because, despite garnering more votes than the Republicans, they lost the Electoral College count.

This time it is not, for consistent with theory the dependent variable is V2, not whether the incumbent won or lost in the Electoral College. What is most remarkable is that these changes had minimal effect on the overall distribution of predictive success: 80% in 1880-1980 and 83% in 1880-2020.

Next, in Table 3 we explore whether there is any relation between fiscal policy on election outcome by party. Since 1880, 16 Democrats and 20 Republicans have filled the presidency. Twenty-two (61%) have implemented a cutback policy, while 14 (39%) have applied an expansionary one. By party, the ratios are 11/16 (69%) and 11/20 (55%) on cutback, and 5/16 (31%) and 9/20 (45%) on expansion, respectively. That is, historically Republicans have been somewhat more likely to expand than Democrats (even though the Chi Square of 0.70 is far from statistically significant), a finding that is contrary to conventional opinion. As for electoral success by fiscal policy and party, 10/11 (91%) of Democrats and 9/11 (82%) of Republicans who refrained from fiscal expansion were re-elected while only 1/5 (20%) Democrats and 2/9 (22%) Republicans who grew the federal budget retained control of the White House. Thus, it does not appear that party makes a difference: Both parties are more or less as likely to get reelected when policy is cutback as they are to be defeated when it is expansionary.

Turning to the six prediction errors, three each by cutback and expansion, Table 4 organizes them by year, president and party and assays a possible explanation for each. The 1884 error could well be an instance of a "time for change" factor after six consecutive Republican presidents (Abramowitz, 2016; Norpoth, 2014). The scission of the Republicans easily accounts for President Taft's defeat in 1912. Also understandable are the war-time victories of Franklin D. Roosevelt in 1944 and George W. Bush six decades later (Norpoth, 2007; Weisberg and Christenson, 2007). No readily generalizable explanations come to mind regarding T. R Roosevelt's 1908 re-election or Carter's defeat, on the other. The fact is, though, that a 100% prediction rate would be an unreasonable standard in social science.

Table 3. Fiscal policy, election outcome, and predictive success by party, 1880-2020

Party	Election Outcomes	FISCAL		Election Wins	Correct Predictions
		Cutback	Expansion		
Democrats					
	Wins	10	1	11	10/11
	Losses	1	4	5	4/5
Sub-total		11	5	16	14/16
Republicans					
	Wins	9	2	11	9/11
	Losses	2	7	9	7/9
Sub-total		11	9	20	16/20
Total		22	14	36	30/36

Table 4. Accounting for prediction failures

Fiscal Policy	Year	President and Party	Explanation
Cutback	1884	James Garfield[a]/ Chester Arthur, R	Time for a change after six consecutive Republican administrations.
Cutback	1912	Wm. Howard Taft, R	A split in the Republican Party when Taft's coreligionist predecessor, having failed to wrest the nomination from Taft, ran as the candidate of the Progressive (Bull Moose) Party.
Cutback	1980	Jimmy Carter, D	Many other failures, including run-way inflation, foreign policy failures (Afghanistan, Iran, Nicaragua).
Expansionary	1908	Theodore Roosevelt, R	Succeeded his predecessor following the latter's assassination. Reputation as hero deriving from his exploits in Cuba during the Spanish-American War. Foreign policy successes, including in Panama, Winner of Nobel Peace Prize in 1906 for successfully brokering Russo-Japanese peace treaty.
Expansionary	1944	Franklin Roosevelt, D	World War II.
Expansionary	2004	George W. Bush, R	War against the Taliban, Al Qaeda

Note:

[a] Assassinated less than half a year after his inauguration.

Summary and Conclusion

We revisited our 1984 fiscal model of presidential elections, this time with a longer data series from a single source. We tracked the ratio of federal expenditures to GDP from one presidential election year to the next, as well as the change in this ratio and the change in the change of the ratio. Most of the time, increases in spending cost the incumbents the White House while reductions in the budget or its rate of growth enabled re-election. The model predicts 83% of election outcomes since 1880. There is little or no difference in fiscal policy or electoral success by party. Republicans have been somewhat more likely than Democrats to spend more, but both parties are as likely to be rewarded for fiscal restraint as they are punished for expansion. Given these findings, it would seem that fiscal policy as we have defined and measured it appears to be an under-appreciated factor in the analysis of presidential elections.

References

Abramowitz, A. 2016. "Will Time for Change Mean Time for Trump?" *PS: Political Science and Politics* 49(4): 659-660.

Clark, C. 2013. *Political Science Research Methods: Exploring America at a Crossroads*. Hackensack, NJ: World Scientific.

Cuzán, A.G. 2013. "Fiscal Model Failure: A Measurement Problem? A Preliminary Assessment." *PS: Political Science and Politics* 46(1): 42-43.

Cuzán, A.G. 2019. "Five Laws of Politics: A Follow-Up." *PS: Political Science and Politics* 52(3): 457-464.

Cuzán, A.G. 2021. "The Campbell Collection of Presidential Election Forecasts, 1984-2016: A Review." *PS: Political Science and Politics* 54(1): 99-103.

Cuzán, A.G. 2022. *Laws of Politics. Their Application to Democracies and Dictatorships*. New York and London: Routledge.

Cuzán, A.G. and C M. Bundrick. 1992. "Selected Fiscal and Economic Effects on Presidential Elections." *Presidential Studies Quarterly* 22(1): 127-134.

Cuzán, A.G. and C.M. Bundrick. 1996. "Fiscal Policy and Presidential Elections, 1880-1992." *Polity* 29(1): 141-156.

Cuzán, A.G. and C.M. Bundrick. 1999. "Fiscal Policy as a Forecasting Factor in Presidential Elections." *American Politics Quarterly* 27(3): 338-353.

Cuzán, A.G. and C. M. Bundrick. 2000. "Fiscal Policy and Presidential Elections: Update and Extension." *Presidential Studies Quarterly* 30(2): 275-289.

Cuzán, A. G. and C.M. Bundrick. 2005. "Deconstructing the 2004 Presidential Election Forecasts: The Fiscal Model and the Campbell Collection Compared." *PS: Political Science and Politics* 38(2): 255-262.

Cuzán, A.G. and C.M. Bundrick. 2008. "Forecasting the 2008 Presidential Elections: A Challenge for the Fiscal Model." *PS: Political Science and Politics* 41(4): 717-722.

Cuzán, A.G. and C.M. Bundrick. 2009. "Forecasting the 2008 Presidential Election: The Challenge Met." *PS: Political Science and Politics* 42(1): 23.

Cuzán, A.G. and R.J. Heggen. 1984. "A Fiscal Model of Presidential Elections in the United States." *Presidential Studies Quarterly* 14(1): 98-108.

Cuzán, A.G. and R.J. Heggen. 1985. "Expenditures and Votes: In Search of Downward-Sloping Curves in the United States and Great Britain." *Public Choice* 45(1): 19-34.

Cuzán, A G., R. J. Heggen and C.M. Bundrick. 2009. "Fiscal Policy in American Presidential Elections: A Simulation." *Simulation* 85(1): 17-32.

Erikson, R. and C. Wlezien. 2016. "Forecasting the Presidential Vote with Leading Economic Indicators and the Polls." *PS: Political Science and Politics* 49(4): 669-672.

Erikson, R. and C. Wlezien. 2021. "Forecasting the 2020 Presidential Election: Leading Economic Indicators, Polls, and the Vote." *PS: Political Science and Politics* 54(1): 55-58.

Fair, R. 1996. "Econometrics and Presidential Elections." *Journal of Economic Perspectives* 10(3): 89-102.

Graefe, A., J.S. Armstrong, R.J. Jones, Jr., and A.G. Cuzán. 2014. "Combining Forecasts: An Application to Elections." *International Journal of Forecasting* 30 (1):43–54.

Horwitz, S. n.d. "Hoover's Economic Policies." *The Library of Economics and Liberty*. https://www.econlib.org/library/Enc/HooversEconomicPolicies.html.

Lichtman, A. 2020. "The Keys to the White House: Forecast for 2020." *Harvard Data Science Review* 2(4): https://doi.org/10.1162/99608f92.baaa8f68.

Niskanen, W. 1979. "Economic and Fiscal Effects on the Popular Vote for President." in D.W. Rae and T.J. Eismeier, Eds. *Public Policy and Public Choice.* Beverly Hills: Sage Publications.

Norpoth, H. 2007. "Mission Accomplished: The Wartime Election of 2004." *Political Behavior* 29(2): 175-195.

Norpoth, H. 2014. "The Electoral Cycle." *PS: Political Science and Politics* 47(2): 332-335.

Peacock, A.T. and J. Wiseman. 1961. *Growth of Public Expenditure in the United Kingdom.* Princeton: Princeton University Press.

Peltzman, S. 1992. "Voters as Fiscal Conservatives." *Quarterly Journal of Economics* 107(2): 327-361.

Tankersley, W.B. and A.G. Cuzán. 2010. "Fiscal Policy and Vote-Getting Efficiency in Presidential Elections: A Data Envelopment Analysis, 1880-2008." pp. 137-159 in C. Putcha, Ed. *Methods of Forecasting American Elections Outcomes. Studies in Strategies and Prediction.* Lewiston, NY: The Edwin Mellon Press.

Weisberg, H.F. and D. P. Christenson. 2007. "Changing Horses in Wartime? The 2004 Presidential Election." *Political Behavior* 29(2): 279-304.

APPENDIX: DATA TABLE

Year	F	F'	F"	FISCAL[b]	VOTE	V2	Election	Prediction	Party
1880	0.0291	-0.18	-0.16	CB	48.31	50.05	W	Correct	R
1884	0.0245	-0.16	0.02	CB	48.28	49.71	L	Incorrect	R
1888	0.0232	-0.05	0.11	CB	48.85	50.29	W[a]	Correct	D
1892	0.0256	0.10	0.16	E	43.01	48.31	L	Correct	R
1896	0.0283	0.11	0.00	E	46.71	47.80	L	Correct	D
1900	0.0303	0.071	-0.03	CB	51.66	53.16	W	Correct	R
1904	0.0243	-0.19	-0.27	CB	56.42	60.01	W	Correct	R
1908	0.0251	0.03	0.23	E	51.57	54.51	W	Incorrect	R
1912	0.0245	-0.02	-0.06	CB	23.2	35.69	L	Incorrect	R
1916	0.0208	-0.15	-0.13	CB	49.3	51.68	W	Correct	D
1920	0.076	2.65	2.80	E	34.12	36.12	L	Correct	D
1924	0.0418	-0.45	-3.10	CB	54.03	65.21	W	Correct	R
1928	0.0373	-0.11	0.34	CB	58.22	58.80	W	Correct	R
1932	0.0717	0.92	1.03	E	39.65	40.85	L	Correct	R
1936	0.1081	0.51	-0.41	CB	60.8	62.46	W	Correct	D
1940	0.0978	-0.09	-0.60	CB	54.72	55.00	W	Correct	D
1944	0.448	3.58	3.68	E	53.39	53.78	W	Incorrect	D
1948	0.1297	-0.71	-4.29	CB	49.55	52.37	W	Correct	D
1952	0.1948	0.50	1.21	E	44.33	44.55	L	Correct	D
1956	0.1691	-0.13	-0.63	CB	57.37	57.75	W	Correct	R
1960	0.1794	0.06	0.19	E	49.55	49.91	L	Correct	R
1964	0.1732	-0.03	-0.09	CB	61.05	61.34	W	Correct	D
1968	0.1894	0.09	0.13	E	42.72	49.59	L	Correct	D
1972	0.1803	-0.05	-0.14	CB	60.67	61.79	W	Correct	R
1976	0.1985	0.10	0.15	E	48.01	48.94	L	Correct	R
1980	0.2068	0.04	-0.06	CB	41.01	44.69	L	Incorrect	D
1984	0.211	0.02	-0.02	CB	58.77	59.17	W	Correct	R
1988	0.2033	-0.04	-0.06	CB	53.37	53.90	W	Correct	R
1992	0.2119	0.04	0.08	E	37.45	46.54	L	Correct	R
1996	0.1933	-0.09	-0.13	CB	49.23	54.73	W	Correct	D
2000	0.1745	-0.09	-0.00	CB	48.38	50.26	W[a]	Correct	D
2004	0.1877	0.08	0.17	E	50.73	51.25	W	Incorrect	R
2008	0.2027	0.08	0.00	E	45.6	46.31	L	Correct	R
2012	0.2177	0.07	-0.01	CB	51.01	51.97	W	Correct	D
2016	0.2059	-0.05	-0.13	CB	48.02	51.11	W[a]	Correct	D
2020	0.2869	0.39	0.45	E	46.8	47.73	L	Correct	R

Notes:

[a] Lost in the Electoral College.

[b] E=Expansion; CB=Cutback

Sources:

Fiscal policy: https://www.usgovernmentspending.com/

Elections: Wikipedia

In: Political Economy
Editors: Caleb M. Clark et al.
ISBN: 978-1-68507-106-6

Chapter 10

Workforce Development in the Age of COVID-19: Implications for Policymakers

Nicholas Bolden
Department of Politics, Philosophy, and Public Administration, Columbus State University, Columbus, GA, USA

Abstract

Since the beginning of the 21st Century, America has been engaged in an ongoing attempt to overturn the effects of deindustrialization and a waning middle class with innovative policy strategies aimed at restoring America's workforce to its global position following the Cold War. Unfortunately, the 21st century has produced more educated citizens than previous decades but has turned out to be much less favorable than the industrial period for maintaining a viable middle-class. In particular, the period of de-industrialization left many local economies victim to the impact of capital flight and unprepared to attract and retain jobs for their citizenry. Manufacturing jobs have declined more over the past two decades than during the Great Depression of the 1930s. This is especially harmful because manufacturing has a larger multiplier effect than any other economic sector. A more positive trend is building up with state and federal workforce development policy. Over the past decade, there has been a growing interest in work-based learning in the US. Through bi-partisan efforts, American states have embraced the need for modern workforce development strategies to mitigate the effects of capital flight and respond to the demands of 21st-century technological advancements. However, the novel COVID-19 virus introduced new complexities to modern workforce development efforts in the US.

Keywords: apprenticeships, COVID-19, deindustrialization, education, workforce development

INTRODUCTION

Since the beginning of the 21st Century, America has been engaged in an ongoing attempt to overturn the effects of deindustrialization and a waning middle class with innovative policy strategies aimed at restoring America's workforce to its global position following the Cold War. Unfortunately, the 21st century has produced more educated citizens than previous decades but has turned out to be much less favorable than the industrial period for maintaining a viable middle-class. In particular, the period of de-industrialization left many local economies victim to the impact of capital flight and unprepared to attract and retain jobs for their citizenry.

Manufacturing jobs have declined more over the past two decades than during the Great Depression of the 1930s. This is especially harmful because manufacturing has a larger multiplier effect than any other economic sector. According to the U.S. Bureau of Economic Analysis (2020), in the fourth quarter of 2020, manufacturing nominal value-added was 10.9 percent of GDP and valued at $2,347.7 billion. As a counteractive approach, the US has aggressively mobilized its efforts to expand work-based learning across all industries. Traditionally, work-based learning programs, such as apprenticeships, were predominately in the skilled trades. Recently, states are tasked with creating ways to increase educational attainment levels of middle-class America, meet the modern demands of high-tech occupations, and compete in the era of globalization. Over the past decade, this reality has been an upward battle for American workforce development efforts, as they attempt to address the 21st-century skill gap and prepare for the advancement of advanced robotics and technology.

A more positive trend is building up with state and federal workforce development policy. Over the past decade, there has been a growing interest in work-based learning in the US. Through bi-partisan efforts, American states have embraced the need for modern workforce development strategies to mitigate the effects of capital flight and respond to the demands of 21st-century technological advancements. However, the novel COVID-19 virus introduced new complexities to modern workforce development efforts in the US. At the beginning of 2020, the global workforce was severely impacted by the unexpected spread of the novel virus COVID-19. In the US, stay-at-home orders prevented non-essential companies from operating and focusing on individual workforce needs, thus creating a severe disruption in individual earnings and career development initiatives. Also, America's education was interrupted and force down an unchartered path of distance learning. This reality is twofold. First, a huge percentage of educators, both k-12 and post-secondary, had no significant experience with teaching online. Second, The American digital divide became an instant explanatory variable to education access and quality. Thus, America is left with several fundamental questions.

Has COVID-19 impacted America's ability to develop, implement, and financially support workforce development policies? Has Covid-19 reduced the feasibility and sustainability of modern American education reform in the short-term? Does America have enough broadband internet infrastructure and 5-G capability to accommodate the technology demands of distance learning? Can government mitigate the pre-existing digital divide from worsening? These realities are most apparent for marginalized communities across the US. This chapter explores the effects of COVID-19 on modern workforce development efforts in the US, the status of workforce development programs during COVID-19, and the government's policy position and financial commitment to work-based learning programs. The first section describes the effects of COVID-19 on workforce development and education; the second examines both federal and state policy responses to supporting workforce development; and the third discusses the status of modern work-based learning programs across America during the COVID-19 era.

COVID-19 Impacts

Despite America's remarkable workforce development efforts of the past decade, the COVID-19 pandemic exposed some serious vulnerabilities in the American workforce and its ability to address the growing 21st Century skill gap. First, it has introduced new complexities to the modern era of displaced workers, especially those in the services sector. Since March 2020, millions of workers have been laid off temporarily or permanently, thus their economic mobility relies heavily on the welfare state. This sector of the workforce is susceptible to being displaced or underemployed long-term, even after full recovery of the US economy. (Alderson, 1999; Arulampalam, Gregg, and Gregory, 2001; Bluestone, 1984; Couch and Placzek, 2010; Iversen and Cusack, 2000). This reality is problematic for low-skill workers because they lack transferable skills or training, are not employed in occupations that are sustainable through work from home agreements, and lack resources to relocate to less impacted regions. In comparison to the period of deindustrialization, business closures due to COVID-19 produced short-term and potentially long-term effects within localities. In particular, COVID-19 severely impacted the service industry that employs most of the low-skilled workers within communities. On February 5, 2021, the U.S. House of Representatives Committee on Education and Labor stated "Millions of people are still without work, and at least 7 million of the jobs lost during the COVID-19 pandemic may never come back. We must use every tool we have to help workers find jobs and prepare them for high-quality employment opportunities, particularly while our country faces a historic economic downturn."

Cowie and Heathcott (2003:158) echoed this sentiment following capital flight in an analysis of the effects of Capital Flight in America:

> As industries flee, middle- and upper-income families began to migrate elsewhere, taking their tax dollars with them. Capital flight freezes localities' mobility and leaves a high collection of debt. Throughout the past half-century, capital flight, population loss, and persistent poverty have left deindustrialized cities to face a single constant: an inadequate property base to balance their budget at acceptable levels of taxation. Government lacks the necessary tools to deal with the fiscal crisis and the effects of disinvestment. In this case of having too little money, politics matters, and to date deindustrialized communities have yet to be served sufficiently well to assure their long-term recovery (Cowie and Heathcott, 2003: 158).

Second, the COVID-19 pandemic expanded the need for advanced workforce development ideas and policies that accommodate the interruptions and limitations due to social distancing guidelines and policies. Most apprenticeships, internships, and career and technical education often take place inside the classroom. Some industries, such as finance, banking, and insurance, were able to quickly transfer their work-based learning efforts online. However, other industries that connect on-the-job learning with related technical instruction are tasked with satisfying the work-based learning agreements that require specified amounts of in-class instruction. Federal and state governments must ascertain ways to progress modem work-based learning programs, financially support their infrastructure and implementation, undergird industry demands, and support the US post-secondary and k-12 education system. One of the immediate challenges of COVID-19 was the need to transfer apprenticeship and pre-apprenticeship instructional modality. On March 16, 2020, the US Department of Labor released bulletin 2020-51, "Flexibilities Available for Delivery Method of Related Instruction" that allowed more flexibility of registered apprenticeship program instruction modality. The use of technology is the way of the future, however, creating equitable and feasible asynchronous online work-based learning is not an easy task. In most cases, the continuation of work-based learning during the COVID-19 pandemic is a local decision made in partnership with the participant, parents, local educational institution, and employers (NGA, 2020).

Third, the COVID-19 pandemic has reduced America's progression in closing the 21st-century skill-gap and highlighted the broadband crisis in America. The broadband infrastructure debate and policy discussion in America has become more apparent due to COID-19. In the public sphere, sufficient broadband is needed to compete in the era of globalization and actively participate in society. Thomas Freidman (2005) argues that the world is flat and no longer run by states. His analysis of globalization asserts that the evolution and advances of the internet allowed companies from more and more countries of the world to compete in the global economy. Moreover, broadband internet leveled the playing field and became a determining factor in developed countries' position, dominance, and participation in the global market. Over the past two decades, broadband access and speed have become a business and household necessity. According to the Bloomberg 2021 Innovation Index, America is ranked in first place for both patent activity and high-tech density, with the highest share of domestic high-tech public companies in the world. Despite the US global ranking for innovation, it lags behind many developed countries in terms of speed, affordability, and adoption. According to the Organization for Economic Cooperation and Development (OECD), the United States is the world leader in broadband subscriptions but ranks 9th in broadband subscribers per 100 inhabitants (OECD, 2020). Mossberger, Tolbert, and Franko (2013) describe the state of broadband in the United States:

> Historically, broadband development in the United States has been left to the private sector, in a thin market that is dominated by few firms, with little pressure to compete over costs or develop faster networks (Berkman Center, 2010; West, 2011: ch. 5). Economists define thin markets (with few providers) as a form of market failure related to monopolies, in thin markets providers set costs too high, resulting in undersupply and market inefficiency or deadweight loss (Munger, 2000). Cable dominates the U.S. market, and many regions have a single able provider (Crawford, 2011). Open access requirements are one policy solution that has been shown to introduce greater competition (Berkman Center, 2010). Without addressing the problems of cost, monopoly supply, and universal access

will remain an elusive goal in cities and the rest of the country (Mossberger, Tolbert, and Franko, 2013: 8).

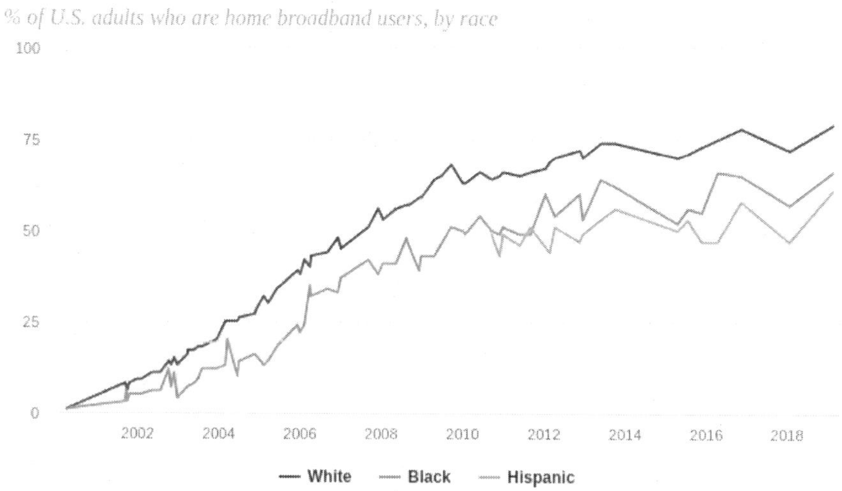

Note: The Center has used several different question wordings to identify broadband users in recent years, which may account for some variance in broadband adoption figures between 2015 and 2018. Our survey conducted in July 2015 used a directly comparable question wording to the one conducted in January 2018.

Source: Surveys conducted 2000-2019. Data for Hispanics includes only surveys that included Spanish-language interviews.

Source: Pew Research Center. 2019.

Figure 1. Home broadband use by race.

This reality is mostly realized in marginalized communities due to the lack of technology infrastructure needed to actively participate in society and operate during COVID-19 social distancing guidelines. Marginalized communities lack broadband physical infrastructure and modern technology to compete equally in the 21st Century. As of 2020, approximately 19 million Americans—6 percent of the population—still lack access to fixed broadband service at threshold speeds. In rural areas, nearly one-fourth of the population — 14.5 million people — lack access to this service. In tribal areas, nearly one-third of the population lacks access. Even in areas where broadband is available, approximately 100 million Americans still do not subscribe (Federal Communications Commission Report, 2020). Despite the remarkable technological advances in the US over the past decade, internet access is still defined by race, education, income, and community, as illustrated by Figures 1-4 on "Who Uses the Internet" which summarizes broadband internet access in the US.

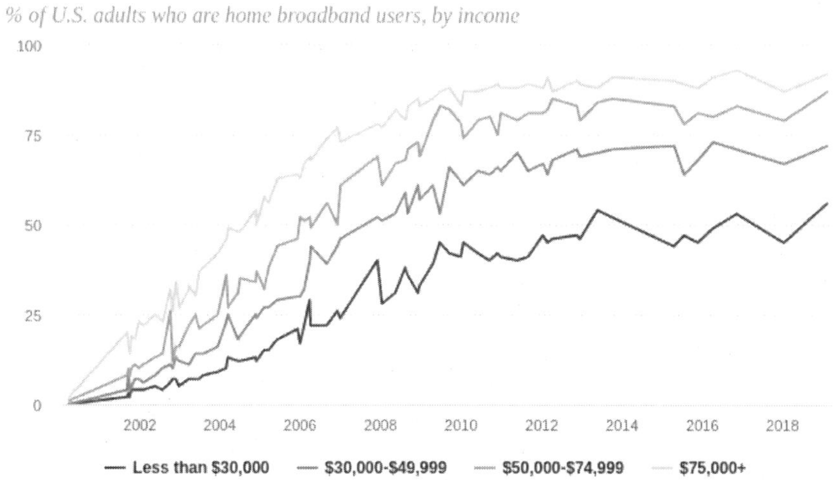

Note: The Center has used several different question wordings to identify broadband users in recent years, which may account for some variance in broadband adoption figures between 2015 and 2018. Our survey conducted in July 2015 used a directly comparable question wording to the one conducted in January 2018.

Source: Surveys conducted 2000-2019.

Source: Pew Research Center. 2019.

Figure 2. Home broadband use by income.

Overall, the COVID-19 crisis has created a growing economic and education problem in the United States, in particular for marginalized communities that experience the most impact of the American digital divide. The COVID-19 pandemic isolated the American poor communities and disconnected its youth from education, the fundamental American workforce development institution. Due to social distancing, many students were asked to participate in classroom instruction, do homework, submit assignments, and take exams in a digital space, while only two-thirds of the US population have broadband internet.

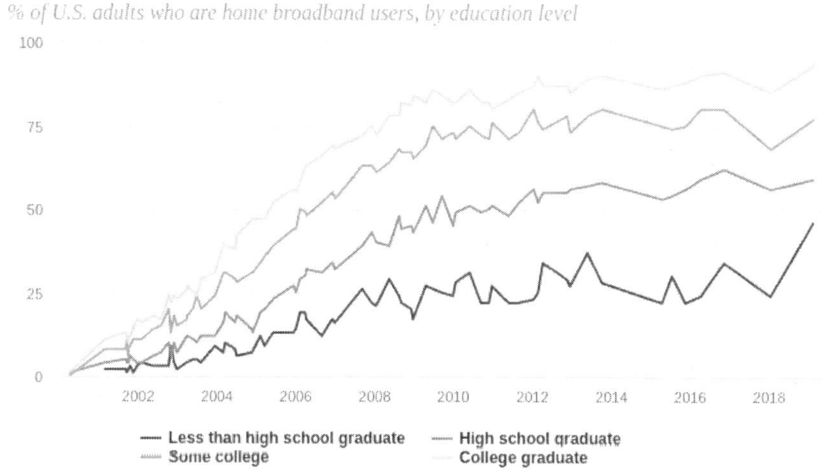

Source: Pew Research Center. 2019.

Figure 3. Home broadband use by education.

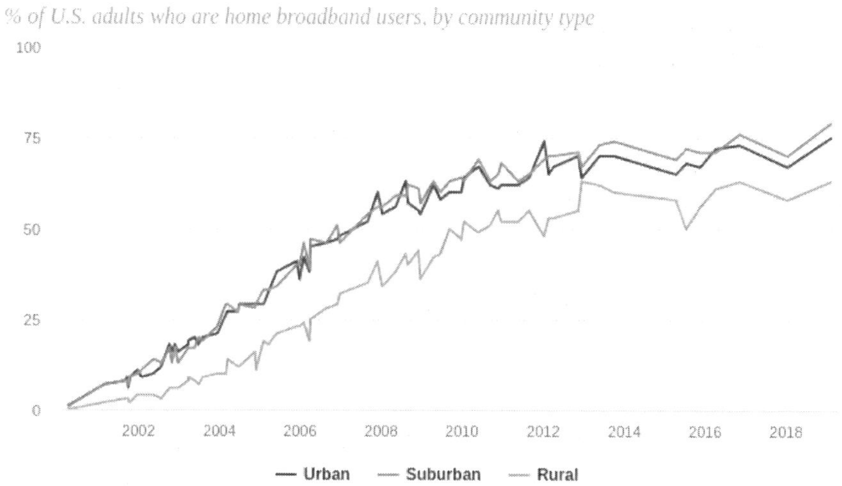

Note: The Center has used several different question wordings to identify broadband users in recent years, which may account for some variance in broadband adoption figures between 2015 and 2018. Our survey conducted in July 2015 used a directly comparable question wording to the one conducted in January 2018.

Source: Surveys conducted 2000-2019.

Source: Pew Research Center. 2019.

Figure 4. Home broadband use by community type.

Moreover, only a small percentage of that population has high-speed internet capable of providing interruption-free video technology on virtual platforms such as Zoom, Google Meet, and Microsoft Teams. In affluent communities, students can continue education and gain further technical skills needed to compete in the global workforce. Thus, there is a growing digital divide between public and private schools within the same community. Taken together, these challenges can devastate middle-class America and further delay career intervention and skill development.

This brings us to the consideration of the workforce and economic condition of poor and marginalized communities across America. Before the Covid-19 pandemic, in many cities, once home to very productive manufacturing, the economic structure was fragile and mostly a proliferation of low-paying service jobs. Most rural American counties' economic structures cater primarily to low-income residents. Deindustrialization scholars contend that regional economies that are unable to address the issues of capital flight are not positioned for a full economic recovery. (Alderson, 1999; Bluestone and Harrison 1982; Brady, 2009; Brady and Wallace, 2001; Kollemyer, 2009; Kollemyer and Pichner, 2013; Sanchez and Green, 2007; Ross and Trachter, 1990; Wood, 1994, 1995). Rural "smoke stacks," especially those that are small and not adjacent to a metropolitan area, lack the population density and size to support a large service sector (Green, 2020). Coupled with COVID-19 interruptions, low educational attainment levels, an aging population, rural America is on the fast track to becoming a community with little or no middle class and continue to be disconnected from 21st century development and prosperity.

Policy Responses to America's Education and Skill Gap Crisis

Before 2020, America's education and training challenge contributed to the declining performance of the American education curriculum and workforce development. Yet, it is easy to apportion blame to problems created by U.S. business and society itself in the other areas of industrial organization, the talents of American managers and entrepreneurs, and a skilled workforce (Bolden and Clark, 2021) Unfortunately, the existence of COVID-19 has painted a grim reality for the progress and success of America compared to other industrialized economies. First, America is the most impacted country world-wide. The presence of COVID-19 has introduced several questions and concerns for the future of workforce development in America. What COVID-19 challenges are here to stay? What COVID-19 challenges differ by sector and region? Are remote work arrangements the new way of doing business? These questions and challenges have stalled the development of industry and America's 21st Century workforce. In particular, many corporations, government agencies, the US healthcare system, education, and training were not equipped or prepared to accommodate an instant shift in operation, functions, and organizational finances. The aforementioned challenges highlighted the fragile elements of the US economy, infrastructure, and education system.

One of the key features of 21st-century workforce development is education. The increasing importance of collaborative governance between the federal and state governments, public education, and industry is one of the most salient components of modern workforce development. The essence of work-based learning rests on the success of collaborative partnerships that supports in-demand high-tech skills for America's workforce. Starting in 2015, America became assertive and aggressive in dealing with government and labor and much more interested in achieving a robust globally competitive workforce. At this point, labor source pipelines and globalization became more apparent to corporations for several reasons. First, globalization and competition created a complex and competitive market that is predominately operated by high-tech, robotics and broadband internet. Second, America's k-12 and post-secondary education performance no longer ranks at the top, compared to other industrialized economies. Third, there was an inherent disconnect between higher education and the specific needs of corporations, especially in high-demand occupations.

K-12 Education

Education, primary and post-secondary, is the primary workforce development institution across OECD countries. Developed nations have recognized the need for contemporary k-12 education curriculum and instruction. Thus, many advanced industrialized nations have proactively aligned their k-12 education curriculum policy with the skill demands of the 21st-Century. Over the past decade, many nations have outperformed American students on international standardized tests, which is an important indicator of the preparation and development of a robust workforce. In 2018, America ranked 38th in math, 19th in science, and 14th in reading on the OECD Programme for International Student Assessment or PISA (OECD, 2019).

Low education performance coupled with COVID-19 closures has introduced a disturbing dilemma for k-12 education in America. First, many school districts lacked the financial resources to instantly and effectively move all instruction virtually. This reality is concerning for early elementary grade levels. On average, elementary school students have lower technology self-efficacy than students in other industrial societies. According to Leech, Gullett, Cumings, and Haug (2020), remote learning presented many new challenges for k-12 teachers and likely presented unique challenges for different content areas and grade levels. Leech, Gullett, Cumings, and Haug (2020) found that 78.5% of teachers had a preference for face-to-face learning; 77.6% of teachers indicated that their students were uncomfortable or unfamiliar with the necessary technologies; 71.4% indicated that students had not been adequately available or responsive; and over 50% said that they struggled with implementing lesson plans remotely and finding adequate replacements for in-person instruction.

Higher Education

Over the past century, higher education has been major leverage for workforce development and creating a work-class economy. Academic rigor and access for all populations have been a major tool used in industrialized economies to foster a more competitive globalized workforce. Despite U.S higher education development or progression over the past decade, universities continue to struggle with varying enrollment rates, financial stability, and retention rates. The intersection of technology and instruction requires universities to have modern facilities with adequate technology infrastructure for 21st century instruction. This reality is more apparent pressing for smaller American universities and colleges.

This brings us to consideration of the immediate impact of COVID-19 on higher education enrollment, retention rates, and financial stability. This crisis is concerning for not only workforce development but the optimal operation of university life. In particular, COVI-19 has introduced instructional design and student course navigation complexities for most US universities. This phenomenon for higher education is two-fold. First, many instructors had no previous experience with online instruction prior to COVID-19. Furthermore, a huge percentage of instructors lacked proper training on online course design, online course curriculum, creating accessible online content, and navigating the online platform used by their institution. According to the *Chronicle of Higher Education*, 85% of lower division and 78% of upper-division faculty currently only teach in-person classes, and 68% of students only take in-person classes. (Gardner, 2020). As a result, many faculties were left with unanswered questions about the continuation of courses and labs that required hands-on instruction. Quality online instruction is essential for successful instructional delivery, easy navigation for students, reducing barriers to student achievement, and successful student performance outcomes. Unfortunately, the quality of education post-COVID-19 closures has not automatically translated into teaching and learning comparable to traditional in-person instruction. Second, many students lack the necessary technology and equipment to actively participate in an online course. COVID-19 limited the number of the availability of free computer labs and technology available to students and faculty. Many institution's technology infrastructures were not suitable for handling large amounts of virtual traffic.

Table 1. University Presidents COVID-19 Survey

How would you rate your level of concern with the following potential long-term issues at your institution in regard to COVID-19?	
% Very Concerned + % Somewhat Concerned	
Overall financial stability	89%
Decline in overall future student enrollment	88%
Ability to afford to employ staff and faculty	81%
Demands for room and board reimbursement	62%
Decline in alumni/donor giving rates	56%
Demands for tuition reimbursement	55%
Decline in international student enrollment	49%
Perceived decrease in the value of higher ed.	48%
Perceived negativity regarding institutional performance	35%
Reduced interest in study abroad programs	33%
Reduced international collaboration	21%
Faculty attrition	16%

Source: Inside Higher Ed. 2020.

Focusing on the nation's universities illuminates the diversity of experiences and perceptions of higher education administrators that must be taken into consideration for increasing challenges due to COVID-19. Overnight, university presidents were tasked with providing fast solutions and policies to address the uncertainty and future of their institution during COVID-19. Table 1 shows university presidents' level of concern with long-term issues at their institution concerning COVID-19.

Federal and State Workforce and Career Development

Over the past decade, several presidential administrations have taken the task of addressing the American workforce problem. The answer to solving this workforce issue is two-fold. First, the amount of appropriations designated to workforce development is a politically divided issue. Second, how to structure nationally recognized programs is multilayered and politically complex. The conservative policy position is that private businesses should be the recipient of work-force development appropriations and lead the definition and implementation of work-based learning programs, such as apprenticeships. Accordingly, government labor divisions should be an academic resource and support to corporate workforce initiatives. Liberal workforce development policy promotes post-secondary institutions and private corporate collaborations as the way of the future. Many scholars and experts are divided on whether private business or education institutions know best the individual workforce and global skills demand.

Trump Administration

Registered apprenticeships and industry-recognized credentials form a bi-partisan strategy to address the American 21st-century skill gap. While Democrats and Republicans both agree on the benefits of apprenticeship programs, they differ on the strategic approach and bureaucratic and administrative authority, distribution, and oversight of government funding. The Trump administration allowed an ad-hoc approach to apprenticeship credentialing. It introduced a decentralized approach to the facilitation and awarding of credentialing. Under the Industry Recognized Apprenticeship Program (IRAP), established by President Trump's Executive Order 13801, the U.S. Department of Labor was charged to assist Industry Recognized programs by "third-party" private corporations:

> On June 15, 2017, President Trump signed Executive Order 13801 charging the Secretary of Labor to establish a process for the U.S Department of Labor to support an Industry Recognized Apprenticeship Program (IRAP). President Trump's Executive Order established a Task Force on Apprenticeship Expansion and appropriated federal funding to promote registered apprenticeships. The task force included representatives of business, labor, educational institutions, trade associations, and public officials. The full Task Force was subdivided into the following subcommittees: (1) Education and Credentialing; (2) Attracting Business to Apprenticeship; (3) Expanding Access, Equity, and

> Career Awareness; and (4) Administrative and Regulatory Strategies to Expand Apprenticeship. The task force's mission was to identify strategies and proposals to promote apprenticeships, especially in sectors where programs were insufficient. Under the order, the Department of Labor established the Industry Recognized Apprenticeship Program (IRAP), which is administered by the US Department of Labor Office of Apprenticeship. Under the IRAP model, the Secretary of Labor promotes the development of apprenticeship programs by third parties. According to the US Department of Labor, IRAPs "represent a new pathway" for the expansion of apprenticeships and do not change requirements for Registered Apprenticeship Programs. Executive Order Section 4 established the regulatory guidelines for new industry-driven programs and outlined the criteria for registering high-quality programs with the US Department of Labor (Presidential Executive Order Expanding Apprenticeships in America, 2017).

President Donald Trump's Executive Order 13801, which established a Task Force on Apprenticeship Expansion and created the IRAP, should serve as a major stimulus for generating new state programs in this area. On May 10, 2018, the Task Force on Apprenticeship submitted its final report. The task force's first recommendation was the expansion of traditional work-and-learn models. In particular, IRAP should expand more traditional work-and-learn models to incorporate the criteria of modern apprenticeship and to ensure better outcomes for workers and employers. The Task Force suggested that employers should focus on implementing competency-based apprenticeship programs. Second, employers should include performance assessment to ensure adequate knowledge, skills, and abilities, as well as earn a recognized credential needed to advance in an occupation. Third, IRAP should establish national recognition and portability of credentials. In particular, IRAP should ensure the integration of the opportunity to earn credentials and provide evidence related to technical instruction gained during a WBL experience. The Task Force recognized that any meaningful expansion of the American apprenticeship framework requires the collaboration of many critical stakeholders, including the private sector, state and local governments, academia, unions, and trade associations. While the federal government can establish the framework for a successful apprenticeship program and provide support, substantial change must begin with industry-led partnerships playing the pivotal role of creating, managing, and certifying apprenticeship programs. The Taskforce on Apprenticeship conveyed the need for robust collaborative governance to facilitate effective workforce development. It brings together multiple stakeholders to develop consensus-oriented programs. In particular, this approach narrows the interpretation of apprenticeships and encourages synchronized curriculums and establishes the need for national credentials (Task Force on Apprenticeship Expansion, 2018). In this context, we may avoid the high cost of adversarial policymaking, expand democratic participation, and restore rationality to public management (Bolden and Clark, 2021).

Biden Administration

On November 3, 2020, the election of Joe Biden, the 46th President of the United States, changed the structure and administration of registered apprentice credentials. Biden's approach to stimulating the American workforce is through a centralized approach to US apprenticeship programs and industry-recognized credentialing. The Biden administration's aim is to validate the US Department of Labor Apprenticeship certificate as the gold standard. On February 17, 2021, the Biden administration took steps to bolster registered apprenticeships that would stimulate the middle-class through work in good-paying union jobs. President Biden's American Rescue Plan will focus on major infrastructure development, such as building roads, bridges, transit, electric vehicle charging stations, broadband, and water infrastructure.

Ultimately, Biden's administration changed the nature and approach to nationally registered apprenticeships and streamlined the application process. Most notably, Democrats contend that a new centralized approach to apprenticeships will rebuild America's workforce with diverse, local, and well-trained workers. The emphasis of Democratic policy has been on the creation of a workforce development policy that addresses the 21st-century skill gap, the rising cost of college, pay equity, and access for all communities. The Biden administration is very optimistic about achieving this goal through several policy actions. First, Biden reaffirmed his commitment to expanding registered apprenticeships to reward work, rebuild the middle class, and connect a diversified workforce to family-supporting, living-wage jobs. Second was reinstating the National Advisory Committee on Apprenticeships. This advisory committee will focus on expanding apprenticeships in new employment industries and sectors like clean energy, technology, and healthcare. In addition, the advisory committee has been charged with ensuring that apprenticeship training and jobs are accessible to black and brown Americans, immigrants, and women. Finally, Biden reversed industry-recognized apprenticeship programs (IRAPs). Despite the recent success of Executive Order 13801, President Biden rescinded the order and asked the US Department of Labor to slow financial support for IRAPs and end funding for Standards Recognition Entities.

The shift in workforce development priorities and credentialing is largely in a response to the Democratic Party's ideal of free two-year education for all. COVID-19 highlighted this policy priority, as education institutions struggle to operate, experiencing declines in revenue and enrollment and difficulty in transitioning to online learning. According to the Biden Administration, this strategy will attract millions of new revenues for two-year community and technical colleges while increasing their visibility and position in training America's future workforce.

Apprenticeships during COVID-19

Post-COVID, apprenticeships are making gains but there remains a concern for program availability, equal access, and financial feasibility. According to the National Governor's Association or NGA (2020), many employers, who have apprenticeship or pre-apprenticeship programs, closed their businesses temporarily or permanently. This reality mirrors the sentiment of other types of work-based learning programs such as internships and co-ops. This phenomenon is an unprecedented challenge for workforce development due to the large scale of closures as a response to social distancing guidelines. In particular, On March 30, 2020, Governor Gretchen Whitmer of Michigan issued a memorandum that ordered the closure of all state-approved work-based learning programs run by intermediate school districts and local education agencies. Conversely, several states provided infrastructure support and new guidelines to apprenticeship programs and participants to mitigate the effects of COVID-19 closures. In particular, California governor, Gavin Newsom, implemented a cross-sector partnership to support the transition to distance learning programs and help bridge the digital divide.

This brings us to the consideration of the financial stability of programs and the increasing number of work-based learning students eligible for unemployment. According to the Department of Labor, companies are required to pay participants in registered programs. Many corporations struggled to maintain both social distancing operations and funding to operate any level of work-based learning programs. This reality is more prevalent in labor-intensive industries that require hands-on training. As a result of layoffs, many work-based participants became eligible for unemployment insurance benefits and dependent on the welfare state.

Conclusion

The current workforce development trend has introduced a new dynamic to America's human capital development efforts. Post COVID-19 workforce development policy is critical to the vitality of the American 21st Century Workforce. Many employers are substituting technology for employees, a trend that is being accelerated by the economic side-effects of COVID 19 (Bolden and Clark, 2021). The challenge, faced by many industrialized economies, is to develop a larger educated pool of workers who are competent with the advances in technology used in all occupations. The significant mismatch between the skills that employers need and the attainment of the current American workforce, coupled with the challenges of COD-19, indicates that innovative workforce development efforts should be given priority. Work-based learning is widely seen as an effective means of pursuing this goal. However, some important issues must be considered. First, America must respond to the changing nature of higher education instruction, affordability, and student needs. According to the 2020 Student's College Plans Survey, 69% of the respondents indicated a change in their financial situation, and 24% indicated that they are rethinking their college location preference due to COVID-19.

Second, America must ascertain the growing percentage of displaced workers and properly train its workforce in high-skill technology and advanced robotics. (Brynjolfsson and McAfee, 2014). According to Manyika, Lund, Chui, Bughin, Woetzel, Batra, Ko, and Sanghiv (2017), one-third of the global occupational change will be in the US – 166 million workers. Current work-based learning efforts should equally focus on the training and development of low-skill workers who are at risk of being replaced by robotics. According to Frey and Osborne (2013), 8.5% of global manufacturing employment will be lost to robotics. According to Muro, Maxim, and Whiten (2019), 36% of American workers will face medium-level exposure to these disruptive technologies by 2030, while 39% or 59 million jobs will face low-level exposure. Richard Florida (2011) concludes that building great communities and economies requires a density of educated and skilled workers, an alignment of skills to jobs, and local leadership. Unfortunately, COVID-19 and global competition have introduced an unsettling reality for industrialized democracies, social distancing, and the internet.

The leading edge of the modern globalized economy is the internet. Broadband Infrastructure has become a 21st business and personal necessity. Peter Drucker (1989) and Robert Reich (1991) argue that the world is flat and that globalization and new technology have changed core economic concepts. This fact, coupled with COVID-19, illuminate the reality, placement, and necessity of broadband infrastructure and access across America. In particular, broadband infrastructure development and access in rural America are critical to economic growth, job creation, education, training, and civic engagement. Continued access to training, professional development, and education offer an efficient method to enable the workforce population to adapt to changing job expectations and/or take advantage of emerging career and occupational opportunities (Sala-I-Martin, Bilbao-Osorio, Batitista, Drezniek, Galvan, and Geiger, 2014). First, America must improve broadband infrastructure across America. Second, America must reform modern work-based learning programs to accommodate the new norm of social distancing. In particular, the utilization of technology in higher education instruction, apprenticeships, and pre-apprenticeships will foster an environment of high-impact learning and 21st century skill development are vital. The utilization of video conferencing, such as Zoom, Microsoft teams, and Google meets, allows corporations, government agencies, and industry experts the avenue to interact with student learning and serve as a modern way of career intervention. In particular, students will be able to virtually meet industry professionals, gain expert advice, obtain constructive feedback, and receive recommendations. The intersection of technology and instruction can be applied to all industries within the American economy. technology and training is essential for addressing the 21st century skill gap, workforce inequality, modern innovation, and creating opportunities for the future, even in the presence of unconventional interruptions.

REFERENCES

A.S. 1999. "Explaining Deindustrialization: Globalization, Failure, or Success?" *American Sociological Review* 64(5): 701-721.

Arulampalam, W., P. Gregg, and M. Gregory. 2001. "Unemployment Scarring." *Economic Journal* 111: 577-584.

Berkman Center. 2010. *Next Generation Connectivity: A Review of Broadband Internet Transitions and Policy from Around the World.* Cambridge: Harvard University, The Berkman Center for the Internet and Society.

Biden, J. 2020. *The Biden Plan for Education Beyond High School.* Biden-Harris Campaign. www.joebiden.com/beyondhs/.

Bloomberg. 2021. *Bloomberg Innovation Index*. Bloomberg. www.media/bloomberg-innovation-index-2021.

Bluestone, B. 1984. *Is Deindustrialization a Myth? Capital Mobility versus Absorptive Capacity in the U.S. Economy. Annals of the American Academy of Political and Social Sciences*. 475.

Bluestone, B. and B. Harrison. 1982. *The Deindustrialization of America: Plant Closings, Community Abandonment, and the Dismantling of Basic Industry*. New York: Basic Books.

Bolden, N. and Clark, C. 2021. *Workforce Development: The Key to Prosperity in the 21st Century*. Hauppauge: NY: Nova Science Publishers.

Brady, D. 2009. *Rich Democracies, Poor People: How Politics Explain Poverty*. Oxford: Oxford University Press.

Brady, D. and M. Wallace. 2001. "Deindustrialization and Poverty: Manufacturing Decline and AFDC Recipiency in Lake County, Indiana 1964-93." *Sociological Forum* 16: 321-358.

Brynjofsson, E. and A. McAfee. 2014. *The Second Machine Age: Work Progress and Prosperity in a Time of Brilliant Technologies*. New York: W. W. Norton.

Couch, K.A. and D. Placzek. 2010. "Earning Losses of Displaced Workers Revisited." *American Economic Review* 100: 572-589.

Cowie, J. and J. Heathcott. 2003. "The Meanings of Deindustrialization." pp. 1-15, 306-307 in J. Cowie and J. Heathcott, Eds. *Beyond the Ruins: The Meanings of Deindustrialization*. Ithaca, NY: ILR Press.

Crawford, S. P. 2011. "Internet Access and the New Divide." *New York Times*. www.nytimes.com.

Drucker, P. F. 1989. *The New Realities*. New York: Harper & Row.

Federal Communications Commission. 2020. "Broadband Progress Report." Washington DC: Federal Communications Commission, www.fcc.gov.

Florida, R. 2011. *The Great Reset: How the Post-Crash Economy Will Change the Way We Live and Work*. New York: Harper Collins.

Friedman, T. L. 2005. *The World is Flat: A Brief History of the Twenty-First Century*. New York: Farrar, Straus and Giroux.

Frey, C.B. and M. A. Osborne. 2013. "The Future of Employment: How Susceptible are Jobs to Computerization?" *Oxford Economics*, https://www.oxfordmartin.ox.ac.uk/downloads/academic/The_Future_of_Employment.pdf.

Gardner, L. 2020. "Covid-19 Has Forced Higher Ed to Pivot to Online Learning." *Chronicle of Higher Education*. March 20, www.chronicle.com.

Inside Higher Ed. 2020. *Responding to the COVI-19 Crisis: A Survey of College and University Presidents.* Hoboken, NJ. Wiley Press.

Kollmeyer, C. 2009. "Explaining Deindustrialization: How Affluence, Productivity Growth, and Globalization Diminish Manufacturing Employment." *American Journal of Sociology* 114: 1644-1674.

Kollmeyer, C. and F. Pichler. 2013. "Is Deindustrialization Causing High Unemployment in Affluent Countries? Evidence from 16 OECD Countries, 1970-2003." *Social Forces* 91: 785-812.

Leech, N.L., S. Gullett, H. Cummings, and C. A. Haug. 2020. "Challenges for K-12 Teachers during COVID-19." *Journal of Educational Leadership in Action*. 7:1.

Manyika, J., S. Lund, M. Chui, J. Bughin, J. Woetzel, P. Batra, R. Ko, and S. Sanghiv. 2017, "Jobs Lost, Jobs Gained: Workforce Transitions in a Time of Automation," McKinsey Global Institute. November 28.

Mossberger, K., T. Tolbert, and W. and Franko. 2013. *Digital Cities: The Internet and the Geography of Opportunity.* New York: Oxford University Press.

Munger, M.C. 2000. *Analyzing Policy: Choices, Conflicts, and Practices.* New York: W. W. Norton.

Muro, M., R. Maxim, and J. Whiton. 2019. *Automation and Artificial Intelligence: How Machines are Affecting People and Places.* Washington, DC: Metropolitan Policy Program, Brookings Institution.

National Governors Association (NGA). 2020a. *Governor's Memorandum June 8, 2020.* Washington, DC: National Governors Association. www.nga.org.

National Governors Association (NGA). 2020b. *Registered Apprenticeship Reimagined: Lessons from the American Apprenticeship Initiative.* Washington, DC: National Governors Association. www.nga.org.

Organization for Economic Cooperation and Development (OECD). 2019. *OECD Statistics*. Paris: OECD, www.oecd.org.

Organization for Economic Cooperation and Development (OECD). 2020. *OECD Statistics*. Paris: OECD, www.oecd.org.

PEW Research Center. 2019. *Internet and Broadband Survey*. Pew Research Center. www.pewresearch.org.

Presidential Executive Order Expanding Apprenticeships in America. 2017. Washington, DC: Office of the President, https://www.whitehouse.gov/presidential-actions/3245/.

Reich, R.B. 1991. *The Work of Nations: Preparing Ourselves for 21st-Century Capitalism*. New York: Alfred A. Knopf.

Ross, R.J. and K.C. Trachte. 1990. *Global Capitalism: The New Leviathan.* New York: State University of New York Press.

Sala-I-Martin, X., B. Bilbao-Osorio, L. D. Battista, M. Drzeniek, H.C. Galvan, and T. Geiger. 2014. "The Global Competitiveness Index 2–14–15: Accelerating a Robust Recovery to Create Productive Jobs and Support Inclusive Growth." in World Economic Forum, Ed. *The Global Competitiveness Report 2013–2014.* Geneva: World Economic Forum.

Sanchez, L. and G.P. Green. 2007. "Does Manufacturing Still Matter." *Population Resolution Policy Review* 26: 529-551.

Task Force on Apprenticeship Expansion. 2018. *Final Report to the President of the United States.* Washington, DC: Task Force on Apprenticeship Expansion. https://www.dol.gov/apprenticeship/docs/task-force-apprenticeship-expansion-report.pdf.

U.S. Department of Labor. 2020. *Flexibilities Available for Delivery Method of Related Instruction.* Washington, DC: U.S. Department of Labor.

U.S. House of Representatives Committee on Education and Labor. 2021. *Report on COVID-19 and Employment*. Washington, DC: U.S. House of Representatives Committee on Education and Labor.

West, D. M. 2011. *Technology and the Innovation Economy.* Washington D.C.: Brookings Institution Press.

Wood, A. 1994. *North-South Trade, Employment and Inequality: Changing Fortunes in a Skill-Driven World.* Oxford: Clarendon Press.

Wood, A. 1995. "How Trade Hurt Unskilled Workers." *Journal of Economics Perspectives* 3(3): 57-80.

ABOUT THE EDITORS

Caleb M. Clark is an Emeritus Alumni Professor of Political Science and MPA Director at Auburn University who received his PhD from the University of Illinois and previously taught at New Mexico State University and the University of Wyoming. He has published widely on the political economy of development. His recent books include the co-authored *Challenging Neoliberalism: The Economic Miracles in China and Taiwan* (Edward Elgar, 2016), *Preserving Basic U.S. Industries: The Implications of Trumponomics* (Nova Science Publishers, 2020), and *Workforce Development: The Key to Prosperity in the 21st Century* (Nova Science, 2021); and the co-edited *A Discourse on Economic Development* (Nova Science Publishers, 2019).

Evelyn A. Clark Benavides is the Chair and Associate Professor of Sociology at the State University of New York, Oswego, who received her PhD from the University of Kansas. Her major fields of teaching and research include globalization, feminism, and social inequalities. She is the author of *Victims of Time, Warriors for Change: Chilean Women in a Neoliberal Society* (Cambridge Scholars Publishing, 2013) and co-author of *Challenging Neoliberalism: The Economic Miracles in Chile and Taiwan* (Edward Elgar, 2016) and *Preserving Basic U.S. Industries: The Implications of Trumponomics* (Nova Science Publishers, 2020).

About the Authors

Marcus Bell is an Assistant Professor of Sociology at SUNY Oswego in Upstate, NY. He received his PhD in sociology from Syracuse University in 2017 and he previously taught at Onondaga Community College. He has published on a number of topics, including white racial identity, racial socialization, racialized discourse, the neoliberalization of higher education, and the intersection of race, crime, and punishment. Professor Bell also has a book manuscript, *Whiteness Interrupted: White Teachers and Racial Identity in Predominantly Black Schools*, that is forthcoming with Duke University Press.

Nicholas Bolden is an Associate Professor of Politics, Philosophy, and Public Administration at Columbus State University who received his PhD from Auburn University. His major fields of interest include economic and community development, the policy process, and state and local government. His recent article "Manufacturing Matters: An Alabama Case Study" was published in the *Journal of Economics and Sustainable Development*. His recent book is the co-authored *Workforce Development: The Key to Prosperity in the 21st Century* (Nova Science, 2021).

Alfred G. Cuzán is a Distinguished University Professor of Political Science (or, as he prefers to call it, Politology), at the University of West Florida. He is the author of *Laws of Politics. Their Operations in Democracies and Dictatorships* (Routledge, 2022).

Rosita Dellios, PhD, is Associate Professor of International Relations and a founding member of the Centre for East-West Cultural and Economic Studies at Bond University in Queensland, Australia. She lectures and writes on the themes of peace and war in international relations, geopolitics, and China's strategic and defence philosophy. Her more recent works include two co-authored books: *China's Quest for Global Order* (Lexington Books, 2013) and *The Politics and Philosophy of Chinese Power: The Timeless and the Timely* (Lexington Books, 2017). She has since published on a range of topics, including several security articles for *The Palgrave Encyclopedia of Global Security Studies*; and chapters on the theme of Confucian concepts applied to security and development, some of which have been published in edited books by Nova Science Publishers, Inc.

R. James Ferguson is *Director of the Centre for East-West Cultural and Economic Studies* and Assistant Professor of International Relations in the Faculty of Society and Design, Bond University, Australia. He has been engaged in research, writing, teaching, and publication roles, and is a member of several international relations and strategic studies organizations. He is actively involved in research and teaching in International Relations, Eurasian Studies, the Indo-Pacific Region, and global governance processes. He has a background in history, cultural systems and Asian affairs. He has presented papers on these issues in Australia, Singapore, Malaysia, China, Japan, India, Austria, Serbia, Indonesia, and the UK. Recent books include *China's Eurasian Dilemmas: Roads and Risks for a Sustainable Global Power* (2018) and the co-authored *The Politics and Philosophy of Chinese Power: The Timeless and the Timely* (2017), as well as several chapters and articles published on environmental diplomacy and non-traditional security issues. He regularly visits Asia to assess new trends in regionalism and international relations. His current project is *Greening China's New Silk Road: The Sustainable Governance of Belt and Road* (forthcoming).

Richard Heggen, Professor Emeritus of Civil Engineering, University of New Mexico, received his PhD from Oregon State University. In addition to his field of water resources engineering, he has published on such topics as econometrics, systems analysis and simulation. He is the co-author of *Voters and Presidents: a Fiscal Model*, (XLibris, 1992). Disciplinary boundaries are cast aside in his *Underground Rivers, from the River Styx to the Rio San Buenaventura with Occasional Diversions* and *Floating Islands, An Activity Book*, both freely available on the web.

Charles E. Menifield is Dean of the School of Public Affairs and Administration (SPAA) at Rutgers University–Newark, who received his PhD from the University of Missouri, Columbia. Dr. Menifield's current research interests lie primarily in the areas of budgeting and financial management, public health and welfare, and policing. He has two books on minority politics and two books on public budgeting and financial management – his fourth edition of *The Basics of Public Budgeting and Financial Management: A Handbook for Academics and Practitioners* (Hamilton Books) was published in Fall 2020. His co-edited 2005 book, *Politics in the New South: Representation of African Americans in Southern State Legislatures*, won the V.O. Key Award from the Southern Political Science Association for best book written on Southern politics that year. His co-authored article, "Do White Law Enforcement Officers Target Minority Suspects?", appearing in *Public Administration Review,* won the Best Paper Award from the Conference of Minority Public Administrators (COMPA) in 2019. He has been selected as a 2021 recipient of the Donald C. Stone Service to ASPA Award from the American Society of Public Administration (ASPA). In 2019, he was awarded the Chester A. Newland Presidential Citation of Merit from ASPA and the Jewel Prestage Award from Conference of Minority Public Administrators (COMPA). He is a fellow in the National Academy of Public Administration (NAPA) and serves as a board member on the New Jersey Martin Luther King Jr. Commemorative Commission. He has served on the Executive Council of the Network of Schools of Public Policy, Affairs, and Administration (NASPAA) and as president of the International Conference on Local Government. He currently serves as Editor-in-Chief of the *Journal of Public Management & Social Policy*.

Katie Mills is a Supplemental Instruction Coordinator and Youth Liaison Officer at the University of Canterbury. She graduated with a Masters of International Relations and Diplomacy in 2021 from the University of Canterbury.

Katarzyna Anna Nawrot is a Polish economist and a member of the Committee for Future Studies, Polish Academy of Sciences. She has been with Poznan University of Economics and Business (2007-2019), the Graduate Institute of International and Development Studies in Geneva (2011–2012) and J.F. Kennedy School of Government at Harvard University (2013–2014). Her research interests include development economics, cultural economics, development studies, international economics, the history of economic thought and the world economy at large. Her recent books include *Economic cooperation and integration of East Asia. Theoretical and empirical study* (Polish Economic Publisher, 2021); the co-edited *The Rise of Megacities: Challenges, Opportunities and Unique* (World Scientific, London 2018); *Economic Potential and Developmental Opportunities of Africa. Polish perspective* (Polish Economic Publisher, 2017); and she is currently writing a book on culture systems and development.

Miguel D. Ramirez received his Ph.D. in economics from the University of Illinois at Urbana-Champaign in 1984 and has been at Trinity College in Hartford CT since 1985. He has held several visiting positions, including at the University of Illinois at Urbana-Champaign (1991 and 1992), Haverford College (Spring 1992), Vanderbilt University (Spring 1999), and Yale University (Spring 2006). His teaching and research interests are primarily in the areas of Latin American economic development, open economy macroeconomics, and the history of economic thought. His latest publications include: "Credit, Indebtedness and Speculation in Marx's Political Economy," *Economic Thought* 8 (2, 2019): 46-62; and "Marx and Ricardo on Machinery: A Critical Note," *The European Journal of the History of Economic Thought* 26 (1, 2019): 81-100.

Alexander C. Tan is Head of Department and Professor of Political Science and International Relations at the University of Canterbury, Honorary Professor of the New Zealand Defence Force Command and Staff College, Fellow of the John Goodwin Tower Center for Political Studies (Dallas, USA), and University Chair Professor of Political Science (adjunct) and Taiwan Institute of Governance and Communications Research at the National Chengchi University (Taiwan). He received his PhD from Texas A&M University, MA (Economics) from University of California-Santa Barbara, and AB (Economics) from the Ateneo de Manila. He has published extensively in the areas of political parties and elections, political economy, Asian politics and international affairs.

INDEX

C

D

E

F

G

H

I

J

K

L

M

N

Q

R

S

T

U

$$[10\, p_w + 20p_c + 50 \text{ x } 0.4\, (p_w + p_c)]\, (1 + r) = 100p_w \qquad (7a)$$

$$[20\, p_w + 30p_c + 50 \text{ x } 0.4\, (p_w + p_c)]\, (1 + r) = 100p_c \qquad (7b)$$

N

O

P

Q

R

S

T

U

V

W

X

Y

Z